Growth, Equality, and the
Mexican Experience

Latin American Monographs, No. 16
Institute of Latin American Studies
The University of Texas

GROWTH,
EQUALITY,
and the
MEXICAN
EXPERIENCE

by Morris Singer

37788

PUBLISHED FOR THE INSTITUTE OF LATIN AMERICAN STUDIES
BY THE UNIVERSITY OF TEXAS PRESS, AUSTIN AND LONDON

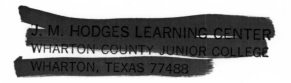

Type set by G&S Typesetters, Austin
Printed by Capital Printing Company, Austin
Bound by Universal Bookbindery, Inc., San Antonio

To my family,
Hilda Leah
Lawrence Raphael
Paul Everett,
I gratefully dedicate
this book

PREFACE

I have written this book about Mexico in the hope that it will throw some light on the relationships between growth and the several components of equality. The era of Mexican history which it covers is primarily post-Revolutionary, with particular reference to the period 1939–1961.

My major proposition is that *the concepts of equality and inequality must be disaggregated.* In some respects a movement toward greater equality may promote economic development, while in others more inequality may be preferable given the growth objective; this, at least, is the hypothesis being tested in these pages. The main task which I have undertaken is that of identifying the components of equality, or inequality, which have been compatible with the economic growth which Mexico has experienced.

I must confess to one added objective, one concerned with method rather than content. I am aiming for a study that combines the analytical approach with the institutional one in a relatively judicious fashion. There is probably too much of a tendency in the growth and development field either to employ formal, highly simplified models or to present data with the very minimal use of theory. These are extremes which I hope to avoid. I am interested in resorting to analyses to clarify Mexico's economic development, while simultaneously appealing to Mexico's experience in order to contribute to formal theory.

The Social Science Research Council gave impetus to my project when it granted me financial aid for independent study in Mexico for a period of six months. This assistance, combined with sabbatical leave and pay from the University of Connecticut, made it possible for me to become a peripatetic scholar. Armed with my questions (actually this is not completely true, since my research helped bring the issues into focus), some background reading, hopes for a sound work, and the moral support as well as physical presence of my family, I made my way to Mexico. There I occupied my time collecting arid statistics from libraries and enjoying animated interviews with Mexican economists and economic practitioners. The libraries in which I studied included those of the United Nations Economic Commission for Latin America, the Benjamin Franklin, the Nacional Financiera, the Bank of Mexico, and the National University of Mexico, all of which were staffed by helpful, knowledgeable and exceedingly patient professional persons. Except for the Benjamin Franklin (which does not offer such services), I also had the pleasure of interviewing persons who were associated with each of these institutions. My interviews further included talks with representatives from The Center for Latin American Monetary Studies, several government agencies, labor unions, commercial banks, the Chamber of Commerce, the Chamber of Manufacturers and the American Embassy. The Center for Latin American Monetary Studies was also gracious enough to arrange many of these interviews. Upon my return to the United States, the University of Connecticut was kind enough to supply funds for research assistance as well as for most of the necessary typing.

While several scholars read fragments of the manuscript, I am particularly indebted to Robert R. Edminster of the Economics Department at the University of Utah and Frederick C. Turner of the Political Science Department at the University of Connecticut for their counsel and encouragement. Any errors to be found in these pages are evidently not theirs. I am further grateful to Calvin P. Blair of the Institute of Latin American Studies at The University of Texas for directing me to several sources in Mexico who were in a position to assist me. My wife, Hilda Leah Singer, not only performed the usual unsung uxorial functions, but as a trained social worker she gathered some of the material for Chapter Nine. She in turn wishes to express her appreciation to those at the Mexican Institute of Social Security who aided her.

This book has been several years in the making. While it thus does not contain references to some of the most recent publications on Mexico, I trust this will not greatly detract from the reader's interest in the work.

CONTENTS

Growth, Equality, and the
Mexican Experience

CHAPTER ONE

Introduction

1. If anything is oft repeated in economic discussions these days it is the proposition that the peoples of the underdeveloped, or developing, nations impatiently seek economic advancement. Economic growth is frequently regarded merely as an increase in per capita income, however, and this leaves some observers and many participants dissatisfied in that this index simply reflects the average change. The concern here is of course with the distribution of income, with the problem of whether there is a mass sharing of the fruits of economic progress.[1] This latter orientation gives rise to some of the most intriguing questions in the area of economic development. Suppose that the growth objective is to be pursued —one hesitates to say, maximized. What then happens to the degree of equality in the system, with respect not only to income distribution but to certain broader dimensions as well? Does the stimulation of growth lead to a sacrifice of equality, or does the implementation of the one result in progress toward the other, or are the two simply neutral and divorced from each other? What, in sum, are the relationships between growth and equality?

The study of a single country, undertaken in some detail, seems highly advisable if one is to focus upon the intricate relationships between economic growth and the various elements of equality. Such an approach at least reduces, though it does not eliminate, the dangers of superficiality. In turn this means that the reader cannot, and will not, find any definitive answers in these pages to

---

[1] See Jacob Viner, *International Trade and Economic Development*, p. 127.

the questions that have just been posed. The opposite is in fact the case. Any generalizations or conclusions are intended simply as hypotheses subject to much further test; one could hardly claim more in the light of the case study approach pursued herein.

Of the several nations eligible for study, Mexico presents herself as a likely candidate. Her growth record is good and of relatively long duration,[2] so that the various relationships introduced above have had an opportunity to exert themselves. Less germane to this study, but of intrinsic value nevertheless, is the point that the United States readers who are unfamiliar with Mexico may become more acquainted with an immediate neighbor. The worth of this possibility is brought out by James Reston's remark, "Sometimes I think we'll do anything for Latin America except read about it."[3]

Of particular relevance, however, is the nature of Mexico's experience with growth and the various aspects of equality. In Frank Tannenbaum's view, Mexico has aimed for both economic growth and egalitarianism. While he does not entirely approve of combining these objectives, he little doubts that Mexico has adopted them. In his words:

It needs to be noted that Mexico is attempting to do two things at the same time: lay the foundation for a rapid capital accumulation, and maintain a high degree of social security and economic equity. This has not been done before, and these two objectives may, in fact, prove incompatible.

It remains to be proved that it is possible to develop, with the speed that the Mexican economy seems to require, a rapidly cumulative body of capital equipment and at the same time place upon it in its initial stages the cost of social security and an elaborate body of trade-union rules and regulations.[4]

Yet the record does not suggest that the Mexican authorities have dedicated themselves to furthering equalities of various sorts. Early in the twentieth century Mexico experienced a revolution

2 See chapter 2 of the present work.
3 "The Biggest Story in the World," *The New Republic*, 148 (May 4, 1963), 16.
4 Frank Tannenbaum, *Mexico: The Struggle for Peace and Bread*, pp. 222–223.

which swept away many of the privileges of the old regime. Thereupon the Revolution served as a unifying force and as a source of national pride; Mexico was after all the first Latin-American country, and one of the few nations in the world, to have experienced so momentous an event.[5] If the authorities were to appeal to the Revolution to further national pride and unity, they could not be entirely neglectful of its egalitarian ideals. Thus no chief executive has persistently acted in violation of these ideals. Beyond this it is difficult to generalize. Some administrations were highly interested in enhancing equalities; others were less enchanted with this objective. Tannenbaum's proposition can perhaps best be stated in negative fashion: the authorities were not actively committed, as are so many other governments in the underdeveloped world, to warding off a more democratic society. Despite their utterances, they tended to handle egalitarian problems less as matters of ideology, whether to the Left or Right, and more along *ad hoc* lines. But they all have been dedicated to the nation's economic advancement. This interest in growth, combined with a flexibility regarding egalitarian measures, renders Mexico an extremely good case for examining the issues raised above.

Thus we turn to questions such as the following (without imputing any significance to the order): What is Mexico's record regarding discrimination against classes of people on racial, sexual, religious, or other ethnic grounds? Does the country possess a genuine political democracy? Does she have an economic pluralism? How is the income distributed? What course have real wages taken? What is the pattern in the ownership of property; in particular, what is the land tenure? How have the authorities dealt with problems of monopoly? Has investment tended to take the form of contributions to human capital (that is, the education, skills, and health of the work force) to any significant degree? How regressive has the tax system tended to be? To what extent has Mexico already turned to a welfare state; are some characteristics of such a state incompatible with growth while others are

[5] This helps explain why Mexico has been more favorable to Cuba under Castro than have most other Latin-American nations. To be strongly opposed to Castro is to be untrue to the spirit of revolution, and of course most particularly to the spirit of *the* Revolution. Moreover, firm opposition might suggest subservience to the United States.

consistent with economic advancement? What has actually been the pace and character of that advancement itself?

Before we proceed with the record of Mexico's economic growth, the changes in its income distribution, and sundry matters, a word on Mexican statistics seems highly advisable. The point is simply that anyone inclined to purism in the gathering and use of data must pack his bags and journey elsewhere. Despite her considerable—in some respects remarkable—development, Mexico in the early 1960's was still a poor country, and this impoverishment extended to her official statistics. Mexican statistics have been largely approximations and guesses—informed ones, it is hoped.

Of the various types of national income data, those pertaining to national income at factor cost are among the most reliable, primarily because of the relatively good figures on payrolls. The data regarding agricultural and industrial production are felt to contain errors of 5 per cent even in census years, while the evaluation of commercial activities presents dreadful problems because of the incidence of petty trading. Banking probably yields the best available statistics. The data on imports, fixed investment, and public expenditures are relatively good, but changes in inventories are virtually impossible to handle. Gross fixed investment does pose difficulties in that imports of capital items are frequently included under construction at the same time that the labor cost of installing capital goods may be excluded. Net investment is further handicapped by the usual difficulties surrounding depreciation procedures. Behind the poor quality of many of the business statistics of course lurk fears that the data may be exploited either by the tax officials and/or one's competitors; word has it that most companies tend to maintain at least two sets of books for diverse purposes. In addition, smaller business units may often not be able to report adequate statistics because of sheer technical inability, perhaps because of illiteracy. What Sanford Mosk wrote in 1950 thus continued to be true in the early 1960's, namely: "It will be many years before the investigator will be able to accept any set of official figures at their face value."[6]

[6] Sanford A. Mosk, *The Industrial Revolution in Mexico*, p. 111. See also UNESCO, Economic Commission for Latin America, *Recent Events and Trends in Mexico* (1950), 8–9.

Yet it is conceivable that the primary danger in the use of these data is not one of uncritical acceptance. An investigator is trained to be cautious and conservative in the handling of information, and if his training has been inadequate in this respect or has somehow eluded him, the community of scholars generally remedies this limitation in his make-up. Possibly the greater danger is that he has learned inflexibility as well as caution and that he will insist upon a degree of excellence that is unattainable in a relatively poor country. If virtually everyone discards the admittedly inadequate data and foregoes action, few will be in a position to cope with the pressing problems of the developing nations. An alternative, conceivably the more reasonable one, is to acknowledge the probable presence of statistical error and yet to utilize the available statistics to further economic growth. The quantitative discrepancies notwithstanding, the various data on like activities tend to yield qualitatively similar results and they tend to be reenforced by a priori expectations. Hence the data will be reviewed, as indicated.

2. Before proceeding with the examination of Mexico's record, a few more comments regarding the general nature of this work seem in order. One of Hollis B. Chenery's pieces on investment criteria[7] provides the point of departure.

Chenery has drawn up a function in which social welfare is made to depend upon income (Y), the balance of payments position (B), and income distribution (D). Given an act of investment, each of these variables may change, with consequent effects upon utility. Chenery drops the income distribution variable almost immediately, however, giving as his reason the unavailability of the relevant data. His decision to neglect D, he emphasizes, is not related to an unwillingness to make interpersonal comparisons; in fact he indicates that it would be difficult to ignore the equity criterion completely in an underdeveloped country. Conceptually, therefore, distribution continues to have a place in the sun. Further, if one were interested in measuring an investment's effect upon distribution, then, given the pronounced structural unemployment in many developing nations, the impact on employment

[7] Hollis B. Chenery, "The Application of Investment Criteria," *Quarterly Journal of Economics*, 67 (February, 1953), pp. 76–96.

might be taken as a rough estimate.[8] Presumably income and distribution (or employment) would be competing items. A community would surrender income when it reached for greater equality, and contrarily.

Yet it seems much too simplified to permit employment to act as a measure of income distribution. Too many other factors—inflation, agricultural productivity, the degree of competition—affect the equality of income distribution. Actually, the relative shares of labor and capital might very well serve as the single most accurate reflection of a country's income distribution. Beyond that it is probably valid to assume a negative relationship between growth and distribution (or employment) in a developing nation during that long interval when the factor shortage is primarily one of capital rather than labor. Nevertheless, this would tend to be true on balance only, as in the case of the relationship between income growth and changes in the balance of payments which Chenery explores so carefully.[9] Inequality of income distribution does bear a relationship to such phenomena as land tenure, the degree of social mobility, the size of the middle class, the extent of training of the labor force, the adequacy of the domestic market, the type of government, and so on. These factors have to be weighed against the various growth-stimulating features of a skewed income distribution.

The foregoing enumeration does more than merely call attention to the complexities of income distribution. It indicates further that the question of the relationships between growth and equality is not limited to income distribution alone. Many additional facets of equality are of relevance and significance for the subject of economic growth. Moreover, a student of economic development must indeed experience consternation as he seeks guidance in the literature for the factors in a social system which may be conducive to the economic development of the poor countries. He then becomes conscious of the considerable ambiguity that surrounds the interrelationships between "democracy," an "open society," "egalitarianism"—call it what one will—and growth. On the one hand there is a tendency to regard the following as being condu-

[8] *Ibid.*, p. 80, n. 1.
[9] *Ibid.*, pp. 87–93.

cive to development: the rule of law rather than by oligarchy; vertical mobility and an integrated society as opposed to dualism or pluralism based on unequal opportunity; a strong middle class; a free labor force; reliance on contract rather than status; and a mass market. Investment in primary education is acceptable to a limited extent. The degree of progressiveness permissible in the tax system is questionable. Labor unions, welfare measures, and equality of income distribution are generally suspect.

All this points to the value of focusing upon the *components of equality or inequality* and of endeavoring to ascertain the relationship between *each of them* and economic development. Many of these components are intangible and immeasurable, but this renders them no less significant. Somewhat more formally, let D_1, D_2, $D_3 \ldots D_n$ each represent an element of a democratic or egalitarian system. Changes in some of the D's should be compatible with a growing income, while the contrary would be true in other instances. One also strongly suspects that the reporting of a positive or negative correlation depends upon the range under observation. The same component, such as the equality of income distribution, may be negatively related to growth at one level of economic achievement and positively related to it at some higher level. This change in sign needs to be explained, and ideally it should be dated.

It is further noteworthy that the types of equality or inequality which may be compatible with growth depend not only on a particular country's development but also on the period in world history in which the development occurs. Important illustrations of this can be found in the ideas of welfare statism and social security; these were hardly entertained in pre-World War I days, but they are given serious consideration in the countries currently experiencing development. As long as nations are exposed to the influence of other countries during the growth process, that which is regarded as a necessary or desirable sequence in one era need not at all be so in another.

The "utility function" implied by these remarks is a complex one.[10] Aggregative utility may alter because Y changes independent-

---

[10] The function would assume the form:

$$\Delta U = \Delta Y + \Delta D_i + \frac{\delta D_i}{\delta Y} \Delta Y + \frac{\delta Y}{\delta D_i} \Delta D_i + \frac{\delta D_j}{\delta D_i} \Delta D_i$$

ly of any particular D or when a D changes independently of Y. Further, it may vary if Y changes and thereby affects a D or if any D shifts and hence influences Y. These terms involve competing relationships and costs when accompanied by minus signs and compatibility when the signs are positive. In any instance, they may each be zero. It is a major contention of this work, however, that growth and the several equalities or inequalities continually influence each other and that zero results are generally unlikely. Finally, the various components of equality also tend to influence and play upon each other, and here, too, the signs may be positive or negative.

So much for the major questions that are posed in this work. Two final points of a general nature need to be made. One concerns the orientation toward growth which will be adopted in these pages. It is assumed that a poor country is interested essentially in promoting increases in its income. Where arguments in favor of approaching some equality do appear, it is generally because such steps are conducive to growth and not because they may be desirable for their own sake. As we have seen, this constitutes yet another reason for selecting Mexico for a case study.

The second point concerns method and the means of presenting the various propositions. Despite the mild flirtation with a more formal approach in some of the preceding paragraphs, this type of exposition does not appear again until the concluding chapter. Most of the work employs the more traditional literary and tabular tools. Also most of it—again excluding the final chapter—is not general, but rather, as the title indicates, it addresses itself to a single nation's experience.

In what follows we shall first consider Mexico's economic growth, one of the major concerns in this work. However, the path of Mexico's growth has been oft traversed, and the treatment will be only moderately detailed relative to all one might say about the subject. The data regarding equality cover less familiar ground and these will be examined comprehensively, especially in Chapter Five, which deals with changes in income distribution. Later chapters take up public policies in Mexico which have been concerned with distribution as well as other aspects of equality. The concluding chapter offers a more theoretical and general approach to the various problems discussed in these pages.

CHAPTER TWO

Mexico's Record of Economic Growth

Changes in money income and the price level. The year 1939
serves as a significant point of departure in Mexico's economic
history: not only did the most rapid and sustained economic development in Mexico begin with World War II, but 1939 marks
the beginning of the country's more reliable income statistics. The
first table indicates the behavior of the gross national product in
current prices and national income at factor cost from 1939
through 1964. Advances in prices, population, and planes of living
have led to thirty-three– and thirty-six–fold increases in gross
product and net income, respectively, in the intervening period
and to annual output-income levels in excess of 200,000,000,000
pesos per year.

However, mounting prices contributed considerably to these
advances in money income and output. The modern rise of prices
in Mexico had its inception in the 1930's, under the presidencies
of Rodríguez (1932–1934) and Cárdenas (1934–1940), when the
authorities decided that deficit financing and inflation were to be
preferred to the low income and employment of the time. If the
year 1959 represents 100, the cost of living index, based primarily
upon price data for Mexico City, rose as follows after 1933:[1]

---

[1] United Nations, Economic Commission for Latin America, UNESCO, *Inflation and Growth: A Summary of Experience in Latin America*, Fig. 1, facing
p. 28.

Year	Cost of Living Index
1933	12
1934	16
1935	17
1936	18
1937	21
1938	24
1939	25

These data indicate a doubling of the price level in the years under consideration, which in turn implies an annual rate of increase approximating 13 per cent. However, the selection of dates tends to overstate the inflation that occurred. In 1929 the wholesale price index stood at 21; it then dropped to 17 in 1932, and rose to 24 in 1937 and 25 in 1939.[2] The increase in prices therefore approximated only 20 per cent for the whole decade. During that time the exchange rate declined more sharply, from 50 U.S. cents a peso in 1929 to 20 by 1940.[3]

For some suggestions concerning the increases in prices after 1939 we can consider three of the indices available for the period: general wholesale, general cost of living (comprising food, clothes, coal, and soap), and food costs only. Each of these series reveals a rise in prices for every year, with the sole exception of the rather mild decline that occurred in 1953. Taking 1953 as the base year for each series, a comparison of the years 1939 and 1958 shows the wholesale price index increasing from 25 to 142, the general cost of living index rising from 22 to 150, and the index for the price of food climbing from 23 to 155.[4] The two cost of living indices thus increased almost sixfold during the twenty-year span, while the wholesale price index rose by a slightly smaller margin. Wholesale price indices, based on 1939 and 1954, are produced in Table 2. They imply price increases approximating 9 per cent per year from 1940 through 1959, or almost 1½ times the rate of

[2] United Nations, Statistical Office, *Statistical Yearbook, 1957*, p. 463, t. 160.

[3] United Nations, Economic Commission for Latin America, UNESCO, *Inflation and Growth*, p. 31, t. 31.

[4] United Nations, Statistical Office, *Statistical Yearbook, 1957*, pp. 463 and 476, tables 160 and 161; and *ibid* (for 1959), pp. 437 and 444, tables 164 and 165.

TABLE 1. Mexico's National Output and Income, 1939–1964*
(millions of pesos)

Year	Gross National Product	National Income at Factor Cost
1939	6,800	5,900
1940	7,300	6,400
1941	8,800	7,700
1942	10,700	9,500
1943	13,700	12,300
1944	17,700	16,100
1945	20,500	18,600
1946	26,100	23,700
1947	29,000	26,300
1948	31,700	28,800
1949	35,200	31,700
1950	40,577	36,630
1951	52,311	47,289
1952	58,643	52,967
1953	58,437	52,601
1954	71,540	64,432
1955	87,349	78,718
1956	99,323	89,743
1957	114,225	103,077
1958	127,152	114,688
1959	136,200	122,820
1960	154,137	139,084
1961	163,757	147,802
1962	177,533	160,476
1963	192,200	173,800
1964	224,600	203,200

* The data for 1939–1949 are taken from Banco de México, *Informe anual, 1960*, p. 73, t. (table) 1. The 1950–1964 figures are from *Informe anual, 1964*, p. 75, t. 1; they are preliminary revisions.

growth of the real GNP over the period. Over the entire period 1940–1964, wholesale prices increased at an annual rate of 7.5 per cent.

A breakdown into subintervals shows a decline in the rate of

TABLE 2. Indices of Wholesale Prices, 1939–1964*

Year	Index (1939 = 100)	Index (1954 = 100)	Annual Rate of Increase
1939	100.0	. . .	. . .
1940	104.0	. . .	4.0
1941	109.3	. . .	5.1
1942	120.6	. . .	10.3
1943	145.7	. . .	20.8
1944	178.5	. . .	22.5
1945	198.7	. . .	11.3
1946	222.7	. . .	12.1
1947	242.3	. . .	8.8
1948	260.0	. . .	7.3
1949	284.8	. . .	9.5
1950	311.2	72.5	9.3
1951	386.0	89.9	24.0
1952	400.0	93.2	3.7
1953	392.5	91.4	−1.9
1954	429.4	100.0	9.4
1955	487.9	113.6	13.6
1956	510.5	118.9	4.6
1957	532.7	124.0	4.3
1958	556.3	129.5	4.4
1959	. . .	131.0	1.2
1960	. . .	137.5	4.9
1961	. . .	138.8	1.0
1962	. . .	141.3	1.8
1963	. . .	142.1	0.6
1964	. . .	148.1	4.2

* The data for 1939–1958, based on 1939, are from Víctor L. Urquidi, "La Inflación en México," p. 2, t. 1. In turn, Urquidi has used statistics from Banco de México, Departmento de Estudios Económicos. The figures for 1950–1964, based on 1954, are from Banco de México, *Informe anual, 1964*, p. 81, t. 6. The Bank's index covers the wholesale prices of 210 commodities sold in Mexico City.

inflation over the twenty-five-year period, as revealed by the wholesale price index. During 1940–1945 it averaged 12.25 per cent, whereupon it decreased somewhat to 11.8 per cent for 1946–1951 (note the special influence of 1951) and then dropped considerably to 5.4 per cent during 1952–1958. Since 1956 the Mexican economy has been especially less subject to inflationary pressures. From 1956 through 1964 the wholesale price level rose at a rate approximating only 3 per cent a year, while the cost of food rose only by one-third over the nine-year period.[5] By the same token the real growth rate declined in several of these years.

Changes in real income, 1895–1940. During the latter part of the nineteenth century and in the first decade of the twentieth, Mexico was more advanced economically than most other Latin-American nations. She nevertheless remained "the archetype of an underdeveloped country."[6] Technological dualism, domination of the advanced sector by foreign interests, an exceedingly small middle class, quasi-feudalistic agriculture, and a large, backward, poverty-stricken rural sector characterized her economy. Nor were the three decades following the Revolution years of pronounced economic growth. During this period certain institutional changes, such as those relating to land tenure, the dispersion of political and economic power, and political stability, had to be consummated in order to lay the groundwork for later economic advance; and of course during the 1930's Mexico, like other suppliers of primary goods, found herself handicapped by declines in revenue from sales abroad. Yet there is a great danger that the concept "industrial revolution" may be misapplied in the case of Mexico, as elsewhere. The Mexican economy could not and did not blossom forth suddenly with the firing of the first shot of World War II. Investment coefficients (investment/income) and capital-output ratios were generally low during the war years, which suggests that Mexico had to rely rather considerably on existing plant and equipment for her industrial production. Some economic, particularly industrial, progress obviously must have taken place by 1939.

One Mexican economist has compiled gross national product data going back as far as 1895, and he has corrected for price changes by utilizing 1950 price indices.[7] As is to be expected, the

---

[5] Banco de México, *Informe anual, 1964*, p. 84, t. 8. The index is based upon the cost of food in Mexico City.

[6] Robert Edminster, "Mexico," in Pepalasis, Mears, and Adelman, *Economic Development*, p. 337.

[7] Enrique Pérez López, "El producto nacional," in *México: Cincuenta años de revolución, I, La economía*, p. 587, t. 2, and p. 588, t. 3.

period includes cyclical, intermediate, and secular changes. From 1895 through 1902 the impression is one of modest growth. National output at constant prices grew about 15 per cent during these years. From 1903 through 1910 the rise was more sustained and more impressive. Income rose from 11,092,000,000 to 13,524,000,000, almost double the growth rate of the preceding period. All of this is consistent with the conclusions many Mexican economic historians are now likely to reach about Mexico's development during the regime of Díaz, which ended in 1910. Díaz was a dictator who supported the privileged few at home, assured foreign enterprise favorable treatment in Mexico in order to win foreign support for his rule, brutally repressed opposition at home, and prevented the vast majority of Mexicans from realizing any improvement in their welfare. On the other hand, his government encouraged developments in mining, transportation, commerce, banking, and textile production within Mexico. The average Mexican scarcely enjoyed the fruits of this activity, but the economic plant which Díaz helped create was to provide some of the background for Mexico's economic achievements after 1940.[8]

It is pointless to speak of the economic developments which occurred during the 1910 Revolution. In the ensuing struggle approximately one million Mexicans lost their lives, many of them as victims of atrocities. On comparison the attendant decline in national output is of minor import. The year 1920 is usually designated as the terminal year of the Revolution, although unrest continued through much of the twenties and Obregón, the last of the major Revolutionary heroes to lose his life through violence, was assassinated in 1928. The Mexican economy recovered from the Revolution in a fashion typical of nations that regress for a time because of the devastation of war or internal disorder and then build upon a given stock of capital, a certain level of technology, and a backlog of demand. Thus Mexico's real income expanded 20 per cent from 1921 to 1926. For the remainder of the decade, however, the economy stagnated, so that its performance during the twenties was only moderately good. Over the course of the decade industry experienced modest growth, activity in petro-

[8] This agrees with the conclusions reached in Daniel Cosío Villegas, ed., *Historia moderna de México*, Vol. 7, Parts 1 and 2, *El porfiriato: La vida económica*.

leum declined, agriculture was retarded often to the point of causing widespread hunger, and national income in 1950 prices advanced merely from 14,560,000,000 pesos in 1921 to 17,240,000,000
and 16,666,000,000 pesos in 1928 and 1929, respectively. Several
years of depression followed, with minerals especially suffering
because of the decline in foreign sales. The low point during this
period occurred in 1932, when national income in constant prices
fell to 13,494,000,000 pesos.   •

The recovery began the following year.[9] In part, nature took a
hand, for the crops were good in 1933. In addition, the authorities
adopted several types of expansionary policy. The official agencies,
primarily the Bank of Mexico, extended credit vigorously. The
government undertook a series of public works which were generally financed by current revenues but which were also supported
by bond issues and funds from government controlled credit institutions. In her foreign trade Mexico was able to obtain higher
prices for silver, petroleum, and industrial metals. In addition she
devalued the peso and enjoyed a growing tourist traffic, so that
her total export sector experienced a growing prosperity. National
output in constant prices expanded from 13,494,000,000 pesos in
1932 to 20,505,000,000 pesos in 1939. Yet the latter rate of flow was
not much higher than the income of 17,335,000,000 pesos in 1926.
The impression is once again one of moderate economic advancement over a longer period, with the relatively high growth rate of
1932–1939 reflecting a cyclical upswing. One student of the thirties
has pointed out, in private conversation, that there was relatively
little private fixed investment during the decade, the increase in
industrial output notwithstanding. The government under Cárdenas was undoubtedly more oriented to the small farmer and
labor, and less concerned with business interests, than any other
post-Revolutionary administration. Further, revolutionary movements were strong abroad; fears of leftism, even communism,
dominated the business community and tended to interfere with
private capital formation.[10] It thus appears that much of the

[9] This paragraph owes much to George Wythe, *Industry in Latin America*,
rev. ed., p. 277.

[10] Yet Wythe reports that according to the Industrial Census, the number of
establishments in manufacturing increased from 6,904 in 1935 to 12,954 in
1940. *Ibid.*, p. 278, t. 15.

capacity which was utilized during the war, certainly during the initial years, was inherited from the pre-1930 period, and perhaps a significant portion of that had survived even the Revolution and the ravages of time. A great deal of this capacity was in textiles, which also helps account for the fairly low capital-output ratios of the late thirties and early forties.

During this moderate economic growth from 1895 to 1940 manufacturing served as a leading sector. This is of course fairly typical of economic development, but in Mexico it especially tended to be the case after 1910 because of the retarded state of agriculture. Various sources generally agree on the industrial growth that occurred between 1895 and 1940, but they differ somewhat on the subintervals. Nathan Whetten sees little trend until 1899 but an approximate doubling of industrial production from 1899–1909.[11] Pérez López reports a much steadier annual increase, with production doubling from 1895 to 1910.[12] Whetten further cites index numbers approximating 70 at the outset of the twenties, 100 in 1929, and 160.5 in 1939.[13] Henry Aubrey reports the volume of industrial production as doubling between 1922 and 1936 and again between 1937 and 1946.[14] Pérez López' figures show a doubling between 1922 and 1938 and then a renewed doubling experienced by 1948.[15] These data are in turn consistent with Mosk's summary statistic that the annual rate of increase in industrial production averaged about 5 per cent during the twenties and thirties.[16] Considering the stagnation in output during the latter part of the twenties and the actual decline in the early years of the thirties, this was a most respectable though not brilliant performance. By comparison the current economically advanced European countries averaged about 6 per cent a year when they began to transform themselves into industrial societies.

The general outlines of Mexican economic development from

[11] Nathan L. Whetten, *Rural Mexico*, p. 273, t. 52.

[12] Pérez López, "El producto nacional," p. 587, t. 2.

[13] Whetten, *Rural Mexico*, p. 273, t. 52.

[14] Henry G. Aubrey, "Structure and Balance in Rapid Economic Growth: The Example of Mexico," *Political Science Quarterly*, 69 (December, 1954), 530–531.

[15] Pérez López, "El producto nacional," p. 588, t. 3.

[16] Sanford A. Mosk, *The Industrial Revolution in Mexico*, p. 120.

1895 to 1940 have now made themselves fairly clear. The rate of increase in the real GNP approximated 2 per cent a year while industrial output advanced at an annual rate of some 4 per cent; this in turn implies that the former series more than doubled while the latter at least quadrupled during the period. There is no record of any sharp spurt in general economic or in industrial development except in those instances when the economy was recovering from a political crisis, as in the early 1920's, or an economic one, as in the later 1930's. Yet there was a steady stream—somewhere between a trickle and a current—of economic improvement that helped prepare the economy for the rapid advance that ensued in the forties.

The national income in constant prices after 1939. With some resort to the jargon it is possible to say that Mexico was technically and institutionally preconditioned for sustained growth by 1940 and that she merely awaited some favorable shock to move forward. During World War II she experienced that once-for-all favorable economic benefit which a nation not heretofore industrialized and remaining free from devastation can receive from warfare. The onset of war particularly brought with it a balance of payments position highly favorable to Mexico. Except for 1941, when imports of goods greatly increased (to $199,200,000, compared to $131,900,000 in 1940) in anticipation of the United States entry into the war, exports surpassed imports each year from 1939 through 1943. Because of the heightened demand for Mexico's exports and some reduction in the availability of imports, Mexico's "favorable balance" in merchandise came to $42,800,000 over the five-year period, and her foreign reserves rose by $48,700,000 as a result of all current transactions during that time. Moreover, the use of net figures may well understate the impact of World War II, for the advance in exports did create reserves for the purchase of imports, which climbed regularly throughout the war.[17] Beginning in July 1941 the United States purchased virtually all of Mexico's products of strategic value at market prices, thereby providing her with a guaranteed market. In return Mexico was to have received raw materials and machines. Actually, much of

[17] Based on The Combined Mexican Working Party, *The Economic Development of Mexico*, pp. 348–349, t. 122.

Mexico's dollar reserves was devoted to the purchase of food, since the United States was subsequently unwilling to part with capital goods; after the war, however, Mexico was able to use some of her reserves to add to her stock of real capital. Finally, it is important to note that the commodities enjoying the greatest boom in exports were produced by Mexican, not foreign-owned, firms.

During the forties, Mexico experienced the highest rate of economic growth in her history for a like period (see Table 3). The total national output nearly doubled from 1939 through 1949, the result of an average increase of 7 per cent per year. The war years especially contributed to this record. From 1939 through 1945 the growth of real output attained annual rates of increase of 8.2 per cent, as compared with a moderately satisfactory 4.2 per cent per year from 1946 through 1949. For the whole period 1939–1952 industrial output expanded at a rate of 6.8 per cent per year, while during the years 1939–1945 its annual rate of increase reached a very impressive 9.4 per cent. This implies, interestingly enough, that in the seven years after the war the industrial sector advanced less rapidly than the remaining sectors. The industrial achievement was also marked by a considerable shift to the production of capital goods and consumer durables. These two components rose from 17 per cent of the value of industrial output in 1939 to 29 per cent in 1951; yet this measure may even understate the shift because of the greater than average rise in textile prices.[18]

The rate of growth of the GNP in real terms slackened somewhat during the fifties, averaging 6.2 per cent a year. During the whole 1946–1959 period Mexico's economic achievements were sufficient to permit a near doubling of the national product. For the five years 1960–1964 the growth rate came to 6.5 per cent. There were of course considerable differences in the income increases of particular years. The rates of advance in 1950–1951 and 1954–1955 approached those attained in the best years of World War II, while the rates of increase in 1952–1953 were negligible. Mexican economists are disturbed not only by these fluctuations as such but by the reason for their occurrence—obviously the continuing economic dependence of Mexico on the United States. One

---

[18] Aubrey is the source for the 1939–1952 industrial data. See his "Structure and Balance in Rapid Economic Growth," p. 531.

TABLE 3. GNP in 1950 Prices, 1939–1964*

Year	GNP (millions of pesos)	Annual Rate of Growth (per cent)
1939	20,505	. . .
1940	20,721	1.05
1941	23,289	12.39
1942	26,373	13.24
1943	27,358	3.73
1944	29,690	8.52
1945	31,595	7.64
1946	34,084	6.64
1947	34,517	1.44
1948	36,080	4.53
1949	37,627	4.28
1950	40,577	7.84
1951	43,621	7.50
1952	45,366	4.00
1953	45,618	0.56
1954	50,391	10.46
1955	54,767	8.68
1956	58,214	6.29
1957	62,708	7.71
1958	66,177	5.53
1959	68,119	2.93
1960	73,482	7.87
1961	76,038	3.48
1962	79,691	4.80
1963	84,700	6.29
1964	93,200	10.04

* The 1939–1949 data in column 1 are from Secretaría de Industria y Comercio, *Memoria, 1959*, p. 910, t. 414. The 1950–1964 figures in column 1 can be found in Banco de México, *Informe anual, 1964*, p. 75, t. 1. The growth rates in column 2 have been computed as $\frac{Y_t - Y_{t-1}}{Y_{t-1}}$.

factor, for example, in the great rise in export proceeds in 1955 was the devaluation of the peso in 1954, which turned out to be unnecessarily sharp because of an underestimation of the United States recovery in late 1954 and in 1955. Moreover, after 1957 the performance of the Mexican economy frequently did not match that of the preceding years, with the annual rates of growth from 1958 through 1963 averaging 5.2 per cent. This retardation in the growth rate begs for analysis, particularly of aggregate demand, which will be essayed in later chapters.

Be that as it may, a review of Mexico's economic development for the 2½ decades beginning in 1939 tends to become the occasion for plaudits. Table 4 indicates that the GNP in constant 1950 prices more than quadrupled during that span. The average annual growth rate associated with this performance approximated 6.5 per cent. This development may fall just short of the spectacular, and it was certainly not without blemish, but it does reflect a good, sustained performance—certainly one of the best in the underdeveloped world.

Capital formation after 1939. Given the emphasis on capital formation in the literature, it seems advisable to look at the investment series before taking leave of aggregates. Aside from considering the data on investment, we shall also take note of some of the relationships between capital and income which have been stressed in growth theory. These relationships may be regarded as criteria for judging the appropriateness of given rates of capital formation.

Table 4 presents data on public, private, and total investment in current prices and as percentages of GNP. The investment concept is that of fixed gross domestic capital formation. Additions to inventories have been excluded because of the aforementioned difficulties of obtaining the data. The total investment coefficients tended to rise until the late forties, but thereafter stabilized at levels approximating 13 or 14 per cent. If inventories were included, gross domestic investment would probably have approached 16 per cent of the GNP during the fifties. At times private investment has reached two-thirds of total investment, but it has not clung to this ratio persistently. At the end of the period covered in Table 4—that is, 1959–1961—private investment/total investment slipped to less than three-fifths, or approximately the ratio it had attained two decades earlier.

Table 5 is of value in presenting the Mexican version of the notorious incremental capital output ratios. The annual fluctuations of these ratios have not been very marked in Mexico, except for the high values experienced during the years of relatively low

TABLE 4. Public, Private, and Total Gross Fixed Investment,
1939–1961*

Year	(millions of pesos)			(per cent of GNP)		
	Public Invest- ment	Private Invest- ment	Total Invest- ment	Public Invest- ment	Private Invest- ment	Total Invest- ment
1939	248	401	649	3.7	6.0	9.7
1940	316	457	773	4.5	6.4	10.9
1941	362	608	970	4.3	7.2	11.5
1942	481	524	1,005	4.6	5.0	9.6
1943	618	659	1,277	4.6	5.0	9.6
1944	714	1,016	1,730	4.1	5.9	10.0
1945	928	1,348	2,276	4.4	6.6	11.0
1946	1,105	2,156	3,261	4.1	7.9	12.0
1947	1,378	2,726	4,104	4.6	9.2	13.8
1948	1,635	2,917	4,552	5.0	9.0	14.0
1949	2,030	3,087	5,117	5.7	8.7	14.4
1950	2,643	3,294	5,937	6.5	8.1	14.6
1951	2,981	4,676	7,657	5.7	8.9	14.6
1952	3,434	4,732	8,166	5.9	8.0	13.9
1953	2,940	4,600	7,540	5.0	7.9	12.9
1954	4,028	5,400	9,428	5.6	7.5	13.1
1955	4,229	7,600	11,829	4.8	8.7	13.5
1956	4,675	9,060	13,735	4.7	9.0	13.7
1957	5,420	10,124	15,544	4.7	8.9	13.6
1958	6,516	10,770	17,286	5.1	8.4	13.5
1959	6,872	10,944	17,816	5.0	8.0	13.0
1960	8,768	12,435	21,203	5.6	8.1	13.7
1961	10,523	12,324	22,847	6.4	7.5	13.9

* Sources of investment data: (a) 1939–1950: Combined Mexican Working Party, *The Economic Development of Mexico*, p. 183, t. 12, and p. 186, t. 14. (b) 1951–1961: Secretaría de Industria y Comercio, *Anuario estadístico de los Estados Unidos Mexicanos, 1960–1961*, p. 628, t. 16.4. Source of income data: see Table 3.

growth rates. One would of course expect the latter relationship from the familiar formula for the growth rate—that is, the average propensity to save divided by the marginal capital-output ratio. When the saving propensity remains relatively constant,

TABLE 5. Incremental Capital-Output Ratios, 1940–1961*
(millions of pesos)

Year	(1) ΔGNP (constant prices)	(2) Fixed Gross Investment (constant prices)	(3) ΔK/ΔO (Col.[2] ÷ Col.[1])
1940	69	754	10.9
1941	851	888	1.0
1942	1,019	833	0.8
1943	323	877	2.7
1944	770	970	1.3
1945	747	1,145	1.5
1946	698	1,425	2.0
1947	158	1,694	10.7
1948	515	1,751	3.4
1949	514	1,796	3.5
1950	972	1,908	2.0
1951	3,044	6,175	2.0
1952	1,745	6,350	3.4
1953	252	5,975	23.7
1954	4,773	6,827	1.4
1955	4,376	7,539	1.7
1956	3,447	8,370	2.4
1957	4,494	9,080	2.0
1958	3,469	9,673	2.8
1959	1,942	9,854	5.1
1960	5,363	11,177	2.1
1961	2,556	11,924	4.7

* For both output and investment the 1940–1950 data are in 1939 prices, whereas the 1951–1961 statistics are in 1950 prices. The 1940–1950 incremental output data are derived from the growth rates presented in Table 3, column 2, beginning with a GNP of 6,800,000,000 pesos in 1939. The 1940–1950 investment statistics are from the Combined Mexican Working Party, *The Economic Development of Mexico*, p. 204, t. 26. The 1951–1961 incremental output figures are derived from the GNP data presented in Table 3. The investment statistics for 1951–1961 are based upon Secretaría de Industria y Comercio, *Anuario estadístico, 1960–1961*, p. 628, t. 16.4; these data have been deflated by the wholesale price indices presented in Table 2.

as it particularly did during the fifties, the negative relation between the remaining two variables stands out clearly.

The values assumed by the incremental capital-output ratio seem at first glance to be low, or, stated alternately, the productivity of capital (not *ceteris paribus*) appears to be relatively high. In ten years the value of the coefficient was 2 or less. Part of this follows from the use of only fixed capital formation. If net investment in inventories were added to investment, the values of the ratios might rise by about 15 per cent.[19] Further, extreme values in years of poor performance have raised the average considerably. The mean value for twenty-one years excluding 1953 and including only fixed investment was 3.2. With the further inclusion of additions to inventories, the ratio would approximate 3.7. In addition, the employment of gross investment and gross product data yields lower results than would be obtained with net investment and output figures. Probably the most useful conclusion is simply that the productivity of capital was satisfactorily high in Mexico during the years of good growth performance.

While world statistics for propensities to save and marginal capital-output ratios generally abound, there have been fewer computations of the rates of growth in investment. Given the role of investment in development, this is somewhat surprising. The popularity of the Harrod-Domar formulation may be partially responsible for this relative neglect of a rather significant series. In the Harrod-Domar world the rates of increase in investment and in the capital stock each equal the rate of growth in income whenever the latter pursues a steady expansion path. Thus $\frac{\Delta K}{K}$, the rate of growth in the capital stock, equals $\frac{\Delta Y}{Y}$ because of the assumption of a constant capital-output ratio. In turn, $\frac{\Delta I}{I}$ equals $\frac{\Delta Y}{Y}$ as a result of assuming that the average propensity to save does not alter and that it therefore equals the margin. The division of the numerator in $\frac{\Delta I}{I}$ by the marginal propensity to save and of the denominator by the average propensity then yields $\frac{\Delta Y}{Y}$.[20]

Others, however, see the development process as characterized by the relationship $\frac{\Delta I}{I} > \frac{\Delta Y}{Y}$.[21] The rate of growth in investment is

[19] Secretaría de Industria y Comercio, *Anuario estadístico, 1960–1961*, p. 628, t. 16.3.

[20] Evsey D. Domar, *Essays in the Theory of Economic Growth*, pp. 90–92.

[21] Cf. Domar's description of Feldman's model in *ibid.*, Essay 9, esp. pp. 233–234. Also see Celso Furtado, "Capital Formation and Economic Development,"

given by $\frac{\Delta Y}{\Delta K} \cdot \frac{\Delta S}{\Delta Y}$, as opposed to the Harrod-Domar formula for the rate of growth in output, $\frac{\Delta Y}{\Delta K} \cdot \frac{S}{Y}$. As long as $\frac{\Delta S}{\Delta Y} > \frac{S}{Y}$, then $\frac{\Delta I}{I} > \frac{\Delta Y}{Y}$. This also implies that the capital-output ratio would rise over time. Since there have been limits to the rise in this ratio historically, and since in addition there is evidence that the saving function tends to be linear after a time, this suggests that $\frac{\Delta I}{I} > \frac{\Delta Y}{Y}$ for transitional economies and that the two growth rates may be more nearly equal thereafter.[22]

Table 6 presents the rather impressive rates of increase in investment for the Mexican economy, 1940–1961. Over this period $\frac{\Delta I}{I}$ averaged 8.5 per cent a year. As just noted, an important aspect of this growth concerns its relationship to the rate of increase in output. This is given in column 3 by the expression $\frac{\Delta I}{I}/\frac{\Delta Y}{Y}$. At the risk of being insufferable, this term can be assigned the name of the "income elasticity of investment demand." The rate of increase in income appears in the denominator not only because of the familiarity of the income elasticity of demand concept but also in order to designate the dependence of investment upon income, or aggregate demand, even in a relatively poor country. Irrespective of the nature of the relationship between income and investment, however, the noteworthy point is that over the course of twenty-two years of economic advancement in Mexico, $\frac{\Delta I}{I}/\frac{\Delta Y}{Y}$ averaged 1.3. For Mexico it was true that $\frac{\Delta I}{I} > \frac{\Delta Y}{Y}$ and hence that $\frac{\Delta S}{\Delta Y} > \frac{S}{Y}$. Further, $\frac{\Delta I}{I}$ averaged 10.3 per cent during the first half of 1940–1961 but only 6.7 per cent during the second half. Given the rates of growth in output over the same intervals, $\frac{\Delta I}{I}/\frac{\Delta Y}{Y}$ declined from 1.4 in the first period to 1.1 in the later one. This is consistent with the tendency of the investment coefficient to stabilize itself during the fifties; that is, the margin then approached the average. The Harrod-Domar framework thus seems more appropriate for the second subperiod.

Beyond these major points some interest attaches to the relationships between $\frac{\Delta I}{I}$ and $\frac{\Delta Y}{Y}$ for particular years. Clearly the "income

---

in A. N. Agarwala and S. P. Singh, eds., *The Economics of Underdevelopment*, pp. 309–337.

[22] However, in the United States economy $\frac{\Delta I}{I}$ approximated 1.75 $\frac{\Delta Y}{Y}$ from 1953 to 1963.

TABLE 6. Comparative Rates of Increase in
Fixed Investment and GNP, 1940–1961*

Year	$\frac{\Delta I}{I}$	$\frac{\Delta Y}{Y}$	$\frac{\Delta I}{I} / \frac{\Delta Y}{Y}$
1940	16.2	1.1	14.7
1941	17.7	12.4	1.4
1942	−6.1	13.2	−0.4
1943	5.2	3.7	1.4
1944	10.6	8.5	1.2
1945	18.1	7.6	2.4
1946	24.6	6.6	3.7
1947	18.9	1.4	13.5
1948	3.4	4.5	0.8
1949	2.6	4.3	0.6
1950	6.2	7.8	0.8
1951	4.0	7.5	0.5
1952	2.8	4.0	0.7
1953	−5.9	0.6	−9.8
1954	14.3	10.5	1.4
1955	10.4	8.7	1.2
1956	11.0	6.3	1.7
1957	8.5	7.7	1.1
1958	6.5	5.5	1.2
1959	1.9	2.9	0.7
1960	13.4	7.9	1.7
1961	6.7	3.5	1.9

* The $\frac{\Delta I}{I}$ series for 1940–1950 is taken directly from the Combined Mexican Working Party, *The Economic Development of Mexico*, p. 203, t. 25; while the 1951–1961 figures for $\frac{\Delta I}{I}$ have been computed from the investment data presented in column 2 of Table 5. The $\frac{\Delta Y}{Y}$ series is from Table 3.

elasticity of investment demand" fluctuated considerably. As a first approximation it may be suggested that the ratio assumed values ranging from 1 to 1.5 during the years of rapid growth; these magnitudes tended to be associated with a good over-all performance. However, 1947 and 1958 defy this generalization because of low rates of growth in output attended by similarly low advances in investment. Four other results fall outside the designated range despite high rates of growth in output. The first approximation must be modified, largely to allow for intertemporal relationships. The burst of capital formation that occurred in the immediate post-World War II period contributed to the relatively low growth rates in investment from 1948 through 1953. Thereupon the rate of increase in investment performed respectably in the mid-fifties, but fell off during the later part of the period. The "income elasticity of investment demand" thus tends to depend upon, and to be inversely related to, the rates of increase in income and in investment in the recent past—from two to six years in Mexico's case.

Population growth. Thus far no mention has been made of the increases in Mexico's per capita income. To derive these we can turn to Mexico's population growth and then allow for the contribution of this factor to the rise in aggregate real income.

The usual correction of national income figures for population changes probably fails to yield an adequate picture of per capita incomes over long time spans. A country that may have for one or two decades realized income and population gains, each of 3 per cent a year, differs importantly from a country that has not experienced increases in either. The first country possesses a certain momentum. An economic and technological dynamism has been built into its structure. Undoubtedly it is in the process of accumulating a stock of physical and intangible capital and of shedding traditional modes of behavior. The community is "developing" despite the rise in numbers, and a rise in per capita income may well occur in due time, particularly if income growth induces a decline in population growth.

An increase in population may further contribute to the dynamic characteristics of the system through its effect on aggregate demand. In the economically advanced countries population growth may constitute an important source of aggregate demand, particularly because of its effects on the consumption of staples. In the poorer countries population growth can also stimulate effective demand, but largely because of the reaction of the public sector. That is, an increase in population may well create intolerable pressures, political and otherwise, which necessitate further action.[23] By the same token it is not legitimate to assert that a

[23] See Albert O. Hirschman, *The Strategy of Economic Development*, pp. 176–182.

country has been unfortunate in experiencing a 2.5 per cent increase in population in the face of a 4 per cent growth in income, as if the population increase merely restricted the rise in per capita income to a relatively low 1.5 per cent. Without the rise in population we have no guarantee that the increase in income would have approached 4 per cent.

In other respects as well the relationship between population growth and the dynamics of development is an uncertain one. If capital-labor ratios are extremely low, an increase in the labor force can result not only in a more conservative use of capital but in a conservation of capital formation as well. However, if labor is scarce relative to land and only moderately plentiful relative to capital, the economy may still be in a phase of increasing returns, and a high rate of population growth then assists the struggling young economy. Further, the structure of population growth is such that it tends to increase the inequality of income distribution. Whether this is conducive to further economic advancement then depends on the relationship between the current degree of inequality and propensity to save.

Finally, there is the factor of free consumer choice. Rapid population growth is associated with so many intense satisfactions and dissatisfactions that we must further question the validity of deflating advances in aggregate output for increases in population and regarding only the remainder as improvements in welfare. When a population grows because of a reduction in deaths and the diseases associated with them, there is surely something inadequate about an accounting system that reports this as an unqualified deterioration in the plane of living. Very many people, particularly parents of young children, receive psychic income not only from the lower death rate but also from the very knowledge that death rates have declined. Much the same may also be said of increases in population due to higher birth rates. On balance children give pleasure, and as such they may be regarded as substitutes for the gratifications received from goods and services. While the jargon repels, one could speak of marginal rates of substitution between changes in economic welfare and in the number of offspring. Among other things, children, like goods and services, are subject to diminishing marginal utilities, particularly when each newborn child implies a reduction in the plane of living of each existing child. These propositions support the view that an economy experiencing equal rates of growth of population and income can be regarded as enjoying economic development. On the other hand many dissatisfactions attend added numbers. Unfortunately for overcrowded regions, the pleasures associated with larger families are immediate, personal, and more controllable than the diffused general dissatisfaction associated with larger numbers. If one limits the size of his own family he may greatly reduce his own satisfactions while contributing hardly at all to an alleviation of the over-all problem of crowding. This is a notorious case of a clash between private and social interests.

In sum, these arguments suggest the difficulties of judging population growth in the abstract. In some instances an increase in population serves various economic and noneconomic ends and brings added gratification; in others the converse is true. Undoubtedly the reported changes in per capita income can misrepresent the underlying changes in welfare by a considerable margin.

In Mexico's case the per capita figures probably understate the satisfactions derived from economic development because of the greatly reduced morbidity and mortality as well as the relatively low over-all population density (18 per square kilometer in 1960).[24] Yet the country's high rate of population growth has probably prevented her from maximizing her rate of increase in per capita income because of the effects upon capital formation, labor productivity, income distribution, and the efficiency of land use. Among other things rural Mexico is so overcrowded that the average-size farm is too small to permit the use of more modern mechanical techniques,[25] and nearly one-half of Mexico's population is to be found in the low production age groups of under fifteen or over sixty-five.[26]

During her period of economic advancement, Mexico has ex-

[24] Dirección General de Estadística, *Compendio estadístico, 1960*, p. 12, t. 6.

[25] Michael H. Belshaw, "Aspects of Community Development in Rural Mexico," *Inter-American Economic Affairs*, 15 (Spring, 1962), 79. Also see John M. Ball, "Some Comments on Mexico's Population," *Journal of Geography*, 61 (October, 1962), esp. 299–300.

[26] Robert C. Cook, ed., "Mexico, The Problem of People," *Population Bulletin*, 20 (November, 1964), 178.

perienced a relatively high rate of population growth. From 1922 to 1940 Mexico's population grew at annual rates approximating 1.75 per cent. During the years 1939–1946 the average annual increase in population climbed to 2.25 per cent and from 1947 through 1953, to 2.8 per cent. Beginning in 1954 it reached persistently above, in some years well above, 3 per cent. The annual rate of increase averaged 2.7 per cent during the forties and 3 per cent during the fifties. The latter rate allegedly represents the "biological ceiling," and it implies a doubling of the population in twenty-four years. Given the more recent rates of increase in excess of 3 per cent, Mexico's population of nearly 26,000,000 in 1950 could well be converted to 50,000,000 by 1970. If so, the population would have tripled in the four decades beginning in 1930. For the census years since 1930 Mexico's population has been as follows: [27]

Year	Population (millions)
1930	16.6
1940	19.7
1950	25.8
1960	34.9

It should be noted that these changes involve merely natural rates of increase. Not only does the Mexican government restrict immigration, but the prevailing conditions in the labor markets have probably led to wage rates that have been too low to attract immigrants. [28]

The explanation of this population growth is consistent with the generalizations regarding demographic changes in the developing communities (see Table 7). Mexico's crude birth rate remained well above 40 from the year 1930 onward. Since a rate of more than 40 per 1,000 is among the world's highest and approaches maximum human fertility, the birth rate seemingly could not have responded much to the ensuing economic development, and hence it was hardly responsible for the rise in population which occurred in the following years. One must, however, express some suspicion

[27] *Ibid.*, p. 41 in the 1958 edition and p. 12 in the 1960 edition.
[28] Banco Nacional De México, *Review of the Economic Situation of Mexico*, 37 (November, 1961), 4.

TABLE 7. Selected Population Series, 1922–1960*

| | | (rates per thousand) | | |
Year	Births	Deaths	Natural Increase	Infant Mortality[a]
1922	31.3	25.2	6.1	222.9
1923	32.0	24.4	7.6	222.4
1924	30.7	25.6	5.1	232.2
1925	33.3	26.6	6.7	215.9
1926	31.2	24.8	6.4	209.4
1927	30.5	23.9	6.6	193.0
1928	32.2	25.2	7.0	193.4
1929	38.9	26.8	12.1	167.6
1930	49.4	26.6	22.8	131.6
1931	43.7	25.9	17.8	137.7
1932	43.3	26.0	17.3	137.5
1933	42.2	25.7	16.5	139.3
1934	44.3	23.8	20.5	130.3
1935	42.2	22.6	19.6	125.7
1936	42.9	23.5	19.4	130.8
1937	44.1	24.3	19.8	130.8
1938	43.5	22.9	20.6	128.0
1939	44.5	23.0	21.5	122.6
1940	44.2	23.2	21.0	125.7
1941	43.2	21.9	21.3	123.0
1942	45.0	22.6	22.4	118.2
1943	44.9	22.1	22.9	117.2
1944	43.5	20.3	23.2	113.5
1945	44.2	19.2	25.0	107.9
1946	42.8	19.1	23.7	110.6
1947	45.3	16.3	29.0	96.4
1948	44.5	16.2	27.9	101.7
1949	44.6	17.6	27.0	106.4
1950	45.5	16.2	29.3	96.2
1951	44.5	17.2	27.3	98.8
1952	43.6	14.9	28.7	89.8
1953	44.7	15.3	28.9	95.2
1954	46.1	13.0	33.1	80.5
1955	46.0	13.6	32.4	83.3
1956	46.3 (46.8)	12.0 (12.1)	34.3 (34.7)	71.0
1957	46.8 (47.3)	13.1 (13.2)	33.7 (34.1)	80.1
1958	44.3 (44.8)	12.4 (12.5)	31.9 (32.2)	80.1
1959	... (47.7)	... (11.9)	... (35.8)	74.4
1960	... (44.5)	... (11.6)	... (33.9)	75.5

* Sources: The 1922–1958 data are from Xavier de la Riva Rodríguez, "Salubridad y asistencia médico-social," *Mexico: Cincuenta años de revolución, II, La vida social*, p. 433, t. 8. The 1956–1960 figures, in parentheses, are from Dirección General de Estadística, *Compendio estadístico, 1960*, p. 18, t. 13.

a Column 4 indicates infant mortality per thousand live births, ambiguous though the concept may be.

regarding the increase reported around 1930. When birth rates rise from 32.2 to 38.9 and then to 49.4 within three years, one can only impute some of the fertility to the productive powers of the statistician. Further, the available data indicate that the birth rate has been neither completely exogenous nor constant during the course of Mexico's economic development. It did rise to some extent from the 1920's to the 1930's, and for four successive years during the 1950's (1954–1957) it attained or surpassed the value of 46 per 1,000. This increase could well have been associated with the expansion of the social services,[29] while the mild decline of 1958 would be consistent with the recession which the United States exported to Mexico in 1957. Mexico's experience thus supports the view that stagnant societies typically do not attain their fertility potential, but in fact tend to pursue various customs which prevent the attainment of the maximum.[30] Once economic development provides the incentive, people may relax these practices and realize somewhat higher birth rates.[31]

Mexico's population increase, then, has resulted largely but not exclusively from declines in her crude death rates. The country has not experienced these declines in sharp and exogenous fashion, as has been the case in so many of the underdeveloped areas. Rather her falling death rates have come gradually and have in considerable part been associated with the improvements in health and safety that tend to accompany economic development. Over a period of almost twenty-five years beginning in 1934, the death rate was halved to about 12.5 per 1,000, which is of course extremely close to the rate enjoyed by the economically advanced communities.

It is relatively easy to identify the major sources of Mexico's long-term population increases. As might be expected, a significant improvement has occurred in infant mortality, which has

[29] A Mexican social worker has expressed this view.

[30] See Kingsley Davis, "Institutional Patterns Favoring High Fertility in Underdeveloped Areas," *Eugenics Quarterly*, 2 (March, 1955), 33–39.

[31] However, two investigators believe that the observed rise in urban fertility may have actually resulted from a decline in infant mortality. But they do not foresee a fall in urban fertility. See Warren C. Robinson and Elizabeth H. Robinson, "Rural-Urban Fertility Differentials in Mexico," *American Sociological Review*, 25 (February, 1960), 81.

been steadily reduced to one-third its former rate while the over-all death rate was cut in half. Deaths from smallpox declined from 72.7 and 104.9 per 100,000 inhabitants in 1925 and 1930, respectively, to 53.0 in 1934 and 6.8 in 1940, with no deaths reported after April 1951. In 1943 the government initiated plans for vaccinating the whole country against this disease. This was also the year in which DDT was first used as a disinfectant against typhoid and in which penicillin was employed in the treatment of syphilis. The death rate from typhoid decreased from 7 per 100,000 in 1943 to 0.60 per 100,000 in 1958, while the syphilis death rate fell from 16.2 to 2.5. Malaria has long been one of the very big killers. As late as 1942 the death rate from this disease was 128.6 per 100,000; by 1953 it had dropped to 87.6, and in both years the disease accounted for nearly 6 per cent of all deaths. In 1955–1956 the government instituted a widespread program of spraying and eradication, so that three years later the rate had been pushed down to 9.7 per 100,000. Considerable progress has also been made in reducing the incidence of gastroenteritis. The death rate in this instance fell from 507.3 in 1932 to 196.8 in 1958.[32] Yet by the late fifties it had become Mexico's major killer, followed by influenza and pneumonia, diseases of early infancy, and heart disease.[33] (Mexico City males have apparently made a major contribution to the last of these.) This array still reflects some of the characteristics of a poor country. Further, Mexico seems to have made considerably more headway in disease prevention than in disease cure, another mark of less economic advancement. Given these considerations, the rather low crude death rates of 12 or 13 per 1,000 are undoubtedly explained in part by the exceedingly young age of the population.

For the foreseeable future Mexicans can only expect moderate reductions in both death rates and birth rates. The country is now in the midst of a period of "functionless fertility." Given the influence of Catholicism, the continued inferior status of women, and the remaining high proportion of rural inhabitants (at least 50 per cent in 1960), the birth rates should continue at relatively high

[32] The data regarding specific diseases are from de la Riva Rodríguez, "Salubridad y asistencia médico-social," pp. 400, 401, and 406.
[33] Banco Nacional de México, *Review of the Economic Situation of Mexico*. 37 (July, 1961), 1, t. 12.

levels for several more decades. The wealthier urbanites have begun to think in terms of the quality of their children's upbringing, but this should simply allow a moderate decline in the crude birth rate to offset the expected continued reduction in the crude death rate. Some Mexicans even refuse to admit the theoretical desirability of reducing the rate of population growth; others are prepared to acknowledge that some reduction in the rate of population increase would yield higher per capita incomes. One and all tend to regard the present rate of increase as a parameter for a decade at the very least, and they argue that Mexico must either take advantage of it or adjust to it as best as possible, as the case may be.

Advances in real per capita income. Despite the problems associated with the correction of income changes for increases in population, let us next trace the behavior of per capita income in Mexico. The method pursued is that of subtracting the percentage rate of increase in population from the rate of growth in income for any given year. While this ignores the interaction between the two rates of growth and thereby overstates the rate of increase in per capita income to a limited degree, it is permissible for a period as brief as one year.

The evidence suggests a discontinuous rise in per capita income, beginning in the 1940's. The plane of living could not have expanded secularly very much during the twenties or thirties, for the advances in population then almost matched those in aggregate income.[34] Much was of course achieved during these decades in terms of the recovery from the Revolution and Depression, advances in aggregate output, and preparation for the spurt that was to come. These accomplishments support the point made in the previous section—namely, that important economic developments can occur while population and income advance at approximately the same rates. The per capita income series, however, did not exhibit a sharp rise until the beginning of World War II. According to the calculations in Table 8, per capita income grew at an average annual rate of 3.9 per cent during the forties, 3 per cent during the fifties, and 3.3 per cent during the first half of the sixties. For the period 1958 through 1963, the average annual per

[34] See tables 3 and 7 in the present chapter.

TABLE 8. Percentage Increases in Per Capita GNP, 1940–1960*

Year	(1) $\frac{\Delta GNP}{GNP}$	(2) $\frac{\Delta P}{P}$	(3) $\frac{\Delta Y_P}{Y_P}$ (Col. [1] − Col. [2])
1940	1.05	2.10	−1.05
1941	12.39	2.13	10.26
1942	13.24	2.24	11.00
1943	3.73	2.29	1.44
1944	8.52	2.32	6.20
1945	7.64	2.50	5.14
1946	6.64	2.37	4.27
1947	1.44	2.90	−1.46
1948	4.53	2.79	1.74
1949	4.28	2.70	1.58
1950	7.84	2.93	4.91
1951	7.50	2.73	4.77
1952	4.00	2.87	1.13
1953	0.56	2.89	−2.33
1954	10.46	3.31	7.15
1955	8.68	3.24	5.44
1956	6.29	3.45	2.84
1957	7.71	3.39	4.32
1958	5.53	3.21	2.32
1959	2.93	3.58	−0.65
1960	7.87	3.39	4.48
1961	3.48	3.14	0.34
1962	4.80	3.16	1.64
1963	6.29	3.20	3.09
1964	10.04	3.18	6.86

* The rates of growth in GNP are taken from Table 3, while the rates of increase in population from 1940 through 1960 are from Table 7. The population data for 1961–1964 are derived from the United Nations Department of Economic and Social Affairs, *The Demographic Yearbook, 1964*, p. 123, t. 4. The United Nations staff warns that these population estimates are of questionable validity.

capita income growth declined sharply to 1.9 per cent. The deceleration evidenced in the aggregate income series thus appears even more strikingly in this series, and it caused grave concern in Mexico in the early sixties. Over the entire period 1940–1964 per capita income advanced at a rate of 3.4 per cent per year. This rate of advance implies that per capita income in the last year, 1964, was approximately 2.2 times as high as in 1940.

A division of the 1960 Gross National Product in current prices by the population of that year yields a per capita annual income of 3,840 pesos, or 307 U.S. dollars insofar as a conversion through the exchange rate of 12.50 to one can be trusted. This in turn implies a 1940 per capita figure approximating $160 per year in 1960 prices. These incomes are obviously low by the standards of the economically advanced countries; in 1960 Mexico was still a poor country. An estimated 20 per cent of the Mexican families lived in urban slums, 70 per cent occupied one-room dwellings, and 40 per cent dwelled on farms of twelve acres or less.[35] Yet even the 1940 per capita income was high relative to the truly underdeveloped world, while the 1960 level suggests considerable economic development. Though perhaps painting too rosy a picture and underplaying the tremendous economic differences among Mexicans, particularly in the urban areas, Oscar Lewis has touched on the human aspects of this advance.[36] For many rural Mexicans, growth has meant beds instead of the ground, bread as well as tortillas, travel by bus as well as by burro, and doctors instead of *curanderos*. It is difficult to generalize about the urbanites because of the great differences among them. The low income group has acquainted itself with beer, radios, and tableware; while the middle class has been exposed to such luxuries as gas stoves, electric blenders, whiskey, nylons, television, and automobiles (which they tend to drive in Mexico City in truly frantic and frenzied fashion).

A diversified economic growth. Mexico has been able to approach the cherished objective of most of the developing countries, that of experiencing a reasonably diversified development. In the words of F. Benham and H. A. Holley:

[35] Frank A. Brandenburg, "A Contribution to the Theory of Entrepreneurship and Economic Development: The Case of Mexico," *Inter-American Economic Affairs*, 16 (Winter, 1962), 8.

[36] Oscar Lewis, "Mexico Since Cárdenas," *Social Research*, 26 (Spring, 1959), 20.

Mexico has recorded perhaps the best all-round economic progress in Latin America during the past twenty years. It is nearly self-sufficient in both fuels and foodstuffs; it has developed basic as well as consumers-goods industries; it has a diversified export trade and a large invisible income and has attracted a substantial volume of foreign capital.[37]

Table 9 summarizes both the structural changes and the over-all improvements in labor productivity that occurred in Mexico over three decades. Since the internal net product expanded nearly 5.7 times in 27 years while the work force increased almost 2.4 times in 31 years, this implies an improvement in productivity of about 2½, or perhaps slightly in excess of the rate of increase in the work force. On the other hand, the productivity rise did not match the increase in per capita income. This follows from the general proposition that national income can equal either the population multiplied by per capita income or the number of workers multiplied by the average labor productivity. Mexico's population in 1960 was about 2.1, not 2.4, times the 1930 figure. Since the rate of growth in population failed to match the rate of rise in the labor force, the increase in per capita income per year evidently exceeded the annual advance in productivity per worker. This conclusion regarding the relative rates of change of per capita income and productivity holds also for the United States as long as the productivity measure is in terms of productivity per man-year. However, given the more conventional approach, that of utilizing man-hours and productivity per man-hour, the opposite result appears for the United States; the rate of improvement in productivity per man-hour has exceeded the rate of increase in per capita income. This of course reflects the United States preference for leisure, which has more than compensated for the increased participation in the labor force. In Mexico hours per worker could not have altered a great deal from 1930 to 1960; certainly they tended to remain constant during the fifties. The increased participation in the labor force has apparently continued to be dominant relative to changes in working hours. Hence the increase in per

[37] F. Benham and H. A. Holley, *A Short Introduction to the Economy of Latin America*, p. 135. See also David H. Shelton, "Mexico's Economic Growth: Success of Diversified Development," *Southwestern Social Science Quarterly*, 41 (December, 1960), 304–319.

capita income has tended to exceed the increase in productivity even when the latter is measured in man-hours.

Table 9 also contains information concerning sectoral changes in productivity. Agricultural productivity, as measured by its percentage of the national output divided by its percentage of the total work force, has remained relatively low; nevertheless, a smaller proportion of the work force produced the same proportion of national income that it had contributed in 1934. The commerce data relate the opposite story, that of a continued highly valued product in 1961 but with the same fraction of the total income produced by a proportionately higher work force. The relative declines in minerals and petroleum are both notable. The figures for manufacturing indicate a good performance: a strong relative rise on the product side accompanied by a slight relative increase in the percentage of work force.

Data on average rates of increase in output for different sectors during recent selected years further corroborate these findings

TABLE 9. Sectoral Changes in the Mexican Economy, 1930 or 1934 to 1961*

Activity	Internal Net Product (millions of pesos in 1961 prices)				Work Force (thousands)			
	1934		1961		1930		1961	
	Value	%	Value	%	Value	%	Value	%
TOTAL	22,417	100	126,648	100	5,166	100	12,226	100
Agriculture, livestock, forestry, and fisheries	4,439	20	25,710	20	3,626	70	6,520	53
Minerals	2,847	13	2,660	2	49⎱	1	70⎱	1
Petroleum	762	3	6,332	5	7⎰		50⎰	
Manufactures	3,071	14	32,422	26	570	11	1,541	13
Commerce	4,954	22	26,343	21	274	5	1,124	9
Transportation and communication	941	4	6,459	5	107	2	437	4
Services and other activities (including construction and electric energy)	5,403	24	26,722	21	533	11	2,484	20

* Source: Nacional Financiera, *El Mercado de Valores*, 23 (February 11, 1963), 73.

(see Table 10). Most of the sectors show somewhat higher rates of growth than the average, while agriculture and government are each somewhat below average and mineral production is considerably below. From 1945 to 1955 total manufacturing output increased 79 per cent. Within this category nondurable consumption goods expanded 57 per cent in the aggregate and only 21 per cent in per capita terms, with most of the latter rise concentrated in the years 1950 and 1951. Capital goods and consumer durables, on the other hand, rose 156 per cent. This group included rolled steel products, cement, and engineering equipment, which rose 170 per cent, 158 per cent, and 149 per cent respectively. Chemicals apparently expanded 1,287 per cent.[38] The output of capital goods rose by 130 per cent from 1950 to 1957, while consumption goods, which proved especially vulnerable during 1952–1953 and 1956–1957, rose merely 27 per cent. By 1957 steel output exceeded one million tons for the first time, and relatively strong advances had occurred in cement, glass, heavy chemicals such as sulphuric acid and caustic soda, machinery tools, electrical equipment, transportation equipment, and a wide variety of consumer durable goods including refrigerators, motor vehicle parts, and plastic gadgets. In short, industry had turned away from the pre-1939 concentration on food processing and textiles and had become considerably more diversified. In part this important change could be attributed to excess capacity in the more established industries, in part to the fact that capital goods had previously been imported and now offered greater scope for expansion.[39]

Since World War II did not serve as a major stimulant to agriculture, this sector becomes of particular interest during the period following 1945. Prior to the war agricultural production advanced barely 1.5 per cent per year;[40] from 1946 to 1956 the agricultural

[38] The data which have thus far appeared in this paragraph are from UNESCO, *External Disequilibrium in the Economic Development of Latin America: The Case of Mexico*, p. 47, t. I-15; p. 48; and p. 51, t. I-16. The figures have been rounded.

[39] The remainder of the paragraph is from Benham and Holley, *A Short Introduction to the Economy of Latin America*, pp. 128–129; and Antonio Carillo Flores, "Mexico Forges Ahead," *Foreign Affairs*, 36 (April, 1958), 494–495.

[40] Víctor L. Urquidi, "Problemas fundamentales de la economía mexicana," *Cuadernos Americanos*, 114 (January–February, 1961), 101, t. 6.

TABLE 10. Percentage Rates of Increase in Sector Output, 1940–1958*

Years	Agriculture	Minerals	Petroleum	Energy	Manufactures	Construction	Commerce	Transportation	Government	Others	Total
1940–1958	5.9	0.8	6.3	6.9	7.0	7.9	6.5	6.5	5.6	6.2	6.2
1942–1946	1.9	—3.2	3.9	5.2	8.4	15.0	7.8	9.1	5.5	6.1	6.1
1947–1950	9.4	5.2	8.1	7.0	5.9	2.5	4.0	7.0	8.3	6.0	6.0
1952–1958	7.1	2.5	8.0	9.5	4.5	3.8	4.5	6.8	4.7	5.1	5.1
1956–1958	4.9	0.9	11.3	9.5	5.5	10.5	4.0	5.1	5.5	4.9	4.9

* Urquidi, "La Inflación en México," p. 3, t. 2. The rates of increase have been computed from data for output in 1950 prices.

sector grew at a rate of 6.8 per cent.[41] The following index numbers of the volume of production, based on the year 1940, show a
steady and rapid expansion of all primary activities from 1945 to
1959, with agriculture as such performing especially well during
the 1945–1955 period.[42]

Year	Primary Activities	Agriculture	Livestock
1945	120	132	77
1950	180	206	81
1955	240	305	105
1959	301	336	131

Despite this rather impressive record, Mexican economists have
discerned several weaknesses in agriculture's performance. One
has been the usual declining rate of increase. The index numbers
just reviewed yield increases of 56 per cent and 48 per cent respectively in the periods 1945–1950 and 1950–1955. According to
another source, agricultural production expanded 58 per cent from
1945 to 1950, compared to 38 per cent in the next five-year period.[43]
In more recent years the declining growth has been more marked.
Secondly, as will be noted on many occasions in this book, the development and the attending income distribution were highly
uneven. This becomes evident, for example, when agricultural
output is divided into export crops (particularly cotton and coffee)
and those used for home consumption. The indices, again based on
the year 1940, are then as follows:[44]

Year	Exports	Domestic Sales
1945	143	131
1950	613	169
1955	1164	227
1959	1323	246

[41] United Nations Economic Commission on Latin America, *Human Resources of Central America, Panama and Mexico, 1950–1980, in Relation to
Some Aspects of Economic Development*, p. 82, t. 77.

[42] Urquidi, "Problemas fundamentales," p. 77.

[43] UNESCO, *External Disequilibrium*, p. 36, t. I-10.

[44] *Ibid.*

The astronomical growth reported for the export crops may in large part be the result of relatively low production in 1940, for once 1950 becomes the base year the differences are no longer as striking. This is shown by the following array:[45]

	1956	1960
General index	150.0	171.8
Cotton	163.7	177.2
Coffee	106.8	114.2
All foods	140.7	165.0
Corn	140.3	176.2
Beans	172.8	231.7

Generally, the data reveal both the modest rise in the per capita consumption of food and the very considerable contribution of Mexican farm products to the country's exports. From 1945 to 1955 the expansion in the volume of exports assumed the following forms:[46]

	Total	Primary Products	Mineral	Manufacturers
Percentage increases for decade	111.7	307.5	46.3	−10.3
Percentage increases per annum	7.8	15.1	3.9	−1.1

Students of Mexico's agricultural advances have sought to analyze the sources of the increases in agricultural output. Aubrey has concerned himself with the 1939–1952 period, when agricultural production nearly doubled. He sees an extension of the area under cultivation as accounting for 44 per cent of the increase. This expansion resulted largely from the migrations to new lands which the irrigation programs made available. During this period the number of hectares under irrigation increased from 240,000 to 1,570,000. Second in significance was the influence of structural

[45] Nacional Financiera, *Informe anual, 1960*, p. 133, t. 2.
[46] UNESCO, *External Disequilibrium*, p. 16, t. I-3.

TABLE 11. Rate of Change per Decade for Selected Countries
1925–1929 to 1950–1954*

Country	Population	GDP$_N$	GDP$_{Total}$
Argentina	21.9	4.4	27.3
Brazil	24.4	15.8	44.2
Chile	17.6	15.5	35.7
Colombia	23.5	22.6	51.4
Mexico	24.7	43.2	78.4
Other Latin-American countries	16.7	28.7	49.9

* Simon Kuznets, *Six Lectures on Economic Growth*, p. 23, t. 2. GDP$_N$ represents Per Capita Gross Domestic Product.

changes—that is, shifts to crops offering higher yields. This accounted for some 33 per cent of the rise in production. (It is presumably estimated as a residual.) Of least importance, approximating 23 per cent, was the increase in yield.[47] Here the results were often very disappointing. In the areas of fertilizers, seeds, insecticides, and the like, Mexican agriculture in many instances had still experienced little progress. Fortunately, an analysis of the years from 1945 to 1955 yields more encouraging results. During this period unit yields increased by 37.5 per cent, while the area harvested expanded by 29.6 per cent, and structural changes advanced production by 22 per cent.[48] Richard Parks reports total agricultural crop production as having increased at an average rate of 7.05 per cent a year over the period 1940–1944 to 1955–1959. During that time the weighted index of labor and land expanded at an annual rate of 2.90 per cent while the residual—the improvement in the productivity of these factors, attributable to improved techniques, capital formation, and so on—rose by 4.15 per cent a year.[49] The sources thus agree in imputing roughly 40 per cent of the increase in production to an extension in the area harvested and the remaining 60 per cent to improvements of various sorts.

[47] Aubrey, "Structure and Balance in Rapid Economic Growth," pp. 527–529.
[48] UNESCO, *External Disequilibrium*, p. 38, t. I-11.
[49] Richard W. Parks, "The Role of Agriculture in Mexican Economic Development," *Inter-American Economic Affairs*, 18 (Summer, 1964), 14–15.

A comparative note. In reviewing Mexico's growth record we have occasionally noted the nation's good relative showing. For a final summary we can glance at Table 11, which indicates how Mexico fared compared to other Latin-American countries, largely during the thirties and forties. Aside from Argentina, the other nations themselves experienced rather impressive rates of economic growth relative to the growth records of the past. Yet Mexico shines in their company. During more recent years, 1950–1965, Mexico's total product continued to grow at a more rapid pace than any major Latin-American country other than Venezuela.[50]

[50] Committee for Economic Development, *How Low Income Countries Can Advance Their Own Growth*, pp. 68–69, t. 2.

CHAPTER THREE

The Influence of the Revolution: I

Introductory remarks. What forces serve to account for Mexico's relatively satisfactory growth rate? A few general observations can serve as a point of departure in considering this question.

Since economic development is so complex and data regarding the earlier phases of economic advancement are so difficult to procure, the number of growth theories may at times appear to approach the number of growth theorists. The aggregative and proximate "causes" of economic development seem clear enough, however. Students of development agree that an improved technology and/or fixed capital formation enhance productivity and that these constitute the dynamic factors of economic change. The previous chapter presented data regarding these variables. Investment in human capital is receiving increasing attention. While many textbooks in development fail to give sufficient attention to demand and markets, the literature on the developing economies nevertheless contains many contributions regarding these matters —beginning with Smith and Malthus and continuing with economists who stress external economies, the need for a big push, and the importance of leading growth sectors. Students of economic development further dwell upon the relationships among the various sectors of economic activity, but it is at this point that serious difficulties begin to arise. Virtually all seem to agree upon the desirability of long term balanced growth, however that may be defined. Some, however, would rather dwell upon the need for short term imbalance, brought about perhaps by assistance to the sector with the weakest demand. Economists tend further to offer investment criteria in the forms of social marginal products, rates of return over cost, and benefit-cost ratios, only to find themselves unable to plug in much of the necessary data. Little is more discouraging in development economics than the inability to measure the several indirect and intangible consequences of particular acts of investment. One need only consider, for example, the obstacle of not being able to ascertain the sociological effects of small industry upon the hinterland; similarly, the desired degree of diversification, or industrialization, and the secular composition of foreign trade are not always self-evident, and they give rise to serious controversies. Since the populace must aspire to change if the so-called dynamic variables are to perform favorably, observers further agree on the significance of values for development—but not on the means of altering them. Some cultures evidently make for wealth and others make for poverty, but any number of traits could be emphasized in support of this point.

It is when one delves into the institutional arrangements that affect technological change, investment demand, and "balanced growth" that disagreements and diverse opinions come particularly to the fore. Arguments become most personal at this point, although the scientific ideal still shines through and it is hoped that hypotheses are still subject to whatever evidence can be brought to bear on a particular position. This writer intends to focus upon the following institutional factors because of their growth-inducing effects upon the populace: contacts with foreign cultures, occurring for the most part on a nonexploitative basis; a government that is stable and committed to economic change; and the "right" degree of equality or inequality in the social-economic-political structure. These forces have in common the property of playing upon the wills of people, of motivating them to behave in a growth-promoting fashion, and of helping to make economic change a mass phenomenon. These several factors of course possess important time dimensions. While foreign contacts are generally conducive to change and while governments must always continue to provide both stability and an impetus to growth, these matters are particularly difficult and urgent in the earlier phases of change. Similarly, the appropriate degree of inequality, or equality, certainly tends to alter as economic development takes place.

Many observers would agree that institutional rigidities, particularly those associated with power structures, tend to assume strategic importance among the obstacles to development. A highly publicized case in point in the postwar development literature has of course been the rule of colonial areas by the metropolitan powers. This has become a classic instance of a temporary initial advance that is hamstrung by powerful interests opposed to the further changes (industrial growth, circulation of the elite, diffusion of technological change) necessary for sustained development. Much has also been written about the necessities of land reform, the reduction of the power and wealth of the landed aristocracy, and the elimination of rule by an oligarchy. In a few instances in history, the case of the British being the most noteworthy, the landed aristocracy seems to have behaved with some flexibility and has voluntarily surrendered some power and status. Much more frequently, those in possession of power have managed to remain supreme—with minor economic development or stagnation as a consequence—until a revolution has dispossessed them. These resistances to change must be significant in at least the short run, no matter what the outcome. That is, as long as the defenders of the status quo are successful, their decisions tend to forestall economic change; and yet the very process of removing this blockage tends to delay economic development, since the revolutionary period may well be one of economic retrogression. These, in any event, were Mexico's experiences.

Mexico's pre-Revolutionary social structure. In several respects pre-1910 Mexico needed to move toward a more democratic system if she were to advance economically. The power of those who traditionally dominate a stagnant, essentially rural society, such as the landlords, the church, and the military, had to be reduced, while those with a high potential for economic production, particularly the farmer, the middle-aged entrepreneur, and the urban wage earner, were to be encouraged. Further, though the categories overlap, the position of the Indian relative to that of the Caucasian and of the domestic entrepreneur relative to his foreign counterpart each required strengthening. Social and vertical mobility and greater equality of opportunity had to replace fixed social relationships and the rule of status. That is, adjustments had to occur in many of the imponderables and intangibles—in matters of power, privilege, prestige, and status.

The major case in point involved agriculture.[1] From early colonial times (from 1521, the year of the Spanish conquest of Mexico) two basic forms of land tenure had existed in Mexico: the free semicommunal Indian village and the large estate, or hacienda.[2] In the former, ownership of the land was vested in the village, which allocated some portion to buildings, another to the *ejido* (or pasture and forest land), and the remainder to its residents in the form of small family plots. Because of their low plane of living, the Indians of the village frequently attached themselves to the haciendas, performing various types of work on the estates and generally receiving land to till in return. After Independence in 1821, and particularly during the years dominated by Díaz, 1876–1910, the *hacendados* took advantage of the lapse of the colonial protective legislation and enlarged their properties by expropriating the lands of the villagers. The census of 1910 showed fewer than 11,000 *hacendados* controlling some 57 per cent of the national territory[3] and of this number 834 held 1,300,000 square kilometers.[4] One of them possessed properties equal in size to all of Costa Rica. At the other end of the scale, some fifteen million persons were landless, since the landholding village had virtually disappeared.

The system evidently tended to make for stagnation. It was dominated by absentee landlords interested primarily in security and the relatively stable returns emanating from the tilling of their lands and from the involved system of renting and subrenting of the time. They were little motivated to introduce labor-improving or land-improving innovations; for example, most *hacendados* refused to utilize the services of the agronomists graduated from the National School of Agriculture. The prices of food-

[1] For a survey of agriculture prior to 1910 see Nathan L. Whetten, *Rural Mexico*, chapters 4 and 5 and the bibliography on p. 75, n. 1.

[2] There was also a third form, the rancho or small private holding, but it was relatively unimportant. Less than 3 per cent of the population owned any land at all.

[3] Arturo González Cosío, "Clases y estratos sociales," *México: Cincuenta años de revolución, II, La vida social*, p 47.

[4] Oscar René Cruz, "Estudio comparativo de los principales planes revolucionarios de México," *Revista de Economía*, 23 (June, 1960), 175–176.

stuffs rose some 300 per cent from 1810 to 1910 while money wages remained stationary,[5] but this did not lead to significant increments in capital. After 1890 Mexico actually imported several basic foodstuffs. The system generally discouraged such practices as crop rotation, the application of fertilizers, and forest conservation, thereby leaving as part of its heritage an eroded soil and a declining fertility. It also left in its wake an illiterate, poorly productive work force, constantly in debt to the plantation, with no capital to speak of, and with no motive or opportunity to experiment. The villages that survived similarly stagnated at low levels of productivity and generally remained isolated.

The life of the peon reflected these several aspects of the hacienda system. He was paid in corn, pulque, the right to live rent-free on property, and petty cash. Most of his payments were in credit at the local plantation store, the *tienda de raya*. He was perpetually in debt. The debt could be his or his father's, or it might be even older. His labor was unfree. He or his wife was forced to perform chores on the land, for the livestock, and within the *hacendado*'s household. His working hours were from dawn to dusk. He could be flogged for requesting an auditing of his account at the store, failing to meet quotas, and not kissing his master's hand. He was subject to so much corporal punishment that an adult's finger could frequently be placed in one of his scars. If, in the eyes of his overlord, he became disrespectful, the punishment accorded him could be limited primarily by the sadistic imagination of his master. In the state of Hidalgo peons were once buried up to their necks and horses made to gallop over them.[6]

The industrial worker was not much more successful in controlling his lot. To some extent, as in the cases of the railroad workers and weavers, he was able to participate in labor organizations, and on occasion he engaged in typically abortive strikes. For the most part, however, the public authorities and private employers refused to tolerate labor unions; the Penal Code of 1872, for example, condemned labor associations and strikes. Workers thus had little means for striving for higher wages and improved

[5] This is the estimate of the noted historian, Jesús Silva Herzog. It is reported in Ernest Gruening, *Mexico and Its Heritage*, p. 136.

[6] *Ibid.*, pp. 129 and 138.

conditions.[7] Interestingly, their bargaining power was weak despite a shortage of unskilled as well as skilled labor in industry. Given the hacienda system, there was little push from agriculture to add to the urban labor force. The producers of textiles and other manufactured commodities reacted by employing women and/or impressing people from the streets when they could not prove their reasons for not working. Failing in these, they recruited from the countryside.[8] According to Raymond Vernon the resulting increase in the flow of labor from the countryside possessed political significance, for it created strains on the hacienda and diminished the degree of loyalty and allegiance of the *hacendados* to the Díaz regime.[9]

Modifications were also required in the foreign ownership of Mexican assets, but these are more difficult to assess. Foreign capital contributed considerably to the early developments in mining, petroleum, banking, commerce, railways, hydroelectric power, textiles, chicle, and coffee; the only important export goods dominated by Mexican interests were henequen, cane sugar, hides, and cattle. North Americans held 64 per cent of the railways, 75 per cent of the minerals, and 58 per cent of the petroleum.[10] Of the total fixed gross investment in the fiscal year 1902–1903, 5 per cent was reportedly public, 50 per cent private domestic, and 45 per cent private foreign.[11] An estimated 42 per cent of the national wealth was controlled by foreigners in 1910. Little wonder that the Mexican people have referred to their country as "the mother of foreigners and the stepmother of Mexicans."

While the influence of foreign investment upon the advancement of the poor countries remains one of the moot questions in economic development, much of the literature emphasizes its

[7] For terse accounts of the pre-1910 Mexican labor movement see Guadalupe Rivera Marín, "El movimiento obrero," *México: Cincuenta años de revolución, II*, pp. 253–257; and Moisés Poblete Troncoso and Ben G. Burnett, *The Rise of the Latin American Labor Movement*, pp. 97–98.

[8] Wilbert E. Moore, *Industrialization and Labor*, p. 280.

[9] Raymond Vernon, *The Dilemma of Mexico's Development*, p. 52.

[10] González Cosío, "Clases y estratos sociales," p. 48.

[11] Alfredo Navarrete Romero, "El financiamiento del desarrollo económico," *México: Cincuenta años de revolución, I, La economía*, p. 516, t. 3.

adverse effects.[12] The extent, composition, and general nature of foreign investment in Mexico before 1910 may be cited in support of the negative view. Foreign investors did not concern themselves with an allocation of resources that would stimulate Mexican development, particularly in the case of industry. Of the total value of foreign investment in Mexico in 1911, 15 per cent was indirect (generally public debt) and 85 per cent, direct. Direct investment, in turn, was distributed among the several major categories as follows:[13]

Activity	Per Cent of Direct Investment
Transport	39
Minerals	28
Petroleum	4
Commercial (including banks)	10
Public services (telephones, telegraphs, electric energy)	8
Agriculture and livestock	7
Industry	4

Perhaps more seriously, these investments often did not foster the development of a skilled Mexican labor force, to say nothing of the appearance of indigenous entrepreneurship and managerial ability. Generalizations regarding human investment tend to be exceedingly difficult because of the differences among the various sectors. Mexican workers remained virtual serfs and an exploited proletariat in foreign-owned agricultural and mining firms;[14] but foreign companies in utilities, merchandising, and manufacturing frequently trained their employees and paid them higher wages.[15] Then, too, remittances and the servicing of the foreign debt apparently placed constraints upon Mexico's development by affecting her capacity to import. As late as 1940 direct investment serv-

[12] Perhaps the most celebrated case in point is Hans W. Singer, "The Distribution of Gains Between Investing and Borrowing Countries," *American Economic Review: Papers and Proceedings*, 40 (May, 1950), 473–485.

[13] Navarrete R., "El financiamiento del desarrollo económico," p. 513, t. 1.

[14] René Cruz, "Estudio comparativo," pp. 176–178.

[15] George Wythe, *Industry in Latin America*, 2nd ed., pp. 288 and 293.

ice totaled twice the value of Mexico's favorable trade balance in merchandise.[16]

Considerations such as these have led many Mexicans to express adverse judgments concerning foreign investment. According to one moderate appraisal: "Before the Revolution foreign investment was the principal source of capital, but it encouraged production primarily for export and touched only isolated sectors of the economy."[17] Another Mexican economist has concluded that foreign investments contributed to the development of the industrial countries and thereby accentuated the economic inequalities and differences among countries.[18] Undoubtedly, considerable truth lies in this view. Let us also recognize that irrespective of its degree of validity this orientation can lead to tensions that adversely affect a country's capacity to develop.

By turning next to the *científicos* we can focus upon another aspect of Mexico's pre-1910 society greatly in need of reform. These were men who gave extensive counsel and support to Díaz.[19] They constituted a rather unusual combination of aristocratic arrogance, middle-class aggressiveness, and intellectual detachment. Typically they were from well-to-do families and had received superior educations. As they developed their views they came to identify themselves with the positivism of Comte, the liberalism of the Manchester School, and the Social Darwinism of Spencer; the term *científicos* was then applied to others who shared their position. Some *científicos* rose to important positions with the government, such as the ministries of Finance, Interior, and Education, while others were private entrepreneurs who fared well under the Díaz dictatorship.

The *científicos* saw the middle class as the appropriate agency

[16] Combined Mexican Working Party, *The Economic Development of Mexico*, p. 348, t. 122.

[17] Antonio Carillo Flores, "Mexico Forges Ahead," *Foreign Affairs*, 36 (April, 1958), 497.

[18] José Domingo Lavin, *Inversiones extranjeras*, p. 226.

[19] For the observations regarding the *científicos* I have drawn from a personal interview and from the following sources: Howard F. Cline, *The United States and Mexico*, pp. 51–55; Gruening, *Mexico and Its Heritage*, pp. 58–63; Henry B. Parkes, *A History of Mexico*, pp. 299–300; Joseph H. L. Schlarman, *Mexico: A Land of Volcanoes*, pp. 389–390; and Robert E. Scott, *Mexican Government in Transition*, pp. 57–58, 78, and 83.

of change and as trustee for the nation. This class supplied the elite who would allocate resources in a rational, scientific fashion and thereby spur the social and economic development of the country. If domestic resources and skills were insufficient for the task, foreign investment was to be encouraged to do the job. By the same token free international trade and private enterprise were each highly desirable as vehicles for economic improvement; but if these yielded unsatisfactory results, tariff protection and governmental intervention were justified. Under Díaz and his *científicos* harbors and telegraph facilities were developed, railway mileage increased from four hundred to fifteen thousand (albeit in unplanned fashion), and many of the leading manufacturing industries in existence as late as 1940 were launched at that time. The last included some 146 cotton mills and 437 tobacco manufacturing plants, as well as facilities for iron, jute, silk, wool, sugar, brewing, meat packing, paper, and soap. Exports expanded fivefold and imports eightfold. Just prior to the Revolution, 4 per cent bonds of the Mexican government sold at 97 per cent and Mexico was able to borrow abroad all she wished.[20]

The *científicos* further advocated a greater degree of intellectual freedom for those in a position to gain from it. In time, they felt. a liberal democracy might be possible but that for the present it was pointless to expect such a system or to squander resources on humanitarian programs. Particularly was this so for the Indians, whom they regarded as biologically inferior and worthy only of serving the Creole oligarchy.[21] Dreams of freedom and equality merely constituted a naïve utopianism. "A rudimentary social organism like that of Mexico, they used to say, could no more absorb freedom than a sponge could absorb beefsteak."[22]

Yet the *científicos* helped introduce a dynamism into Mexico's society which proved beyond their control. The expanding middle class, made up largely of the mestizos (mixed bloods), sought more power and status in the national life. This group had much to resent. Díaz ruled by bribing the politically serviceable and the

20 Gruening, *Mexico and Its Heritage*, p. 62.

21 The Creoles were those of Spanish descent who had been born in the Western Hemisphere.

22 Parkes, *A History of Mexico*, p. 299.

politically dangerous, so that those outside the favored cliques found concessions or privileges difficult to obtain. The government interfered with the press and held many political prisoners. Disorder and violence were frequent. The *Ley Fuga*, designed presumably to protect the citizen against banditry, actually served as the legal pretense for murdering about 10,000 persons during Díaz's regime. The superior status of the foreigner provided yet another major source of antagonism. Eventually the middle class turned these several resentments into a revolution. It is instructive that after 1920 all of the country's presidents had their origins in this group. The Revolution was essentially a middle-class uprising against the old order—in effect, of the same type as the classical French Revolution. This class in turn received support from the lower income groups, who could not manufacture a revolution by themselves but who nevertheless had many serious grievances of their own.

The revolution in agriculture. With discontent so widespread, the liberal leader, Madero, discovered that he had opened the proverbial Pandora's box when, in 1910, he successfully led a movement to dispose of Díaz. He had intended to introduce the mild political reform of assuring presidential succession, but his revolt led to profound changes in the socioeconomic realm. As the Revolution evolved many of its leaders sought a new Mexico free from exploitation, in control of her own destiny, and with the lower income groups integrated into her national life.[23] In part these views were reflected in the new functional theory of property, which appears in the Constitution of 1917 in the relatively famous Article 27. Ownership of private property became conditional, subject to limited use and to changing legal prescriptions as dictated by the public interest. Thus: an owner now has a moral but not a legal claim to compensation for damages; the state cannot alienate subsoil and waters to a private person except by concession and specified limitations of use; commercial stock companies cannot own or hold rural properties; foreigners can acquire ownership in lands and waters or concessions to exploit sub soil min-

[23] Stanley E. Hilton, "Church-State Dispute over Education in Mexico from Carranza to Cárdenas," *The Americas*, 21 (October, 1964), 165.

erals and fuels only if they surrender claims to protection from their home governments.[24]

The functional theory of property has been applied to the *ejido*, or semicommunal village organization. Any lands presented to an *ejido* are the property of the village; yet the latter cannot sell, mortgage, or lease the land. If the *ejido* is of the individual type, as is usually the case, the village must pass the tillable portions on to the farmers who will work them. The farmers are then subject to the same constraints regarding alienation; they cannot hire workers, and they must return the land to the village if they fail to utilize it for two successive years. If they work the land as prescribed they can pass it on to their heirs. Their holdings are quite small, usually five hectares or less. At various times, especially under Cárdenas (1934–1940), the government has also sponsored the larger cooperative *ejido*. This calls for a collective effort and a sharing of the product, and it typically produces commercial crops through the use of more capital intensive modes of production. The hacienda has persisted, but in a greatly modified form. The agricultural worker is now free and he is absorbed in the market. If he works for the hacienda, he is paid in money wages, not in kind or in script; if he functions as a small peasant, he can sell a portion of his produce in the market.[25] Subject to changes of this type, the hacienda has survived, especially where the population has been sparse. The *hacendado* has existed in an atmosphere of considerable uncertainty, however, for the law sanctions small holdings only and his estate can be legally dismembered at any time.[26]

These comments serve to introduce one of the most important consequences of the Mexican Revolution, one that has in fact received considerable study in other countries seeking economic development: Mexico has served as a rewarding case study in the errors as well as the achievements of land reform.

The purposes of the land reform were both to restore and to grant land to the villages. Further, the law of 1920 sought to en-

[24] See Frank Tannenbaum, *Mexico: The Struggle for Peace and Bread*, chapter 6.

[25] Robert Edminster, "Mexico," in Pepelasis, Mears, and Adelman, *Economic Development*, pp. 338–339 and 346–347.

[26] Tannenbaum, *The Struggle for Peace and Bread*, pp. 150–152.

sure that the average *ejido* holding would be of proper size; the minimum plot was to be sufficiently large to provide a family head with a daily income equal to twice the wage per day in a given district.[27] Nevertheless in its conception as well as inception the program was unpredictably conservative. It was neither retaliatory nor confiscatory, and it was in fact most considerate of the old order.[28] According to Article 27 (no less), compensation was to be 10 per cent above the assessed value. The peasant's land hunger and the functional theory of property notwithstanding, the plantation was not to be destroyed in its entirety. The program was so conceived that the *hacendados*' main objection to it lay not in the parting with acreage but in the loss of serfs. The authorities also moved very slowly in the implementation of the program. The emphasis at the very beginning was on restitution to the villages that had surrendered property during the Díaz regime, and this was subject to the delays and complications attending identification, proof, and judicial review. When land was redistributed, petty government officials tended to cut into the effectiveness of the program by exacting their traditional tributes.

Since *ejidos* are established by presidential order, the outlook and energy of the chief executive can clearly be critical in affecting the success of land reform. Having floundered under Carranza and Obregón, two heroes of the Revolution, the program picked up momentum under Calles (1924–1928) and under Portes Gil (1929), when for the first time more than one million hectares were granted to *ejidos* in a single year. A highly rapid pace was experienced under Cárdenas, who distributed some 70 per cent of the land made available to the peasants from 1916 to 1940. In 1937 alone the number of hectares transferred came to over five million. Cárdenas was also responsible for the Agrarian Code of 1934, which simplified procedures of transfer and promoted the distribution of higher value land by providing that the boundaries of an *ejido* lie within seven kilometers of the center of the neighboring village. Under Avila Camacho (1940–1946) the redistribution dropped to an annual average approximating one million

[27] United Nations, Department of Economic Affairs, *Progress in Land Reform*, pp. 81–82.
[28] See Gruening, *Mexico and Its Heritage*, pp. 141–166.

hectares,[29] while from 1946 to 1952 Alemán, Mexico's most business-oriented president, distributed merely four million hectares in all.[30] The next two heads of state, Ruíz Cortines and López Mateos, greatly stepped up the pace of reform. López Mateos was responsible for the distribution of ten million hectares in the first four years of his administration alone and ultimately surpassed Cárdenas' effort. According to estimates in 1962 the land belonging to *ejido* farmers totaled 53,000,000 hectares, or nearly one-third of the country's farming area.[31] The feat had been considerable, but it had taken half a century to accomplish and the process was still continuing.

The program has undoubtedly succeeded in introducing greater equality. What, however, have been its effects upon productivity, efficiency, and the growth of the economy and the agricultural sector?[32]

Of the two major types of *ejido* holdings, the collective seems designed to yield a relatively high efficiency. Potentially at least, it possesses the several buying, production, and marketing advantages of larger units. Financing calls for less appraisal per person by the financing agency, greater specialization in production is possible, farm machinery can be employed more readily, and marketing economies can be realized. Yet this mode of organization is vulnerable in its reliance upon top-level leadership. Because of poor management and inadequate organization of production, the collective *ejido* has not been much more efficient than the individual type *ejido*. The collective has also not proved popular because it calls for considerable discipline and a subordination of the individual's interests to those of the group. Since it gives only limited expression to aspirations of land ownership, most *ejidatarios* have preferred the individual *ejido* to it.[33]

29 For annual figures see Whetten, *Rural Mexico*, p. 125, t. 19.

30 United Nations, Department of Economic Affairs, *Progress in Land Reform*, p. 83.

31 Octaviano Campos Salas, "Economic Panorama of Modern Mexico," *Comercio Exterior de México*, Supplement, 9 (February, 1963), 3.

32 For a general survey of these issues see Whetten, *Rural Mexico*, esp. pp. 144–151 and 203–214.

33 In the Tarascan culture area, for example, the rural inhabitants have been ego-oriented. See Michael H. Belshaw, "Aspects of Community Develop-

However, the individual type tends to yield as low, or lower, a product. The individual *ejidatario* suffers considerably as a result of the typically miniscule plot he is forced to cultivate. In 1940 his farm averaged only 4.6 hectares, or about 11 acres. Given adequate rainfall, small size can lead to a relatively high efficiency; but in Mexico only 12 per cent of the land is tillable, about 7.5 per cent is actually cultivated, perhaps 80 per cent of the cultivated land suffers from insufficient rainfall, and approximately three-quarters of the crop failures are due to a lack of rain. The Mexican government has long been aware that these conditions call for larger *ejidos*, and it has sought to modify its redistribution accordingly. In 1929 each *ejidatario* received an average of 2.8 hectares for cultivation, but in 1945 the average grant came to 8.3 hectares. A 1946 amendment of the Constitution increased the standard grant of land to ten hectares of naturally watered or irrigated land, or twenty hectares of seasonal land. Since a limited supply of land is available for redistribution, such increases in unit size of course tend to reduce the number of ultimate beneficiaries of the program. In effect, the redistribution of land tends to promote both income growth and equality in land holding as long as the beneficiaries receive plots sufficiently large to permit efficient production. If land is further redistributed in response to widespread land hunger, growth and equality objectives clash.

Studies of agricultural production generally reveal the continuing weakness of the small *ejido*-type production. The work by Whetten shows that in 1940 the *ejidos* outperformed the small private holdings in the production of only three out of seven principal crops. In each of these seven instances, moreover, the *ejidos* produced less than did the private holdings of more than five hectares.[34] In 1949 the individual *ejidos* received less net income and a smaller return on capital than either the large or small privately held plots (see Table 12). According to a survey taken in the mid-fifties of seven municipalities in the state of Guanajuato in central Mexico, the *ejidatarios* lagged in seven out of nine commodities and they did not produce three remaining ones (see

ment in Rural Mexico," *Inter-American Economic Affairs*, 15 (Spring, 1962), 85–86.

[34] *Ibid.*, p. 248, t. 43.

TABLE 12. Incomes of the Agricultural Properties Farmed in 1949*
(pesos)

Value	For Individually Held Units Greater Than 5 Hectares	For *Ejidal* Plots	For Individually Held Units 1 to 5 Hectares
Gross sales value	10,391	1,309	1,100
Family net income	3,359	734	695
Value of unremunerated family labor	1,101	220	83
Net income of operator	2,258	514	612
Value of capital	29,004	5,982	2,956
Income of capital	3,604	316	434
Per cent return of capital	12.4	5.3	14.7

* Armando González Santos, *La agricultura: Estructura y utilización de los recursos*, pp. 208–209, t. 95 and t. 96.

Table 13). The private cultivators farmed plots averaging over thirty-seven hectares, compared to an average of less than seven for the *ejidatarios*. The former also utilized capital valued on the average at somewhat more than 53,000 pesos, while the value for the *ejidatario* barely exceeded one-tenth as much.

The influence of size upon efficiency is further suggested by the relative success of *ejidos* in the North Pacific area. In the states comprising this region the individual *ejido* has averaged from ten to fifteen hectares. Here the *ejidatario* concentrates on producing cotton and certain types of fruits and vegetables for export to the nearby United States market. The government has not found it necessary to provide much technical assistance in this area because of the relatively good management already in existence. The collective *ejidos* have functioned here without political intrusions, while the individual ones have operated with a relatively high degree of efficiency.[35] The following array indicates the average real income (in 1930 prices) of the *ejidatario* in the North and in other zones.[36]

[35] González Santos, *La Agricultura*, p. 208, t. 95.
[36] Banco Nacional de México, *Review of the Economic Situation of Mexico*, 35 (May, 1959), 9.

Zone	1930	1950	1958
United Mexican states	81	206	346
Northern	85	361	528
Central	80	150	204
Southern	80	153	249
Southeastern	85	136	381

The record in the North serves to demonstrate that under favorable circumstances the *ejido* farm is compatible with sustained improvements in agriculture.

The generalizations that can be drawn from this account are clear. Land reform programs like the Mexican *ejido* movement can represent a serious clash between the objectives of growth and equality. Or, perhaps less unfavorably, land reform may fail to generate growth and simply result in stagnation. Land reform is a necessary beginning—we shall very shortly focus upon the

TABLE 13. Returns from Agricultural Properties in Guanajuato*
(kilograms per hectare)

Product	Total Returns	Private Cultivators	*Ejidatarios*
Maize	933	1,060	783
Wheat	1,239	1,335	1,132
Kidney beans	164	196	133
Chick peas	427	436	420
Garlic	2,921	4,689	1,022
Tomatoes	6,334	6,165	6,720
Sugar cane	33,566	33,566	...
Alfalfa	35,380	38,449	27,794
Onions	8,076	7,815	8,414
Lima beans	928	928	...
Lentils	266	266	...
Chile	761	1,041	87

* Carlos Manuel Castillo, "La economía agrícola en la región del Bajío," *Problemas Agrícolas y Industriales de México*, 8 (July–December, 1956), 111, t. 105.

adjective—but it can serve only as a point of departure. Unskilled peasants, seeking to function on tiny plots with a minimum of equipment, hardly serve as the ideal agents for agricultural development. While students of Mexican agriculture may argue over the precise course of agricultural production, they tend to agree that the output was higher in each of the years 1908–1910 than in any of the thirty years following. According to the Oficina de Barómetros Económicos the general index of agricultural production, based on the year 1929, stood at 141.9 in 1908–1910 and then dropped to 111.3 during 1925–1929 and 113.9 during 1935–1939.[37] As late as the relatively prosperous 1950's, many peasants continued to work their small plots by the traditional methods, some 20 per cent of them using the pre-Hispanic method of cutting and burning without resorting to plows. Many farmers exploited their land without fertilization, rotation, or catch crops to replenish depleted soils, while others permitted a total of perhaps more than one million hectares to lie fallow. According to the combined Mexican Working Party, writing in the early fifties: "Agricultural methods in Mexico are generally poor. Agricultural implements used in most regions are still primitive, and crop rotation is almost unknown."[38]

In sum, given a land reform program, particularly one designed for regions of relatively high population density, it is incumbent upon the authorities to raise productivity by concentrating on technical, financial, and marketing assistance.

Table 14 indicates the investment that was undertaken in agriculture, for selected years. Private investment as a percentage of total investment has tended to rise, while the ratio of irrigation outlays to total public investment has remained high. Actually many of the irrigation requirements of Mexican agriculture have yet to be met. Of a potentially irrigable 11,000,000 hectares, about 2,700,000 hectares were under irrigation in 1960.[39] This small proportion can be attributed to a slow start in the irrigation program—which in turn was due to the time required to achieve political stability, the faith placed in land reform and redistribu-

---

[37] Cited by Edminster, "Mexico," p. 356.
[38] *The Economic Development of Mexico*, p. 31.
[39] Secretariá de Industria y Comercio, *Memoria, 1960*, p. 63.

TABLE 14. Agricultural Investment, for Selected Years*

Year	Total Gross Investment	Public Investment	Irrigation Works	Private Investment	Machinery
		(millions of pesos)			
1939	86.2	39.7	38.1	46.5	10.4
1943	164.6	86.0	83.0	78.6	24.7
1947	474.3	266.1	228.3	208.2	89.5
1949	1,104.3	504.2	260.7	600.1	205.5
1950	1,098.9	333.0	324.2	765.9	319.7
1954	1,815.4	481.3	466.8	1,334.1	509.9
1955	2,245.8	485.4	469.5	1,760.4	842.6

* Banco Nacional de México, *Review of the Economic Situation of Mexico,* 34 (March, 1958), 5.

tion, and the widespread poverty. Be that as it may, the government did not establish an irrigation policy until 1926, and the average annual increase of irrigated lands for 1926–1946 amounted to all of 38,867 hectares. By the mid-fifties the annual average had risen to well over 200,000.[40] These projects have been most valuable in permitting the cultivation of lands removed from the center, primarily those in the North.

Since the beneficiaries of the land reform were generally bereft of equipment, the provision of credit became another critical policy area. Once again the year 1926 represented a point of departure. The government then re-established the Banco de Crédito Agrícola in order to encourage the development of agricultural cooperatives, particularly those of smaller size. Yet the Bank seems to have lent instead to established farms on the basis of either sound business principles or political favoritism. One decade later the Banco Nacional de Crédito Ejidal arrived on the scene. This bank has been only moderately successful, primarily because of inadequate funds and consequent attempts to operate on a business basis at a time when something more akin to a social agency was required. The Bank has endeavored to increase the funds at its disposal by utilizing private sources for its lending operations and guaranteeing

[40] Banco Nacional de México, *Review of the Economic Situation of Mexico,* 34 (March, 1958), 5–6.

repayment to reduce the element of risk; this has reduced but not removed the inadequacy. As late as 1945 the Bank was serving only 14 per cent of the *ejidatarios* in Mexico, with most of the remainder at the mercy of the *acaparadores* (monopolizers).[41] Coincident with the expansion of agricultural production, a rapid increase in public long term agricultural credit occurred after 1945. Adjusted for price changes, the expansion in the fifties amounted to nearly 70 per cent a year. Moreover a system of crop insurance has placed agricultural credit on a sounder footing in more recent years. According to the 1950 census, hazards such as droughts, floods, hail, frost, and pests have seriously affected 15 per cent of Mexico's total croplands; coverage of these losses has helped to ease the burdens placed upon the agricultural banks.

Technological improvements could also serve to reduce the effects of such hazards, but the government's extension work has been insufficient. Fortunately, private agencies such as the Rockefeller Foundation have greatly contributed to the development of Mexico's agriculture through programs emphasizing technical rather than capital assistance. In addition the government has offered tax exemption to bring new land under cultivation; it has extended price supports to a wide variety of foodstuffs; and it has subsidized agriculture through lower costs of fertilizer and equipment. Nevertheless, according to some observers in the early sixties, the government was still not adopting a sufficiently forceful program for improving productivity and alleviating poverty in the rural sector.

Criticism has also been directed against the pace of the land reform itself. Some argue that the program moved much too slowly in the incipient years, while others claim that it eventually accelerated to the point of irresponsibility, especially under Cárdenas. The first position is certainly valid, and it is also true that the transfer of titles was later made without adequate care. The economic results of these policies were unfortunate. Despite reasonable compensation, the government's behavior resulted in insecurity of tenure, which probably led to a curtailment of production and a search for short run gains. In one writer's view, ". . . this drawback can be avoided by an explicit and precise definition of

[41] Whetten, *Rural Mexico*, pp. 195–196.

the terms of land redistribution and by the swift transference of property rights."[42]

Let us make certain, however, that we do not underestimate the institutional changes introduced into agriculture by the Revolution. *Ejido* literally means "the way out,"[43] in effect the avenue for escaping from peonage, serfdom, insecurity, and attitudes of fatalism. As *ejidatarios* the farmers have lived under conditions of much greater freedom and dignity and with some hope. The freedom of agricultural labor has made at least the "marginal" worker mobile, and this in turn has stimulated the modern commercial farm and augmented the urban labor supply. The Revolution has thus created a more flexible economic structure, an adaptability of the component parts—in effect a much more open society—all of which greatly facilitate an economic development. Freedom and mobility have also contributed to political stability. During the presidency of López Mateos, which began in 1958, violence and eruptions still occurred in the countryside, but they were minor and infrequent (and, incidentally, immediately suppressed by the federal government). The *ejidatario*'s plane of living may not have risen spectacularly, but he tends to be better off economically. If his dwelling itself is little improved it may at least contain a radio or sewing machine; he is likely to visit nearby towns more frequently; and some advances in diet and medical care have served to enhance his longevity.[44] Although the magic of property did not "turn sand into gold," the Revolution has tended to affect incentives favorably. One would expect these several intangibles of enhanced freedom, mobility, security, and political stability to contribute positively, if perhaps vaguely, to economic development.[45]

In addition one Mexican economist views the Revolution as having led to a sequence of Hirschman-like imbalances that cre-

---

[42] Edmundo Flores, "The Significance of Land Use Changes in the Economic Development of Mexico," *Land Economics*, 35 (May, 1959), 116.

[43] This appears in the title of the classic work by Eyler N. Simpson, *The Ejido: Mexico's Way Out.*

[44] Whetten, *Rural Mexico*, p. 333. For a discussion of the issues discussed in this paragraph, see pp. 238–239 and chapter 12.

[45] For a similar view see C. P. Dowsett, "Agriculture and Economic Development: Mexico," *Australian Quarterly*, 34 (March, 1962), 62–68.

ated pressures for further growth.[46] The alterations in agricultural institutions so disrupted Mexican society, he believes, that they compelled further changes. Because of the uncertainty created by the Revolution, many erstwhile *hacendados* moved to the more urbanized center, bringing a significant portion of their wealth with them. By the 1920's this movement had led to a real estate boom, particularly in Mexico City, and to a resulting expansion of the construction industry and of such allied industries as glass, cement, and iron and steel. These developments in turn affected the countryside. The rural areas of the center turned toward intensive grain culture, and the flow of labor from rural to urban areas increased as villagers were pulled in by the hopes of economic opportunity and pushed out by rural poverty. Expanding markets helped stimulate productivity improvement on the part of the nation's more efficient farms, and more farmers were then in a position to purchase goods from the industrial sector. This is, then, a multisector model of economic development, stimulated by institutional reform in agriculture and by a series of imbalances generally subject to correction. Unfortunately the process did not touch much of agriculture, thereby creating imbalances of a dualistic form that were too severe to be relieved automatically.

The last proposition returns us to the area of adverse criticism, and we should not close the section on agriculture in such fashion. Mexico was among the very first of today's poor countries to institute a land reform program, and most of the developing countries have yet to initiate what Mexico accomplished decades ago. Relatively speaking, Mexico performed the task remarkably early and remarkably well.

The effect of the Revolution on organized labor. The Revolution has further served to introduce some significant changes in the house of labor. Because of the rather complicated array of labor organizations in the early sixties, it seems best to approach the subject by reviewing the organizations in existence during that time. A summary of the growth of the labor movement after the Revolution follows, with particular emphasis on the very strong ties between labor and the central government. Final considera-

[46] Flores, "The Significance of Land Use Changes," esp. pp. 120–121.

tion is given to the effects of labor organization upon Mexico's economic development and to the important question of whether unions have tended to further or retard economic change.

Since Mexican labor organizations are largely of the hothouse variety—encouraged and sponsored by the central government— the basic classification of the labor unions is a political one. Most labor organizations cooperate very closely with the government in a system of *quid pro quo* and mutual support. These belong to an association known as the Workers' Unity Bloc or BUO (Bloque de Unidad Obrera). The others tend to stand apart from the government and to be more critical of it, with frequent charges of betrayal of the Revolution. These compose the National Workers' Central or CNT (Central Nacional de Trabajadores). At times, the CNT has led the anti-BUO forces in fairly extensive strikes. In 1959, for example, the government on one occasion used troops to raid union headquarters to arrest the CNT strike leader and several hundreds of his followers.

The latter dissident group is the smaller of the two, with members totaling about 200,000 in the early 1960's. The Unity Bloc is considerably larger, but its membership is determinate only within a very broad range. The Bloc has claimed some four million nonagricultural workers out of a total labor force of nearly thirteen million. However, a top level official with the Labor Secretariat is willing to grant them no more than 2,500,000; the authors of a work on Latin-American labor cite 1,900,000 as the total number of Mexican trade unionists;[47] and a foremost labor authority believes that the figure is closer to 1,500,000.[48] That the Bloc's figures are so lacking in reliability is due in part to the political role of the labor unions. For more bargaining power within the major political party and with the government, it is obviously useful to claim the representation of more workers. As is characteristic of many organizations into which all of us have stumbled from time to time, once a Mexican worker affiliates with a union he tends from that moment on to be considered a permanent member. In fact the membership lists contain the names of those who

[47] Poblete Troncoso and Burnett, *The Rise of the Latin American Labor Movement*, p. 7.
[48] Rivera Marín, "El movimiento obrero," p. 268, t. 1.

might have felt that they would no longer be carried as members once they departed into the hereafter.

These political divisions are evidently unknown to American labor unions, which have generally underplayed their political roles. The remaining organizations, however, are along lines familiar to North Americans. Within each of the political associations is a number of centrals and autonomous unions similar to the AFL, CIO, and the Railroad Brotherhood. The central and autonomous unions contain some confederations (twenty-five in all), which in turn have their federations and locals, or syndicates. Of the centrals within the Unity Bloc, the largest and most powerful is the Confederation of Mexican Workers or CTM (Confederación de Trabajadores de México), created in 1936. One of its strongest unions is made up of the industrial sugar workers. Two older and much smaller centrals are the Mexican Regional Confederation or CROM (Confederación Regional de Obreros Mexicanos), which has the distinction of having been the first labor organization (1918) founded after the adoption of the Constitution, and the CGT (Confederación General de Trabajadores), organized in 1922.

Making up the autonomous unions in the Unity Bloc are the workers in cotton and woolen textiles, mining and metallurgy, petroleum, railways, the theater, and public employment. The last of these, ranking second in membership and influence to the CTM, is known as the Federation of Unions of Government Employees or FSTSE (Federación de Sindicatos de Trabajadores al Servicio del Estado). Finally, a series of confederations appeals to agricultural laborers alone, or to a combination of these and nonfarm-workers. The oldest of these (1938) represents only agriculture and tends to cooperate with the CTM. This is the National Agricultural Confederation of CNC (Confederación Nacional Campesina). The second-oldest (1942) has taken the name of the Confederation of Mexican Workers and Peasants or COCM (Confederación de Obreros y Campesinos de México); it has endeavored to compete with the CTM but its membership has failed to reach twenty thousand. The Union of Agricultural Federations of Mexico or UFCM (Union de Federaciones Campensinos de México) was created in 1950 by political opponents of the business oriented regime; it is also tiny.

The smaller political bloc, the CNT, is composed of a number of centrals and autonomous unions, many of recent origin. Foremost among the centrals are CRT (Confederación Revolucionaria de Trabajadores) and CROC (Confederación Revolucionaria de Obreros y Campesinos). The latter represents the most radical component of organized agricultural labor and, with its membership of close to seventy thousand, is the most powerful union in the anti-BUO bloc. CROC has found its greatest strength in textiles, food and beverages, and trucking. The Communists have also organized a relatively small union of less than twenty thousand members, made up primarily of agricultural and mining workers, who are of course traditionally Mexico's most exploited workers. This is the General Union of Workers and Peasants of Mexico, or UGOCM (Unión General de Obreros y Campesinos de México). Among the autonomously organized workers in the CNT, the electrical workers are probably best known for their militancy. Others include the employees in telephones, hotels and restaurants, and printing.

These organizations notwithstanding, vast numbers within the Mexican work force have remained unorganized. If we accept the highest of the more authoritative membership figures for the Unity Bloc—that is, 2,500,000—we can still conclude that between 75 per cent and 80 per cent of the total work force has been outside the union membership. Predictably, the kinds of workers in this group include the self-employed in or out of agriculture, domestics, employees in petty commercial and manufacturing establishments, and white-collar workers. Women, minors, and the disabled make up a considerable portion of the group. Most of the unorganized workers are under federal jurisdiction, however, so that they are legally entitled to such protection as minimum wages.

The proliferation of labor unions in Mexico has indeed been extensive. Why, it may well be asked, have so many organizations tended to appear? Part of the answer is to be found in ideological differences. Some unions, like the electricians, seem to be Communist-led (and, it is generally agreed, untainted by corruption); while others, such as the influential CTM, are of the Right and lend strong support to the government. Yet the ideological differences among unions are typically minor. The major explanations are again political ones. At various times in Mexican labor history, particularly in the early 1930's, proliferation attended a disagreement between the government and the most powerful union, so that governmental paternalism then no longer offset the divisive tendencies within the labor movement. More generally, the head of a union has political support to sell, in return for which he hopes to receive patronage. As a head he can participate in the political process in a manner denied him if he merely occupied a subordinate position within a larger unified organization. The political leaders in turn tend to cooperate with him because of their interest in internal peace and stability. At the political level they seek consensus and the prevention of any strong overt opposition to the government's policies. At the economic level they desire control over union militancy. The heads of the state are particularly anxious to repress sharp wage increases in order to check further advances in the price level and to avoid the deterioration of nationwide morale which could result if a few economically strong unions received wages that were way out of line. The dispensing of political plums permits the government to achieve its several objectives—thereby illustrating the proposition that the Mexican government has been able to utilize personal favoritism to gain the cooperation required for economic change.

Nor do the rank and file pose any threat to the government's policies and programs, despite the "polyfunctionalism"[49] of the union heads. The membership lacks militancy in a way that seems strange to a student of Western labor movements. Some observers attribute this to a lack of education, in the urban as well as in the rural areas. Then, too, Mexican workers come from a tradition of degrading exploitation, in the Marxian sense, and they tend to live with attitudes of fatalism and the acceptance of a class society. Centuries of experience have taught them to restrain their aspirations and their attempts to better themselves. Despite their background, however, they are experiencing some improvement in their lot. As a result they see their government as an agency dedicated to national economic growth, improved social welfare, and fulfillment of the ideals of the Revolution. The government is not only too powerful to attack; in many respects it is a genuine friend and ally. Hence their demands for higher wages, fringe

[49] The term is from Scott, *Mexican Government in Transition*, p. 25.

benefits, shorter hours, and improved working conditions are limited indeed.

Consequently organized labor, be it the hierarchy or the rank and file, may well be the number one supporter of the government. A labor convention is likely to concentrate on an unveiling of a mural and an enthusiastic reception for the President of the Republic, with only the gentlest introduction of problems and the voicing of complaints. Even the splinter bloc, the CNT, frequently supports the government, though it is opposed to official cooperation. The alliance between government and the unions, in brief, is a close one.

So it has been since the Revolution. From the beginning the government has encouraged and sponsored the labor movement, so that organized labor has found it possible to secure its existence much earlier (at a much lower per capita income) than has been true elsewhere. This has been due both to the ideology and the political attachments introduced by the Revolution. Tannenbaum has also attributed it to the predominance of foreign enterprise and interests. The state was not merely helping workers; it was assisting its nationals against foreigners. Hence the internal opposition to its measures was attenuated.[50]

The government's encouragement to labor was evidenced first and foremost by the celebrated Article 123 of the Constitution of 1917.[51] With the adoption of this Article, often referred to as labor's "bill of rights," a trade union became a legal person with special rights and privileges. Workers now possessed the rights to organize and strike, whereas under Díaz these activities had been regarded as crimes. Collective bargaining became mandatory and the collective labor contract a source of industrial law. The government was to determine the legality of a strike. If its finding was in the negative, as in a case of violence, it could force the workers to return to work; if in the affirmative, it helped enforce the strike. (A strike can legally continue, incidentally, while the workers actually return to the job.) Article 123 further covered minimum wages, participation in profits, discharges and severance pay (of

[50] Tannenbaum, *The Struggle for Peace and Bread*, p. 229.

[51] See *ibid.*, chapter 7; Gruening, *Mexico and Its Heritage*, pp. 336–337; and Whetten, *Rural Mexico*, p. 586.

three months), maximum hours, protection of women and children (particularly expectant mothers and children under twelve), employer accident liabilities, and the collection of debts, which were limited to one generation because of the implications of peonage. These provisions did not possess the full force of law but represented rather the statement of an ideal which, according to the first clause in the Article, was to be approached as quickly as possible through the passage of appropriate legislation. In some instances, as in the provision of an eight-hour day or the prevention of child labor, the achievement has thus far fallen short of the declared policy.

Since the Revolution organized labor has indeed come a long way. In the years just after 1910 it reportedly had about twenty thousand members all told, and by 1917 the figure may have been thirty thousand. The membership was to be found in as many as 506 different pursuits, but it was drawn especially from the printing, shoe, textile, clothing, tile, and railroad industries.[52] The doctrine during those days was extremely radical, with an anarcho-syndicalist orientation and an emphasis upon class conflict. Representing this view and heading the movement were two centrals, the Casa del Obrero Mundial (1912) and the Confederación del Trabajo de la Región Mexicana (1916). These and other labor organizations led a major strike in 1916, which they not only lost but which caused Carranza generally to repress strikes.

Once Article 27 encouraged trade unionism, the moderates, Socialists, and syndicalists combined in 1918 to form the first central, still extant, the CROM. This organization abandoned anarchy as an objective, but it did continue the emphasis on class conflict. The central was to work for the abolition of private property, largely through political action.[53] This departure from anarchism and the embracing of political instruments of course represented the beginning of the long history of cooperation between government and organized labor. CROM helped elect Obregón (1920–1924) to the presidency, and Confederation leaders participated actively in his government. Calles (1924–1928) had in his cabinet the top labor leader of CROM, Luis Morones, a gentleman who was remarkably

[52] Rivera Marín, "El movimiento obrero," p. 276.
[53] Vicente Lombardo Toledano, "The Labor Movement," *Annals*, 208 (March, 1940), 50.

successful in both bringing benefits to labor and, reputedly, carving out a fortune for himself. By 1924 CROM's membership may have exceeded one million. By the end of the twenties, however, a serious rift developed between the Confederation and the government. CROM opposed the return of Obregón to the presidency, and it feared the interference that might result from the government's attempts to standardize the states' social legislation.[54]

When CROM disassociated itself from the government, factionalism struck the labor movement as it has generally affected Mexican labor history during periods of disagreement with the government. The CGT, which in 1922 had been organized as a dissident group opposed to extensive political involvement but had previously offered CROM little effective competition, now gained strength. By returning to a philosophy of anarchism and syndicalism it registered enough appeal in the desperate years of the Depression to attract eighty thousand members. The big labor event of the thirties, however, was the formation in 1936 of the currently powerful and prominent CTM; it originated under the leadership of Vicente Lombardo Toledano and with the blessing of President Cárdenas. The ensuing years have especially witnessed the formation of the several rural-urban labor organizations, formed in reaction to one another. In 1952, for example, the major anti-BUO organization, CROC, was formed through an amalgamation of four smaller groups. In the meantime the membership of organized labor has been growing at a considerably more rapid rate than the total work force. According to Rivera Marín, whose estimates are relatively conservative, the index number for organized labor advanced to 409 in 1958 (1930 = 100), while the numbers for the work force and the economically active population climbed only to 195.[55] The growth rate of organized labor thus more than doubled the growth rate of the entire work force.

The important questions concern the effects of labor organizations upon the workers' welfare and the economy as a whole. How have unions influenced Mexico's economic development and to what extent have they actually assisted the rank and file?

---

[54] The remarks about CROM's history are from Poblete Troncoso and Burnett, *The Rise of the Latin American Labor Movement*, pp. 100–102.
[55] Rivera Marín, "El movimiento obrero," p. 278, t. 7.

The organized workers have undoubtedly fared well relative to the unorganized. The industrial-urban workers have particularly been the beneficiaries, since the favorably placed CTM, with over twenty industrial unions, has frequently set the wage patterns. According to one informant, during a fifty-year period money wages have gone up close to 800 per cent for all organized labor, some 2,000 per cent for the electric power, iron and steel, and telephone workers, and 500 per cent for the textile workers. The wage data for the unorganized are not quite comparable because of differences in skills and the high incidence of agricultural workers among the unorganized. Yet union activity and the accompanying cooperation with the government do seem to act as factors. A case in point is given by the relatively well-trained bank employees, who are not organized and who have sometimes failed to earn even the minimum wage rates assigned them by special statute. Wage rates also tend to be lower in the smaller shops and among casual laborers hiring themselves out by the day. Unions have further managed to obtain a variety of fringe benefits, including vacations with pay, family allowances, severance pay, profit sharing, and *prestaciones* such as purchases from company stores.

Yet the major point is that the organized appear favored only when compared with the remainder of labor. Once allowances are made for price increases, the wage rates of organized labor exhibit little or no upward trend. By the same token those outside organized labor have frequently been forced to accept lower real wage rates. Inflation has reduced the value of the workers' take-home pay to the point where reductions in real income have tended to interfere with the development of a domestic market. While the unions have been instrumental in preventing inflation from corroding real wages, they have not been entirely successful because of lags in collective agreements and in the setting of minimum wages by the authorities.[56] This in turn implies that organized labor has failed to appropriate its share of the improvements in productivity noted in Chapter Two.

Many students of economic development tend to fear labor unions as causing inflation. Whatever merit this argument may

[56] Adolf Sturmthal, "Economic Development, Income Distribution, and Capital Formation in Mexico," *Journal of Political Economy*, 63 (June, 1955), 193.

possess in other contexts, such has not been the case in Mexico. The market has in large part been responsible for this, since the ready supply of labor accruing from the rural-urban migrations has served as a "natural" depressant upon wage rates. Nor have the unions possessed the power to impose severe entrance and apprenticeship requirements to restrict supply and raise wages. In addition the government's policy has supplemented the effects of the market place. Identifying itself with programs for economic development, the government has chosen to live with demand pull inflations when necessary, but it has refused to go along with labor's more militant demands and tolerate cost push inflations.[57] This combination of attitudes toward demand pull and cost push is probably the most felicitous one for economic development, but it has forced labor, particularly the unorganized, to bear the major burden of the nation's growth. That this has happened in a country proud of its revolutionary heritage and inclined to the Left poses the possibility of its being a necessary path to development. In Mexico the humanitarian quality of the regime has led it to undertake special programs to alleviate the suffering occasioned by economic progress, but the unions' wage policies have not increased labor's share of the national income, nor have they hampered the country's economic growth.

The government is hoping that one of its new programs will alter income distribution and encourage economic growth without seriously affecting the price level. The reference is to a new profit-sharing plan which was applied for the first time in 1964 to 1963 company profits. The degree of worker participation is suggested by the 5 per cent of profits claimed by a union in the cotton industry. The Treasury is charged with granting companies a reasonable return on their capital as well as a reserve for reinvestment; this is so interpreted that interest and funds for reinvestment make up 30 per cent of profits after taxes. Of the profits 14 per cent are distributable to capital and labor on the basis of a firm's capital-labor ratio. Some firms are exempt from this procedure. In keeping with the emphasis on industrial development, new com-

---

[57] Horacio Flores de la Peña and Aldo Ferrer, "Salarios reales y desarrollo económico," *El Trimestre Económico*, 18 (October–December, 1951), 617–628, esp. p. 621.

panies manufacturing new products may refrain from profit sharing for four years, as opposed to two years for new firms generally. Small firms and nonprofit institutions are generally exempt. Nevertheless, in the first year of its operation the plan affected about 5,000,000 workers and added at least 500,000,000 pesos to their incomes. (This implies an average increment of eight United States dollars per worker during the year.) The authorities maintain that attendant increases in prices should be minimal in that the profit sharing does not add to unit cost and the installed capacity is sufficient to absorb the added demand.[58]

While the contributions of unionization to workers' incomes have only been moderate, the labor movement has brought with it some important noneconomic advantages. Perhaps above all, it has given greater emotional security to the urban worker. Adaptation to a union may be one additional step in the great process of adjustment to an industrial society, but once made it undoubtedly helps overcome the loneliness and the aimlessness of a new way of life. According to UNESCO, labor unions have assisted in the transition to an industrial society by channeling protests and serving as agencies of social participation. In its words: "There are situations where the union organizations provide an effective bridge between small social structures necessarily left behind by the urban worker and the impersonal anonymous social reality of the large factory and metropolis."[59]

Unionization has also made some apprenticeship in the political process possible, faint though the beginnings may be. The rank and file have generally been denied genuine democratic elections, and they have been dominated by the labor and governmental hierarchy. Yet they are beginning to obtain insights into the working of the government apparatus which they would not have achieved had they remained outside the structure of organized labor and government. There is evidence, for example, of a greater freedom of speech for the membership in recent years. Society as a whole has also benefited from unionization in a number of respects. Organized labor has strongly supported the government

[58] See Banco Nacional de Comercio Exterior, "Profit Sharing Plan," *Comercio Exterior de México*, 10 (January, 1964), 9–11.
[59] UNESCO, *Seminar on Urbanization Problems in Latin America*, p. 44.

and has helped make officialdom the relatively dynamic and progressive force that it has been since the days of the Revolution. Labor has helped institute and then enforce Mexico's social security provisions in the face of frequent employer attempts at evasion. This has been helpful in several ways. Social security has brought in much needed governmental revenue and has made possible a higher plane of living for Mexico's lowest income groups. The prevention of further declines in real wages has helped preserve the political stability so needed for continued economic change, and it has surely prevented the rate of increase of consumption from declining any further, thereby mitigating the rather severe economic problems that disturbed Mexico in the late fifties and early sixties. As we have seen, this has been accomplished with little responsibility for inflationary pressures. These represent considerable benefits.

Somewhat surprising is the finding that Mexican labor has typically supported, or at least has not actively interfered with, technological change. This behavior is of course contrary to the usual belief that labor, in its desire for economic security, tends to oppose technological improvement. Mexican labor has profited not only from history, however, but also from its current contacts with the labor leaders of the advanced countries, most of whom speak not of retarding technological change but of introducing it under controlled conditions. Many Mexican workers are surely aware of the role of machines in the development of the richer countries. There is also the question of the power of the unions, of their ability to retard the introduction of more efficient techniques if they wished to do so. Be that as it may, Mexican industry has generally adopted the most recent techniques ever since the mid-thirties. The plants may be small by United States standards, but they do not tend to be antiquated. The major exception has been Mexico's oldest industry, textiles. In contrast to most other manufacturing industries, textiles, particularly cottons, have experienced little technological change. Cotton textiles have been subject to the vicious circle of limited markets and little improvement in productivity. Their situation has been ripe for the displacement of labor if and when cost-reducing innovations could be introduced; according to some estimates only about 50 per cent of the 100,000 workers would be required if the industry were over-

hauled. Hence, textile workers have continually resisted technological change in their negotiations with management. Some modernization recently occurred in cotton textiles, and it occasioned
a reduction in manpower to which the unions agreed very reluc-
tantly.

Mexican labor unions can thus be given a fairly clean bill of
health in the matters of price stability and technological change.
Another common indictment concerns the control of labor unions
over hiring and firing. What is the record in this case?

Organized Mexican labor has tended toward the union shop, but
not the closed one. The union does the actual recruiting, a pre-
rogative of which it is exceedingly jealous and to which it clings
tenaciously. It finds it relatively easy to locate additional persons
because of the available labor pool. Union workers are likely to
have relatives and friends whom they are pleased to recommend;
union leaders are in continual contacts with the schools; and there
are areas where casual laborers, often carrying their tools with
them, tend to congregate in the hope that someone will make use
of their services. On occasion, management does the actual hiring,
but more frequently its role is to examine the qualifications of
those whom the union has recommended. The government has
endeavored to improve the efficiency of the labor market by introducing national employment agencies, but the unions have refused
to relinquish their right to recruit. The government has thus
worked primarily with the unorganized. In their hiring activities
the unions have not placed artificial restraints upon the supply of
labor to control the prices of labor services. Indeed there is no evidence that they would have any interest in trying to do so, given
the strong political orientation of the labor movement.

More controversial is the discharge rule. In Mexican industry a
worker dismissed without "just cause" receives three months' severance wages plus twenty days' pay for every year of service with
a given company. The initial purpose of the rule was to prevent
employees from combating unionization by discharging more militant employees. This may have been commendable, but the rule
has resulted in considerable friction. The employees resent its
disloyalty feature, according to which a worker is not entitled to
severance pay if he has been unfaithful to the firm or guilty of
insubordination; if management has its way, the unions suspect,

Mexican workers may yet set an international record of disloyalty to their employers. Businessmen, on the other hand, charge that the rule places an undue financial burden upon them, particularly when a company is obliged to close a plant. Business firms cannot even suspend operations temporarily without permission of the appropriate board of conciliation or arbitration. The rule is actually administered in a spirit of compromise, so that a discharged worker frequently receives some fraction of the maximum severance pay for which he may be eligible. Nevertheless, the rule seems ill advised. It adds to the risk and cost of operating a business, and as such it may have an adverse effect upon the marginal investment decision. It probably leads to higher commodity prices. Further, the business group is likely to exaggerate the reports of its bad effects beyond its actual proportions. For purposes of improving relations with the business sector, the rule could well be weakened or abolished, with more reliance on social security in order to protect the jobless. Article 58 of the labor code, which is of the same genre as the United States fair trade laws but less severe, also requires revision. According to its provisions, once a collective labor contract is accepted by two-thirds of the employees in a specified industry in a given area it becomes binding upon all in that industry and district.

In many other respects business and labor are in fairly close agreement. The unions and the new group of businessmen possess the same orientation toward Mexico's economic independence, industrialization, protective tariffs, and government participation in economic growth. While many of the leaders of the major labor organization, the CTM, have been Socialist in ideology, they have been so only in long run, doctrinaire terms. In their everyday affairs they have accepted the principle of industrialization largely through the medium of private property.[60]

Labor organizations did frequently behave in less than exemplary fashion in their earlier years. In their zeal for "workers' rights," unions resorted to violence, frequently with open support from the government. Thus: "Police protection and a friendly courtroom atmosphere enabled CROM to reduce management to accepting most of its demands. Apparently, whenever CROM

[60] Sanford A. Mosk, *The Industrial Revolution in Mexico*, chapter 6.

erected its red and black flag at a striking plant, even the federal army could be counted upon for support."[61] The printers' union possessed sufficient power in the 1920's to insist upon extra help as well as overtime during rush periods, but with no consequent discharges during periods of slack. In addition it imposed censorship and refused to print criticisms of itself and of CROM, to which it then belonged. These excesses, however, tended to occur at a time when the unions were young and inexperienced—and prior to the present power structure in which labor and business play approximately equal roles in influencing government policies. The mellowing of the labor movement is perhaps best revealed in the strike data. In 1944 strikes numbered 887: in 1957, they amounted to only 193.[62] Moreover, since World War II strikes have generally been settled by conciliation or arbitration. As Ernest Gruening observes, the union members come from a group that in a century of national independence seldom organized anything on its own initiative. Viewed in this fashion, the labor movement emerges as "an unprecedented achievement."[63]

Social mobility and the growth of the middle class. The degree of social integration in Mexico has been disappointing in many respects. Despite some fifty years of revolution the lines between the several classes remain quite sharp. The upper class, made up of those with economic and political power as well as the descendants of the old aristocracy, thinks of itself as a distinct elite, highly placed above the struggling middle classes and masses. In the conversations of the upper and the upper middle classes is frequently to be found the very marked disdain of the masses that one tends to associate with a highly regidified feudalistic society.

Nevertheless, social mobility is always a possibility in Mexico, and for some it has proved to be a reality. Indians have been able to climb into the urban lower class as mestizos, so that an initially biological classification has evolved into a sociological one. While the mobility among the other various socioeconomic levels is less marked, sons of unskilled workers can join the ranks of the skilled. technicians can work themselves into white-collar or business occu-

[61] Poblete Troncoso and Burnett, *The Rise of the Latin American Labor Movement*, p. 101.

[62] Howard F. Cline, *Mexico: Revolution to Evolution, 1940–1960*, p. 226.

[63] Gruening, *Mexico and Its Heritage*, p. 390.

pations, and the middle class can penetrate the upper classes. Women have not been able to escape their biological heritage as have the Indians, but the old traditions of genteel ladies dedicated exclusively to their families and homes are beginning to disappear. Lower class women have of course long been in the labor market.

Let us consider these several groups at somewhat greater length.

Development theory has placed special emphasis on the rise and growth of the middle class. This is the group that particularly associates itself with the industrialization and urbanization of a society and that supports a government that tolerates (and, it is hoped, stimulates) economic advancement. In Mexico's case, as we have seen, this group led a revolution—indeed as it has in many other countries. Quantification of the rising significance of Mexico's middle class would thus be highly desirable. Unfortunately, this endeavor is beset by difficulties of definition. One presumably relies on types of occupations and the sources and levels of personal income; such, I take it, are the bases of classification used in Table 15 to show the trends for the various classes. The middle class made up 17 per cent of the population in 1960, not a particularly high figure by mature economy standards but never-

TABLE 15. Class Structure, for Selected Years*

Class	Per Cent of Population			Per Cent Increase in Population	
	1900	*1950*	*1960*	*1900–1950*	*1900–1960*
Upper	0.6	0.5	0.5	79.5	157.4
Rural	0.4	0.2	0.1	9.1	12.1
Urban	0.2	0.3	0.4	301.2	520.7
Middle	8.3	15.5	17.1	255.6	426.0
Rural	6.6	9.8	9.9	184.0	285.5
Urban	1.7	5.7	7.2	527.1	958.4
Popular	91.1	84.0	82.4	74.5	129.8
Rural	74.8	55.4	50.1	40.2	70.0
Urban	16.3	28.6	32.3	232.4	405.0

* González Cosío, "Clases y estratos sociales," p. 55, t. 1.

theless about twice the percentage of 1900. The highest rate of increase in population over the sixty-year period was exhibited by the urban middle class. While the statistics are subject to the usual qualifications, they assuredly confirm subjective impressions of a class increasingly gaining in strength though still in the minority.

Of particular interest in this group is the industrial entrepreneur. Sanford A. Mosk has probably done the best work on the general nature and origin of what he has called the "New Group" of Mexico's industrialists.[64] This New Group is composed chiefly of owners of small manufacturing plants, many of which arose during World War II to supply articles no longer sufficiently available from foreign sources to satisfy the Mexican market. The firms represented by the New Group are thus relatively small and of recent origin. In addition they use Mexican capital, ". . . and last but not least in this list of characteristics, the New Group industrialists do not have good relations with the principal financial institutions in Mexico."[65] In contrast to the industrialists who established themselves before World War II, the New Group is generally prolabor, progovernment and antiforeigner. It has stood for cooperation with labor unions to establish high standards of productivity; it believes in comprehensive economic action by, and a working alliance with, government; and it has been openly hostile to United States participation in Mexican industrialization. Like the other group, however, it has been vigorously protectionist in its tariff policy.

Mosk has also turned his attention to the sociological origins of the new entrepreneurs,[66] arguing that they did not emanate from commercial and mercantile activities. While traders did play some role in Mexico's nineteenth-century industrial development, particularly in cotton textiles, they preferred stability in the 1940's. The new men that appeared during and after World War II tended to be technicians, former politicians, former military men, and refugees from Franco's Spain. This finding by Mosk obviously indicates the value, if any further indication is needed, of social mobility for the development of industrial entrepreneurship.

[64] Mosk, *Industrial Revolution in Mexico*, chapters 2 and 3.
[65] *Ibid.*, p. 21.
[66] Sanford A. Mosk, "Discussion" [of H. G. Aubrey, "Industrial Investment Decision . . ."], *Journal of Economic History*, 15 (December, 1955), 357.

The Mexican handling of the Indian problem deserves at least passing laudatory comment. In contrast to neighboring Guatemala, Mexico has made a determined effort to integrate its Indian population in the national culture and economy.[67] This is hardly to suggest that the change came without a struggle. In 1925, for example, President Calles found it necessary to demonstrate to the people of Mexico City that the Indian was capable of absorbing an urban culture by dramatically importing a group of young Indian men from their native habitats and schooling them in urban ways. So successful was the venture that they had no desire to return home.[68]

As used in Mexico the term "Indian" has come to mean a rural proletariat attached to the old Indian traditions and modes of life. It is a cultural, not a biological, classification. Once one changes one's style of dress, lives in a house rather than a hut, speaks Spanish, and generally surrenders his identification, one is no longer considered an Indian. This transfer to the category of mestizo may occur in rural areas, especially near the United States border, but it tends to be associated with the procurement of work in an urban area.

Those who have remained Indians, culturally, experience varied degrees of contact with the remainder of society. Frequently they exhibit their wares in municipal market places and thereby come into contact with visiting non-Mexicans. In other instances the Indians have lived in isolation and have remained indifferent, perhaps hostile, to change. As such they have made up a surprisingly heterogeneous and diversified world, which includes more than seven hundred tribal groups, twelve distinct linguistic families with fifty to one hundred different languages and dialects, and considerable differences in culture and tradition. Their languages can be as sharp in contrast as English, Chinese, and Hebrew, a fact which helps explain the very little intermixture among the tribes, to say nothing of the minimal contacts with the dominant occidental culture. These characteristics of language reflect the Indian problems of post-Revolutionary Mexico. Many of the Indian communities have preferred to remain unassociated and unidenti-

[67] *Ibid.*, p. 359.
[68] Tannenbaum, *The Struggle for Peace and Bread*, pp. 165–166.

fied with the rest of the nation—which is to say that they have withdrawn from situations which they have not liked, although they have not resisted them. Such communities have apparently remained strongest when their cultures have been most complex and the Indian population most highly concentrated.[69] Others have tended to disappear gradually under the influence of economic development.[70]

Since the Revolution Mexico's women have also managed to experience progress toward greater equality. Anthropologists inform us that Mexicans inherited the concept of male domination from the Spanish conquerers. The Aztecs generally treated their women as equals, though they could neither govern nor inherit a legacy. With the coming of the Spanish, the woman was relegated to the role of drudge in the lower income groups and to that of charming hostess as well as bearer and educator of the children in the upper classes. During the nineteenth century Mexican women, like Spanish, continued to possess a "protected" status and were far behind British and American women in their degree of liberation. Women were not permitted to enter normal school until 1886, while in 1887 the first university woman graduate received her medical degree. In 1904 women teachers passed examinations for school inspectors. Only when the Secretary of Public Education hired the first woman did office work open up as a proper feminine occupation.

During the Revolution local and national heroines participated in the fighting as cooks, porters, and even as soldiers. Women were slow to benefit from the Revolution, however. It was not until 1947 that they were given the right to vote, while the opportunity to govern was limited to municipal councils until 1953. In 1955 four women were elected to the Chamber of Deputies.[71] Discrimination has continued in the economic realm. In the lower economic groups the boy child is given the preference if every pair

[69] Robert Redfield, "The Indian in Mexico," *Annals*, 208 (March, 1940), 135. Also see Philip L. Wagner, "Indian Economic Life in Chiapas," *Economic Geography*, 39 (April, 1963), 156–164.

[70] Antonio Carrillo Flores, "Mexico and the Indian," *Américas*, 16 (February, 1964), 11.

[71] Ana Maria Flores, "La mujer en la sociedad," *México: Cincuenta años de revolución, II*, pp. 329–349.

TABLE 16. Participation of Women in the Labor Force,
for Selected Years*

Year	Total	Numbers (thousands) Men	Women	Per Cent Men	Women
1930	5,352	4,981	372	93.06	6.94
1940	5,858	5,426	432	92.62	7.38
1950	8,345	7,208	1,138	86.37	13.67
1958	9,253	7,707	1,545	83.30	16.70

* Ana M. Flores, "La mujer en la sociedad," p. 339, t. 4.

of hands does not have to earn a living; he is sent to school if a choice can be made, while the girl is kept at home to help run the house and take care of the younger children. In the middle-class home the girl often receives some education for employment as a shop clerk or secretary. The life of the upper-class woman can be highly circumscribed. As the symbol of her husband's status she has several maids to help her run the household, but frequently she has had no education beyond the equivalent of high school. Some have not followed these patterns. In 1940 about 4,000 women constituted almost one-tenth of those in the liberal professions, while 42,000 made up 20 per cent of the public administration employees. Simultaneously, women in the fields of commerce and industry composed 17 and 10 per cent, respectively, of all gainfully occupied persons in these two groups. The 1950 census reported almost 44,000 men and just over 19,000 women in secondary schools.[72] From 1941 through 1958 the male recipients of university degrees outnumbered the female by a multiple of four to one, with the ratio showing fairly little fluctuation.

Since 1930 women have been entering the work force at a more rapid rate than the men. Table 16 indicates that the number of women in the labor force expanded more than fourfold from 1930 to 1958, while the number of men increased by a multiple of about 1½. These statistics do not include women employed at home to

[72] Clementina Z. de Equihua and Ifigenia M. de Navarrete, "El desarrollo económico de México y la mujer," *Revista de Economía*, 20 (May, 1957), 117–120.

work on clothing, shoes, blankets, toys, and similar items, for their number is extremely difficult to determine. One estimate places the figure at thirty thousand for the Federal District alone in 1946.[73]

In sum, the data reflect the rather considerable, albeit not remarkable, changes in woman's status since the pre-Revolutionary days. She is now evidently in a more favored position to contribute to her country's economic development.

[73] Josefina Poulat de Durand, "Trabajo femenino a domicilio," *Revista de Economía*, 20 (May, 1957), 121–124.

CHAPTER FOUR

The Influence of the Revolution: II

The role of government in economic development: public investment and assistance to private industry. The peculiar role of the government in Mexico's economic life renders its economic system virtually incapable of classification. This in fact constitutes a source of national pride to many Mexicans, who attribute a uniqueness to Mexico's politicoeconomic system. The combination of public capital formation and governmental assistance and regulation suggests the German and Japanese models of development; but these countries possessed exceedingly strong totalitarian features which eventually led to fascism and external aggression. While Mexico requires a strong executive for political stability, the political climate is generally one of liberty; the country has virtually no army, and the government's policies frequently take on the trappings of a welfare state. Despite the very great differences in history, politics, size, and population, the developments in the Scandinavian countries and Israel appear analogous to those of Mexico. However, the influence of the business sector upon the government, whether through personal contacts or through the chambers of Industry and Commerce, certainly equals that of labor, and the distribution of income is severely skewed. That is, the welfare aspects do not dominate government decisions. One is thus forced to eschew attempts at classification and to speak simply of a government-directed economy in which large sectors are reserved for private efforts.[1] Presumably some of the poor countries may someday emulate the "Mexican model" of development.

[1] S. Walter Washington, "Mexican Resistance to Communism," *Foreign Affairs*, 36 (April, 1958), 513.

Growth, Equality, and the Mexican Experience

TABLE 17. Public and Private Investment as
Percentages of Total Investment, 1939–1961*

Year	Public Investment (%)	Private Investment (%)
1939	38.3	61.7
1940	40.9	59.1
1941	37.3	62.7
1942	47.9	52.1
1943	48.4	51.6
1944	41.3	58.7
1945	40.8	59.2
1946	33.9	66.1
1947	33.6	66.4
1948	35.9	64.1
1949	39.7	60.3
1950	44.5	55.5
1951	38.9	61.1
1952	42.1	57.9
1953	39.0	61.0
1954	42.7	57.3
1955	35.8	64.2
1956	34.0	66.0
1957	34.9	65.1
1958	37.7	62.3
1959	38.6	61.4
1960	41.4	58.6
1961	46.1	53.9

* Sources: (a) 1939–1950. The Combined Working Party, *The Economic Development of Mexico*, p. 188, t. 15. (b) 1951–1961. Secretaría de Industria y Comercio, *Anuario estadístico de los Estados Unidos Mexicanos, 1960–1961*, p. 628, t. 16.4. Investment is in fixed and gross terms.

Of the two major types of government activities, let us first glance at public investment. What has been the magnitude of this investment? What have been the particular industries affected and what criteria have been adopted by the authorities in planning the public investment programs? Beyond that, what criteria have been adopted and what techniques utilized in assisting private industry?

As noted in Chapter Two, public investment in Mexico has comprised a fairly significant fraction of the nation's gross product and a rather high percentage of total investment. Public capital formation as a percentage of gross national product fluctuated between 4.1 and 6.5 from 1939 through 1961, and over the same period it approached 40 per cent (39.7 per cent) of total investment (see Table 17). The latter series also exhibits considerable variations, but some regularity of behavior is discernible. World War II generally brought the percentages above 40. Thereupon, with the exception of three years, they dropped below 40 from 1946 through 1959. Because of this decrease, many students of the Mexican economy predicted a relatively declining role for government in the investment field. Nevertheless, in 1960 private investment began to lag and public investment once again surpassed 40 per cent of the total. Moreover, it continued to do so through 1964, even though private fixed capital formation expanded nearly 25 per cent that year.[2] In all probability the decrease in private investment to less than 60 per cent of total investment would also prove to be cyclical. As the government continued with its public investment programs and stimulated economic growth and as excess capacity in the private sector was reduced, the 60-40 ratio would undoubtedly be approached once again.

For institutional reasons public investment must be limited to certain fields, frequently the familiar public utilities. Roads obviously arise through public enterprise, and the National Railways of Mexico own some 70 per cent of the total roadbed. Since the famous expropriations of 1938, the production of petroleum and natural gas has been managed by the state-controlled Petróleos Mexicanos (Pemex), while the retail sales of gasoline have remained in private hands. The generation of electricity, more frequently hydroelectric than thermoelectric, has long been a public matter. The government also took over distribution of electricity in 1960, apparently in order to win popular favor through national ownership and through discriminatory pricing based on income differences. Telephones, on the other hand, have remained in private hands, since it has been possible to Mexicanize the owner-

[2] Based on United Nations, Economic Commission for Latin America, *Economic Survey of Latin America, 1964*, p. 103, t. II-58.

ship without also nationalizing it. Public education, irrigation, and municipal construction represent three other obvious areas of government investment. Certain specialties, such as petrochemicals and fertilizers, further qualify. The government also owns and controls portions of iron and steel, auto and truck assembly, sugar refining, meat products, and a host of other activities.[3] Nevertheless, most firms in Mexico are privately owned and operated. A revolution against feudalism together with some highly publicized expropriations have managed to conceal the business-like character of Mexico's economy. But in those areas where it has chosen to operate, the Mexican government, unlike that of Venezuela and many other Latin-American countries, has functioned as a highly dynamic entrepreneur.

Of the several major divisions of public investment, transportation and communication—consisting not only of railroads and highways, but also of airports, harbors and ports, and telegraphy and radiocommunications—have taken the largest share. The share has declined, however, from 60 per cent in 1942–1943 to less than 40 per cent in the 1950's. The investment trends for agriculture, livestock, and natural resources border on the alarming, given the many needs in this sector. During the forties the trend was somewhat upward, from some 15 per cent during the war years to approximately 20 per cent from 1947 to 1951. But during 1951–1957 the percentage once again resided in the neighborhood of 15, and by 1960 it had fallen below 10. By contrast the energy-industrial group has moved up very sharply, from less than 10 per cent during the war to 33 per cent in 1960. The last major division of public investment, for such social benefits as health, education, housing, miscellaneous urban services, and rural development, has climbed gradually but persistently from somewhat more than 10 per cent during the war to some 14 per cent in the early fifties and over 20 per cent by 1960. Construction for miscellaneous purposes, such as administration and defense, has not varied much beyond 2 or 3 per cent of total public investment.[4]

[3] See Frank R. Brandenburg, "A Contribution to the Theory of Entrepreneurship and Economic Development: The Case of Mexico," *Inter-American Economic Affairs*, 16 (Winter, 1962), 10.

[4] This summary of the behavior of the major components of public investment is based upon: Combined Mexican Working Party, *The Economic De-*

Percentages and relative positions scarcely do justice to the pro-
digious rates of growth which occurred in many of these sectors.
According to a statement in 1962 by Secretary of Finance and
Public Credit:

> Investment programs undertaken since the early thirties have made it
> possible to increase by eleven times the country's highways to the
> present network 26,000 miles; and to build a series of dams which
> have raised by 20 times the area of irrigated land (to 7,400,000 acres).
> In electric power, installed capacity has grown six times to 3,400,000
> kw.

In the two decades beginning in 1939 the production of electric
energy and petroleum each tripled. By 1958 petroleum was sup-
plying as much as 85 per cent of the energy consumed, and it
was apparently making significant external economies possible in
many industries through the provision of a low cost fuel, frequently at a price involving a subsidy.

While several criteria have influenced officials in their public
investment decisions, one does emerge as prominent. This is the
relief of bottlenecks or the overcoming of shortages, whether in
public or private fields of endeavor. Mexicans speak of "balanced"
growth in this context. Thus:

> What has been done in our country has been to consider, on the basis
> of public investment need surveys, the damage that would be done if
> certain works were not constructed: for example, electric power re-
> striction in a given zone if an electric plant is not provided for in
> opportune time, or the shortage of fuel for industry in a specified
> area because of the lack of a refinery or adequate pipelines. It has
> been necessary to adopt this criterion in our country, in view of the
> limited investment resources available as compared to public works
> needs; for in this respect the objective consists of distributing what-
> ever investment resources there are among the various sectors with
> the idea of avoiding economic bottlenecks. . . .[5]

---

velopment of Mexico, p. 195, t. 20; United Nations, Economic and Social
Council, *World Economic Survey, 1959*, p. 85, t. 2-17; and Nacional Financiera,
"Mexican Economy: Selected Economic Indicators, 1961," p. 1.

[5] Gustavo Romero Kolbeck, "La inversión del sector público," in *México:
Cincuenta años de revolución, I, La economía*, p. 502; cited and translated by
Miguel S. Wionczek, "Incomplete Formal Planning: Mexico," in Everett E.
Hagen, ed., *Planning Economic Development*, p. 161 n.

The business sector may quarrel with the degree of inclusiveness of "public works needs," but it certainly has tended to approve the relief of transportation and other major bottlenecks, and it welcomes, indeed encourages, investment activities which it believes to be outside the responsibilities of private enterprise. When the government has chosen not to enter certain activities because of adverse reactions from business, as has largely been true in pulp and paper, it has endeavored to work out an integrated policy through financing and persuasion. In other instances, as with fertilizers, it has directly produced the required resources. In recent years many observers have urged that the ideas of balance and the relief of bottlenecks be carried to regional developments. The view has been that near stagnation in the hinterlands could exercise a retardative influence on Mexico's economic advancement and that seriously diverse development rates were highly inequitable.

Yet a single criterion cannot be permitted to dominate the public investment programs. In addition the authorities have weighed the productivity and the earning power of the projects under consideration; one would, however, expect these factors to be highly correlated with the aforementioned relief of bottlenecks. The volume of employment generated by a project upon completion has served as a criterion, as have the fiscal and financial position of the government and the implications for the general price level. As with most underdeveloped countries, the balance of payments position is a critical factor which can under certain circumstances outweigh several of the others. Sometimes Mexicanization has been a prime objective and the Mexican government has stepped in, when Mexican business could not, to prevent foreign business from entering certain fields; this has occurred most frequently in the exploitation of natural resources. To all intents and purposes the authorities have not attempted any vigorous quantification of these several criteria.

In the case of the government's indirect assistance to private industry[6] a somewhat different set of criteria emerges. Industries are eligible for fiscal and/or financial assistance if they are either

---

[6] The secretariats particularly involved are those pertaining to Finance, or Public Credit, and to Industry and Commerce (until recently, Economy).

"new" or "necessary" for the economy. Necessity is generally interpreted in terms of import replacement combined with the need for integration. That is, import replacement designed to further diversification and a sound balance of payments position serves as the prime objective; whatever is then required to help attain this goal—be it raw materials, intermediate goods, and so on—is in turn to be stimulated. The latter again suggests the relief of bottlenecks. In Albert Hirschman's terminology, "necessary" means import replacement plus linkage,[7] and if his views are valid the linkage associated with working backward in this fashion should be considerable. The stress on the "new" similarly serves the interest of long term diversification.

The authorities have of course understood that an adherence to the balance of payments criterion can be highly incompatible with improved productivity, at least in the short run. They have been aware of the opportunity costs, if for no other reason than because of the complaints of business men of higher prices of materials. As a consequence they have seemingly avoided a very excessive import replacement policy. According to one public official, if an industry is to qualify for governmental assistance in the curtailment of imports, the price which it ultimately charges for its marketed product cannot exceed the current price of the imported item by more than 10 or 15 per cent. The government makes no attempt to defend the sanctity of these percentages, but simply maintains that in its judgment this represents a reasonable compromise and not too high a price to pay for fostering economic sovereignty and growth. To paraphrase further the aforementioned official, the 10 to 15 per cent rule has been imperiled by a tendency on the part of some foreign exporters to engage in dumping, particularly of chemicals and also of artificial fibers. This of course results in prices so low that Mexican producers would be completely unable to establish new firms and compete in their own market. To solve this problem the textbooks typically recommend the application of quotas, but Mexico has generally not sought a solution along these lines. Instead the authorities have adopted the relatively high prices in the United States market as the standard for policy, whereupon the prices to be charged by

[7] Albert O. Hirschman, *Strategy of Economic Development*, chapter 6.

assisted Mexican firms may not exceed the United States prices by more than 10 or 15 per cent. These statements are in keeping with the usual governmental utterances about protection: namely, that protective duties should not raise prices unduly for the Mexican public. In practice, however, the authorities have distinguished sharply between capital goods and consumer goods. Investment goods have indeed been subject to duties approximating 10 or 15 per cent, but the duties on consumer items have averaged 50 per cent and even as high as 100 per cent on luxuries.[8]

Still another set of criteria is pursued by the Nacional Financiera. Until the late fifties the Financiera was an industrial bank, generally lending funds to Mexican financial and nonfinancial firms on the basis of profitability. It has since recognized that while a private profit rate may be correlated with social marginal productivity, the one is an imperfect measure of the other. Influenced by the ideas of Tinbergen, it has established a system that embraces four different criteria and assigns a value to each. The criteria and corresponding weights are applied to particular ventures in the following fashion:

(a) The balance of payments effect (30 per cent). The Financiera seeks to determine if an industry is export-generating or import-replacing as well as the import components it might require and whether the net result is a favorable one.

(b) Integration of industries (30 per cent). This represents an attempt to include linkage effects, whether backward or forward. Textiles, iron and steel, automobiles, and chemicals rank high according to this criterion.

(c) The generation of savings (20 per cent). This involves the capability of firms to engage in internal financing and reinvestment. Capital intensive companies tend to perform better according to this criterion.

(d) The effects on employment and regional development (20 per cent). Preference is particularly given to industries on these counts when the required infrastructure has already been introduced. Criteria (c) and (d) can of course conflict sharply.

These values simply provide the working rules which serve as

[8] Rafael Izquierdo, "Protectionism in Mexico," in Raymond Vernon (ed.), *Public Policy and Private Enterprise in Mexico*, pp. 254, 256.

points of departure. There is no rigid adherence to them. The whole orientation is one of flexibility and adaptability to differing circumstances. If, for example, workers may be discharged unless some credit is forthcoming, this can lead to the assignment of a much greater weight to the last criterion. Here, as elsewhere, the Mexican government has not applied its criteria in rigorous fashion.

To further their several goals the authorities have relied upon tax exemption, commercial policy,[9] and credit inducements. Tax exemptions have been in use since 1926, but for thirteen years they were limited to small firms with capital of less than five thousand pesos. In 1939 they were applied to certain new industries and in 1941 to "necessary" ones, primarily in manufacturing. The requirements for eligibility were not at all strict during the war; typically the concession ran for five years and could involve any major tax. After World War II the government made eligibility more difficult, but it permitted firms regarded as "fundamental" for economic development to obtain concessions for ten years, while those of "economic importance" might enjoy seven-year exemptions. From 1939 through 1961 over one thousand companies with capital of several million pesos profited from tax exemptions.

In its tariff policies since the thirties Mexico has swung from a system of duties which possessed both revenue and protective features to one of greater protection, in terms of both the commodities covered and the rates employed. Protection has particularly been offered to agricultural products and to those manufactured items that Mexican firms can produce; moderate duties have been applied to raw materials and equipment required by domestic plants; while the free list has included prime necessities, mining materials, and supplies used by the government. Direct import controls, unaccompanied by exchange controls, have further buttressed the protective features of the tariff measures. Since 1944 the Minister of Finance has been required to list commodities for which import licenses would be necessary. In recent years these

[9] The following survey of tax exemptions and commercial policies is largely based upon: Sanford A. Mosk, *Industrial Revolution in Mexico*, pp. 63–83; and Nacional Financiera, The Department of Financial Studies, "Tax Incentives for New Industry," *Mexican American Review*, 29 (December, 1961), 59.

licenses have been required for about three-quarters of the goods imported into Mexico. Some of these items are in addition subject to annual quotas.[10]

The government has also influenced the extension of credit in order to induce private investment in growth industries. Mexico's central bank (Banco de México) has generally been forced into a fairly tight monetary policy to restrain inflation, but at the same time it has resorted to selective credit controls to stimulate private capital formation. Private commercial and savings banks have had the option of maintaining a proportion of their liabilities with the central bank or of reducing their required reserve ratios by investing in longer term private securities. As a consequence the private banks have exercised less preference for short term loans than heretofore and have built up their holdings of medium (over one year) and long term paper. At the end of 1960 the short term loans of private institutions of credit aggregated 8,347,000,000 pesos, while the longer term investments totaled a relatively impressive 5,603,000,000.[11] In order further to promote growth the central bank has regulated the asset holdings and liability accounts of private financial institutions. This it has done according to a financial scale that assigns top priority to the public sector, a second order priority to productive private investments (particularly in industry and agriculture), and the least significance to "speculative" and "unproductive" ventures. The measures employed by the Bank have included quantitative controls and regulation of the interest rates.[12]

Aside from regulating private banks, the authorities have also established specialized official credit institutions to make funds available to both private firms and public agencies. These specialized banks have been highly active in lending to private firms. In 1950, for example, public loans as a percentage of private fixed investment totaled 28.5, while in 1957 the percentage was still as high as 23.4. During the intervening years public loans for private investment expanded at an annual rate of 27 per cent, so that the

[10] Izquierdo, "Protectionism in Mexico," pp. 254–255.

[11] Dirección General de Estadística, Compendio estadístico, 1960, p. 147, t. 207.

[12] David H. Shelton, "The Banking System: Money and the Goal of Growth," in Raymond Vernon, ed., Public Policy and Private Enterprise, chapter 3, esp. pp. 154–155 and 159.

relative decline in the public financing of the private sector simply resulted from a greater rise in the private financing of the business sector.[13]

Some of the more celebrated of these institutions pertain to foreign trade, agriculture, and urban housing, but the best known has been the Nacional Financiera.[14] This bank initiated its operations in 1934. Since then, aside from financing basic public investments, it has provided the private sector with funds, and it has in addition acquainted the more affluent Mexicans with the workings of a capital market by issuing various types of certificates and bonds. The Financiera's securities have been popular with both individuals and financial institutions, essentially because it has recognized the value of reducing uncertainty in order to stimulate the market. At one point, for example, this bank floated bonds bearing a minimum guaranteed yield of 8 per cent and frequently yielding as much as 10 per cent a year. Yet progress in the development of the capital market has come slowly, so that the major sources of the institution's revenues have continued to be government contributions and foreign loans. In its other major role, that of lending, the Financiera has provided valuable financial assistance to the private sector, though this use of its funds has not matched its outlays on public overhead capital. In 1961 it accounted for about 30 per cent of the total loans extended to industry by Mexico's banking system, private or public. Table 18 shows the distribution of the bank's total financing among 533 public and private enterprises as of June 30, 1961.

These several measures for stimulating growth indicate the very considerable involvement of the government in private capital formation. Mexico's over-all rate of industrial advance has been sufficiently impressive to suggest that the measures may have been

[13] United Nations, Economic and Social Council, *World Economic Survey, 1959*, p. 89, tables 2-19 and 2-20.

[14] The major source of the following comments concerning the Nacional Financiera is a speech delivered by José Hernández Delgado, General Director of the Financiera, entitled "The Contribution of Nacional Financiera to the Industrialization of Mexico" (August 1, 1961). The remaining data come from various issues of this Bank's *Informe anual*. See also Calvin P. Blair, "Nacional Financiera: Entrepreneurship in a Mixed Economy," in Raymond Vernon, ed., *Public Policy and Private Enterprise*, pp. 191–240.

Table 18. Financing of the Nacional Financiera,
by Types of Activities, June 30, 1961*

Activity	Millions of Pesos		Per Cent of Total	
(1) Infrastructure	9,414		61.3	
Transports		2,632		17.2
Electric energy		4,198		27.3
Irrigation and other public works		2,583		16.8
(2) Basic industries	1,872		12.2	
Petroleum and coal		1,014		6.6
Iron and steel		795		5.2
Cement and other building materials		63		0.4
(3) Other manufacturing industries	2,739		17.8	
Food products		490		3.2
Textile, shoes, and other clothing		142		0.9
Paper and pulp		378		2.5
Fertilizers and other chemicals		435		2.8
Metal working and machinery		399		2.6
Transport equipment		780		5.1
Others		117		0.7
(4) Other activities	1,335		8.7	
TOTAL	15,360		100	

* Source: see reference to Hernández Delgado in n. 14.

helpful. Specific instances of apparent success may be also cited. For example, by 1964 Mexico had met her goal of producing vehicles that were 60 per cent Mexican by cost and of a quality equal to the imported items, and her duties forced an American concern to invest in Mexico to produce insecticides.[15] Moreover, many students of economic development would give theoretical support to these and like policies by calling attention to the limita-

[15] "Three-Fifths Mexican," and "Mexican Import Controls," *Economist*, 213 (December 12, 1964), 1282, and 212 (August 8, 1964), 578, respectively.

tions of the price system in the underdeveloped areas.[16] On the other hand it is evident that the application of investment criteria by government officials can be ridden by errors in judgment and by waste and inefficiency.

Of the several measures noted for inducing private capital formation, tax exemption is typically regarded as a rather crude and wasteful mechanism, despite the fact that it may help budge the economy from the status quo. Mexico offers little reason to alter this judgment. The administration of the exemptions has been fraught with problems. "New" and "necessary" have been so broadly defined that they have lost some of their power in affecting the allocation of resources. The degree of red tape has frequently been so strangling that many firms have ignored their opportunities to claim exemptions; in a perverse way a highly complex set of regulations may thus on occasion become something of a virtue. The tax exemptions providing for relief from import duties on raw materials, intermediate goods, and equipment were probably quite effective, for they helped relieve serious bottlenecks. Otherwise, tax relief might well have been an overworked device for stimulating economic growth, especially given the country's revenue requirements.

Accelerated depreciation provides a superior incentive. Fiscal assistance ought to be made contingent upon behavior which promotes economic growth, and accelerated depreciation possesses this property in that firms can use it to their advantage only if they have first engaged in acts of investment. The device does possess a weakness qualitatively similar to the one associated with tax exemption, for an investment might well have been undertaken without the inducement. But the association with capital formation is more direct than in the case of exemptions. Tax exemptions may result merely in greater dividends; by contrast, accelerated depreciation must be associated with capital formation, though not necessarily "causing" it. When tax exemptions apply only to profits plowed back into the firm, they are of course similarly superior to general tax relief because once again they affect behavior more directly. However, when compared to this more selec-

---

[16] For example, see Henry J. Bruton, *Principles of Development Economics*, pp. 105–108.

tive type of tax relief, accelerated depreciation still possesses several virtues. The former tends to involve firms that have already experienced considerable business success, whereas accelerated depreciation is better designed to attract the new, perhaps hesitant, marginal firm. In addition, the exemptions imply tax revenues irrevocably foregone, while accelerated depreciation merely results in a postponement of tax payments by a successful firm. If the firm is moved to postpone its payments indefinitely through continued capital formation, the government has achieved marked success in promoting private investment. For these several reasons it is to be regretted that Mexico has not used accelerated depreciation more extensively. The authorities have resorted to it and they extended its use in the tax reforms of 1961, but they have not been able to move fast or far enough in this direction.

Little need be said here about the use of credit instruments to promote private investment. Undoubtedly the views of the central bank on "productive" versus "unproductive" investments did not find a perfect parallel in the realities of the everyday world. However, if the monetary authorities were denied extensive use of the general instruments of monetary control,[17] what recourse had they but to resort to selective tools? Moreover, despite evidence of some entrepreneurship, the profession tends to mold bankers along rather conservative lines. When possible it would seem advisable to direct them more to longer term loans in industry and agriculture and less to short term extensions of credit in commerce and speculation. Particularly would it seem so when, as in Mexico, commerce enjoys handsome profits over an extended period of time.[18]

Although ". . . the power of commercial policy to accelerate the development of poor countries is likely to be exaggerated,"[19] protective tariffs appear to possess greater theoretical justification than general tax exemptions. As is well known, protective duties are capable of assisting infant industries, promoting external economies, and encouraging foreign firms to leap over tariff barriers, if that is desired. Tariffs can further serve to strengthen the bal-

---

[17] See chapter 7.

[18] See chapter 5.

[19] Gerald M. Meier, *International Trade and Development*, p. 149. See his chapter 6 for a good discussion of commercial policies.

ance of payments position, and they are more likely than general tax relief to influence business decision-making through their direct effects upon the prices and costs of a given commodity. A great deal then depends upon the manner in which the program of protection is conceived and administered. The aforementioned 10 per cent–15 per cent rule for capital goods speaks well for the Mexican system in that it gives every indication of attracting the truly infant, potentially efficient industries. As with the tax relief program, the bureaucratic world has frequently been an irritating one. However, the problems of administration may in this instance actually enhance the effectiveness of the program, since foreigners may be repelled by the various regulations even when they are able to meet the price competition.

While protective tariffs are theoretically superior to tax exemptions as means of promoting private capital formation, the two can on occasion be highly similar. This is true when balance of payments considerations influence the selection of industries eligible for tax exemption and the exemptions involve indirect taxes. Each of these has characterized much, though not all, of Mexico's tax exemption program. The two forms are further alike both in their probable contributions to unequal income distribution and in their staying power beyond the age of infancy. Nevertheless, the two may still be distinguished with respect to their effects on tax revenue. Tax exemptions corrode the tax base. In similar fashion protective tariffs eliminate tax revenues when they perform as intended. But in practice the duties are likely to be partially protective and partially revenue producing rather than completely prohibitive. Moreover, in the case of tariffs the authorities have not opened the doors to widespread tax relief and they are in a stronger position to impose other taxes to raise revenue. In the face of protection these should not interfere unduly with the incentives of domestic entrepreneurs, particularly if they can be shifted. Tariffs, in brief, can be incorporated into a system that does not greatly interfere with the collection of tax revenue, while the waiving of taxes in certain industries is less easily reconcilable with fiscal needs and is in fact likely to spread over much of the economy. This difference can be of some importance in a country like Mexico, where public revenue has fallen considerably short of public expenditure requirements.

In sum, an economically progressive, dynamic government has intervened, in admittedly arbitrary fashion, to advance the nation's economy. Many of its actions can be subject to considerable criticism; the lack of integrated planning, the degree of emphasis attached to particular measures, and the extent of the administrative snarl are some cases in point. Yet the burden of proof falls upon those who maintain that Mexico would have progressed even more rapidly had she engaged in less public investment and had she permitted the market to exercise a much greater influence on her economy.

Toward national economic sovereignty. Finally, the Revolution has been noteworthy because of its influence upon Mexico's international economic position. In several respects it has permitted Mexico to assume greater control over the operation of its own economic affairs.

The effects of other nations, especially those of the United States, upon Mexico's long run growth are of course extremely difficult to assess. They range from the concrete and easily demonstrable to the intangible and diffused, from the highly favorable to the seriously unfavorable. Mexican children become acquainted early in their education with the details of the seizures of 1846 and 1847. It was the "gringo" who stole half of Mexico's territory. It has also been the "gringo" who has invested his dollars in Mexico to his advantage and to the detriment of the Mexican people, who has depleted Mexican resources, who continually interferes with Mexican prosperity whenever he decides to purchase fewer Mexican goods or the same quantities of goods at lower prices, and who frequently appears in Mexico as a tourist, unaware of Mexican history and culture, "flashing" money, clothes, and perhaps cars, and haggling with Mexican venders over a few pesos as if it were a challenging, exciting sport. At the same time, trade and tourism have bolstered the Mexican economy, while foreign investments have more than occasionally introduced Mexicans to new products and new modes of production. From the United States the Mexicans have learned the meaning of political democracy. Juárez, for example, was a close student of the American system and an admirer of Lincoln; and Mexico's labor leaders familiarized themselves with the ideas of Samuel Gompers. North Americans have undoubtedly claimed superiority because of their greater wealth, but from them the Mexicans have also learned to place greater value upon economic attainment.[20] From the United States Mexico has obtained new technical knowledge, despite the frequent lack of cooperation by investors in Mexico. Mexicans have ranked first among Latin-American countries as students in the United States; they numbered 1,185, for example, in the year 1951–1952.[21]

Mexicans have also found work in the United States. By North American standards the bracero (who, unlike the wetback, is legally permitted to work in the United States) is economically exploited, and by any standards he is frequently treated without the respect and dignity that human beings seemingly crave so strongly. Yet at the prevailing wage rates the supply of bracero services has generally exceeded the demand for them. The peak in the employment of braceros occurred during the war years, 1942 through 1944, when nearly 200,000 farm and railroad workers earned approximately $138,000,000 north of the border.[22] From 1942 through 1955, some 1,500,000 Mexicans came to the United States as braceros. In the early sixties the number averaged about 450,000 annually. The braceros have returned not only with savings, but with new skills and consumption habits as well—the stuff economic development is made of. The braceros could not always utilize their new ways in their old villages, whether because of geography, lack of capital, or even psychological problems of readaptation. As a result they might opt for urban employment, thus further contributing to the ferment of change. In turn the migration to the towns and cities probably furthered political stability. The braceros came largely not from the north, where agricultural wage rates were relatively high, but from the central zone, which was densely populated, relatively poor, and a potential source of violence and disturbance.[23]

The flow has of course also been in the opposite direction, as

[20] Washington, "Mexican Resistance to Communism," pp. 510–511.
[21] Howard F. Cline, *The United States and Mexico*, p. 359.
[22] Nathan L. Whetten, *Rural Mexico*, pp. 267–271.
[23] Robert E. Scott, *Mexican Government in Transition*, p. 37. For a different view of the effects of the braceros on Mexico's growth, see Laura Randall, "Labour Migration and Mexican Economic Development," *Social and Economic Studies*, 11 (March, 1962), 73.

United States citizens have come to Mexico for vacationing, business, work, and study. While personal income in the United States and the relative prices in the two countries have strongly influenced the timing of tourist receipts,[24] there can be no doubt about the long term importance of tourism for the Mexican economy. In 1950 Mexico earned 75 per cent of all tourist dollars spent in Latin America. Tourism has just about matched agriculture or the extractive industries in its ability to earn foreign exchange. Further, it has repeatedly rescued the current account in merchandise, which enjoyed an export surplus only during the years 1939, 1942, and 1943 during the entire 1939–1958 period.[25] It has advanced at a more rapid pace than merchandise exports apparently because the price elasticity of demand for tourist services approaches one, while the demand elasticity for Mexico's exports falls below unity.[26] Mexico earned the equivalent of $637,000,000 from foreign tourism in 1959, which compares most favorably with the $534,000,000 earned by Italy and France's $326,000,000.[27] The contribution of the United States to this total is reflected in the fact that, in 1960, transactions at the northern border brought Mexico 78 per cent of all receipts from foreign tourist expenditures. These border transactions contributed to further development because of the exchanges between the border towns and the remainder of Mexico and because the trade with the United States called forth projects, financed jointly by government and private effort, for industrializing and modernizing the northern area.[28] As for the trade in goods, as late as 1959 and 1960 Mexico was still shipping over 70 per cent of its merchandise exports to the United States, with coffee and unprocessed cotton comprising the major items.[29]

24 UNESCO, *External Disequilibrium in the Economic Development of Latin America: The Case of Mexico*, pp. 20–22.

25 Secretaría de Economía, *Memoria, 1958*, p. 236.

26 UNESCO, *External Disequilibrium*, pp. 20–22.

27 Banco Nacional de México, *Review of the Economic Situation of Mexico*, 37 (September, 1961), 19, t. 1.

28 B. Quint, "Cleaning Up the Border," *Mexican American Review*, 29 (September, 1961), 3.

29 One observer has attributed Mexico's economic success to her strong foreign exchange position, traceable in turn to the propinquity of the United States

One can regard these facts with mixed views—and they have been so regarded. On the one hand merchandise exports to the United States combined with United States tourist expenditures contribute some 10 per cent to the gross national product. Mexico would surely like to trade more with the other Latin-American countries, but it is a cold, hard fact that their purchases comprise barely 4 per cent of the Mexican exports and only the minutest portion, less than 0.50 per cent, of Mexico's aggregate product. On the other hand, the data highlight Mexico's continuing trade dependence on the United States, with all the attendant implications for trends and cycles in the Mexican economy. The Mexican government has been endeavoring to reduce this relative significance of United States purchases through the diversification of its economy and through the encouragement of trade with other countries, in Latin America and beyond.

Always conscious of its history and the advantages as well as the dangers associated with private foreign investment, Mexico has further endeavored to steer a sensible middle course between extreme encouragement and discouragement of foreign capital. At its best foreign investment has been a relatively quick and economic way of introducing capital goods, advanced techniques, and additional employment into the economy. Less favorably, it has at times involved business activity but little enterprise. It has then appeared in the tried and true industries, taking on a competitive property and largely replacing, rather than adding to, local activity. Mexican economists have complained that much of United States investment in manufacturing has been in the established consumers goods industries which already possessed adequate productive capacity. Similarly, private foreign investment is not known for its ability to meet over-all national plans and requirements, and from the point of view of a poorer nation this represents a relative malallocation of resources. Thereby the Mexican government has sought the growth of a diversified industrial economy subject to Mexican control. Because of balance of payments considerations it has further preferred to limit its debt charges on

---

and the absence of exchange controls. See Norman Macrae, "Mexico Shows the Way," *Economist*, 216 (September 25, 1965), 19.

all foreign capital, public as well as private, to approximately 10 per cent of its foreign exchange earnings.

Subject to these constraints, which in effect subordinate foreign capital to national needs, private foreign investment is welcome and is in some quarters considered indispensable. The Mexican government has for the most part avoided discrimination, whether in favor of or in opposition to foreign investors. It has not participated in any agreements involving special assurances or guarantees on the grounds that these would place foreign companies in a privileged position. Since the government has generally been encouraging private investment, however, the foreign concerns should find the Mexican business climate an attractive one. Like the Mexican firms, they can take advantage of the favorable profit rates, the relatively low tax rates, the freedom of exchange convertibility, and the fairly high degree of political stability and predictability to be found in Mexico. In the important pre-1940 cases of expropriation—namely, oil and land reform—foreign owners received at least partial compensation for their properties as a result of the negotiated reductions in the government's obligations. Generally, foreign investors are free to participate in any Mexican corporation as long as they agree never to invoke the protection of their respective governments.

However, such policies alone fail to yield the direction and control which the Mexican authorities would like to exert. Hence Mexican firms are favored in some instances and in some respects. A case in point is the 51 per cent rule, designed to assure the cooperation of foreign investors in Mexico's drive toward diversification. In order to invest in Mexico, foreigners must obtain the approval of the Mexican government, and to receive this they will frequently be advised to participate in joint ventures with Mexican capital. The rule has been described as follows:

Only Mexicans can have the control of corporations engaged in auto, air or sea transport; commercial broadcasting and television, aerial photography; colonization of national lands; exploitation of forests, sea products, and a few others. In all these instances, regulations provide that in the capital of the respective corporations the minimum participation of Mexican capital must be 51%.

There is also a tendency to grant special facilities to those mixed-capital corporations in which the majority of the stockholders is

Mexican. This is the case for instance of the Mining Law that provides that new mining concessions can only be granted to Mexican companies or to mixed corporations with a maximum foreign participation of 49%.[30]

The following furthers national sovereignty in another manner:

With respect to the legal capacity of foreigners to purchase land in Mexico, the Constitution has reserved solely to Mexican citizens the right to acquire land within 100 kilometers along our borders and within 50 kilometers of our seashores.[31]

Recently, foreign firms have been subject to additional discrimination in taxation (in the case of mining), the awarding of contracts, and the granting of permits.[32] Yet, these various restrictions and regulations have certainly not impaired Mexico's ability to borrow from foreign sources. By 1964 the supply of foreign capital was in excess of the demand, and the interest rate on bonds had declined to 9 per cent.

As might be expected, the official attitude toward private foreign investment has been attacked from every side. Some critics see it as attracting too much foreign capital, others as attracting too little; some feel that greater economic independence would lead to more rapid economic growth, while others believe that shortages of foreign capital have reduced Mexico's growth rate. The data show that Mexico has succeeded in moving rather significantly toward economic independence. In 1929 United States business investments in Mexico totaled $682,000,000. Thirty years later the figure stood only at $759,000,000 in current prices, so that the United States investment had fallen behind proportionately. During the interval it had also dipped absolutely; in 1950, for example, it was valued at $415,000,000. Moreover, its composition had altered considerably. In 1959 the manufacturing industries made up 47 per cent of the United States business investments, with 18 per cent in mining and smelting, 15 per cent in public service, 11 per cent in commerce, 5 per cent in miscellaneous, and 4 per cent

[30] Mario Ramón Beteta, "Notes on Foreign Investment in Mexico," *Comercio Exterior de México*, 8, Supplement (August, 1962), 5.

[31] *Ibid.*, p. 4.

[32] Raymond Vernon, *The Dilemma of Mexico's Development*, pp. 120–121.

in petroleum.[33] This composition of investment, however, has not served as a source of comfort to those who view the Mexican economy as remaining unduly dependent. They see the all-important industrial sector as dominated by foreign interests and the situation in mining as reminiscent of the exploitative pre-Revolutionary period. In the later fifties, for example, foreign interests controlled 71 per cent of the capacity for ginning cotton, 91 per cent of lead production, 97 per cent of zinc production, and 98 per cent of the copper output.[34]

The data on remittances suggest that Mexico is subject to only limited economic dependency. From 1939 to 1950 remittances of dividends, interest, and royalties as a percentage of the gross product averaged 1.5 per cent.[35] For the period from 1939 through 1957 the servicing of *direct* private investment consumed about 7 per cent of foreign exchange income earned on the current account. During the same time the servicing of long term *credits* from the Export-Import Bank, the World Bank, and private suppliers in the United States and Europe took up less than 3 per cent of the income earned on current account, while the old public debt required an additional 2 per cent.[36] In all, the servicing thus accounted for about 12 per cent of the foreign exchange earnings. In 1938 total service charges as a percentage of foreign exchange income came to 16.8; by 1947, it had gone down to 8.2; and in 1956 it was recorded at 13.5.[37]

Nor do the available data on foreign profits support the view that extravagant rates of return on private foreign investment have seriously curtailed Mexico's economic growth (see Table 19). Only the wartime rates of return in manufacturing appear relatively high. Otherwise, considering the greater risks associated

[33] These data are from Banco Nacional de México, *Review of the Economic Situation of Mexico*, 37 (August, 1961), 15–16.

[34] Guillermo Calderón, "Las inversiones extranjeras y el ahorro interno," *Revista de Economía*, 21 (June, 1958), 148–153, esp. 150–151.

[35] José Luís Ceceña, "Inversiones extranjeras directas en México," *Revista de Economía*, 15 (October, 1952), 317. Ceceña himself is not likely to view these results with equanimity.

[36] Antonio Carillo Flores, "Mexico Forges Ahead," *Foreign Affairs*, 36 (April, 1958), 582.

[37] United Nations Department of Economic and Social Affairs, *The Latin American Common Market*, p. 156, t. 2.

The Influence of the Revolution: II   109

TABLE 19. Profits from Direct Foreign Investment, 1939–1958*

Year	Total Profits (millions of dollars)	Book Value of Direct Foreign Investments (millions of dollars)	Rate of Return (total)	Rate of Return (mfg.)
1939	15.5	401.2	3.9	13.5
1940	15.4	449.1	3.4	10.6
1941	22.6	452.9	5.0	13.5
1942	26.5	477.4	5.6	15.8
1943	33.3	491.2	6.8	18.6
1944	27.7	531.8	5.2	16.4
1945	39.6	568.7	7.0	15.6
1946	48.9	575.4	8.5	15.9
1947	59.5	618.6	9.6	13.2
1948	61.3	608.8	10.1	12.4
1949	47.9	518.6	9.2	11.6
1950	57.9	566.0	10.2	13.7
1951	88.5	675.2	13.1	16.2
1952	83.4	728.6	11.4	15.1
1953	60.5	789.5	7.7	11.2
1954	50.9	834.3	6.1	8.9
1955	73.4	952.8	7.7	10.6
1956	93.4	1,091.4	8.6	10.8
1957	76.8	1,165.1	6.6	9.8
1958	73.2	1,169.5	6.3	8.8

* United Nations, *Private Foreign Investment*, p. 13, tables 7 and 8.

with investment abroad, the profit rates seem quite reasonable—in fact, surprisingly low, given the expectation of Mexican industry of a profit rate of from 20 to 25 per cent after taxes. The conservative conclusion is that foreign investors probably have not enjoyed a higher profit rate than attained by domestic firms.

An analysis of total investment within Mexico further indicates a lack of domination of the economy by foreign investors. Direct foreign investment has constituted a relatively small percentage of all investment. For the few years shown in Table 20 the average percentage was 10.5, and indeed for the entire 1940–1958 period

TABLE 20. Foreign Sources of Investment, 1953–1959*

Year	Total External Investment Funds As a Per Cent of GNP	Total External Investment Funds As a Per Cent of Total Investment	Direct Foreign Investment As a Per Cent of Total Investment	Direct Foreign Investment As a Per Cent of Total External Investment Funds	International Credits As a Per Cent of Total External Funds
1953	...	14.4	8.4	...	...
1954	...	19.8	12.2	...	...
1955	3.2	23.0	11.0	52.4	47.6
1956	3.3	20.9	10.5	53.1	46.9
1957	3.5	22.5	10.5	45.4	54.6
1958	3.7	...	...	29.6	70.4
1959	3.7	...	...	36.8	63.2

* Columns 2 and 3 are taken from Calderón, "Las Inversiones extranjeras y el ahorro interno," p. 149; columns (1), (4), and (5) are from Banco Nacional de México, *Review of the Economic Situation*, 36 (November, 1960), p. 8, tables 1 and 2.

the annual percentage never exceeded 15. Moreover, the ratio of direct investment to total external funds has declined as a result of the expanded operations of international lending agencies. This reflects the preference of the Mexican government for externally financed investments that can be controlled and directed toward over-all development needs.

The following figures summarize the very considerable changes that have taken place in the relative importance of various sources of investment funds since the days of Díaz.[38]

Period	Total Gross National Investment %	Domestic Savings % Total	Domestic Savings % Public	Domestic Savings % Private	Foreign Savings % Total	Foreign Savings % Direct	Lending
1902–1903	100	47	15	32	53	47	6
1950–1959	100	88	28	60	12	7	5

[38] Nacional Financiera, "Mexican Economy: Selected Economic Indicators, 1961," p. 3.

Finally, the amount of net foreign private investment becomes anything but large once the capital flows in both directions are taken into account. This may have little bearing on the issue of whether the Mexican economy is controlled by foreigners, but it does serve to indicate that on balance private capital flows have not contributed materially to Mexico's economic advancement. A comparison of columns (1) and (2) in Table 21 shows that in two years, 1946 and 1954, the outflow actually exceeded the inflow, while in many other years, as in 1947, the outflows reduced the net inflows. Once remittances are added to the other capital outflows (column [4]), the net inflows become negative for most years (column [5])—a result which can be exploited equally by the proponents and opponents of more private foreign investment. Since the data embrace both public and private capital flows and the direction of the former was primarily inward, the picture for

TABLE 21. Total Capital Inflows and Outflows, 1945–1955*

		(millions of pesos at 1950 prices)			
	(1)	(2)	(3)	(4)	(5)
			Remittance of	Total	Net Inflow
		Outflow	Dividends	Outflow	of Capital
	Inflow of	of	and	(Col. [2] +	(Col. [1] −
Year	Capital	Capital	Interest	Col. [3])	Col. [4])
1945	621	94	586	680	−59
1946	509	678	559	1,237	−728
1947	1,190	1,116	760	1,876	−686
1948	431	299	627	926	−495
1949	707	412	478	890	−183
1950	1,091	270	586	856	235
1951	772	322	510	832	−60
1952	1,137	400	684	1,064	83
1953	760	421	759	1,180	−420
1954	637	910	551	1,461	76
1955	1,194	452	753	1,205	−11

* The first three columns are drawn from United Nations, Economic Commission for Latin America, *Economic Survey of Latin America, 1955*, p. 19, t. 18. Column (1) includes reinvestment.

private flows is somewhat darker than indicated. Irrespective of the disagreement regarding the attraction of private foreign funds, there can be little argument over the desirability of reducing the outflow of the capital of Mexican nationals. This can be done, it is hoped, by increasing profit opportunities and reducing risk (essentially through economic growth) rather than by imposing direct controls.

On the other hand the Mexican government has been increasing its acquisition of funds from abroad, both from private and public sources. Perhaps because Mexico has stood in relatively little danger of adopting communism, the United States government has never furnished Mexico with extensive grants in aid. From 1954 through 1958, for example, Mexico received all of $20,000,000 in grants, with only $11,000,000 coming as part of bilateral aid and almost $9,000,000 emanating from UNICEF and the UN technical assistance program.[39] This implies total grants of $.14 a year per Mexican inhabitant, or less than $.08 a year per capita if only bilateral aid is included. The loans to the Mexican government, on the other hand, have been fairly considerable over the years, and they have contributed materially to Mexico's economic growth. In the three year period 1955–1957 the international credits utilized by Mexico averaged about 1.67 per cent[40] of the gross national product and 11.5 per cent of total gross investment.[41] As with most capital assistance, these may have been relatively small proportions of their respective totals but they mattered considerably at the margin.

The magnitude and behavior of public foreign borrowing can best be determined from the records of the Nacional Financiera, since that bank has served as the agent for all such loans extended to the Mexican government. From 1942 through 1960 the Financiera received almost $1,500,000,000 of credits from abroad. Of these 36.6 per cent came from the Export-Import Bank, 14.9 per cent from the World Bank, and the remaining 48.5 per cent from a variety of institutions, national and international, public and private. In 1960 the Financiera handled funds from the United States, Canada, four Western European nations, and the World

[39] United Nations, Statistical Office, *Statistical Year Book, 1959*, p. 423, t. 159.

[40] Based on Banco Nacional de México, *Review of the Economic Situation*, 36 (November, 1960), 8.

[41] Calderón, "Las inversiones extranjeras y el ahorro interno," p. 149.

TABLE 22. Credits of One Year or More Utilized from Abroad
through the Nacional Financiera, 1942–1960*

	(1)	(2)	(3)	(4) Total Servicing Interest (Col. [2] +	(5) Net Borrowing (Col. [1] −	(6) Obli- gations at End of
Year	Utilized	Amortized	Paid	Col. [3])	Col. [2])	Year
1942	10,000	696	167	863	9,304	9,304
1943	. . .	1,105	331	1,436	−1,105	8,199
1944	. . .	1,136	277	1,413	−1,136	7,063
1945	8,300	1,220	269	1,489	7,080	14,143
1946	37,390	4,533	878	5,411	32,857	47,080
1947	30,198	8,781	2,171	10,952	21,417	68,417
1948	20,181	11,979	2,649	14,628	8,202	76,619
1949	31,831	14,463	3,304	17,767	17,368	93,987
1950	30,656	18,839	4,307	23,146	11,817	105,804
1951	35,772	22,549	5,099	27,648	13,223	119,027
1952	58,332	21,066	5,287	26,353	37,266	156,293
1953	48,446	18,953	6,351	25,304	29,493	185,786
1954	49,592	24,800	6,787	31,587	24,792	210,579
1955	51,166	28,375	8,581	36,956	22,791	233,369
1956	66,661	31,933	9,188	41,121	34,728	268,097
1957	90,353	37,937	9,326	47,263	52,416	320,513
1958	125,842	55,950	10,696	66,646	69,892	390,405
1959	152,758	85,747	13,590	99,337	67,011	457,416
1960	286,441	80,804	19,088	99,892	205,637	663,053
TOTAL	1,133,919	470,866	108,346	579,212	663,053	. . .

(thousands of dollars)

* *Informe anual, 1961*, p. 51, t. 13. The statistic in column (6) for any particular year is of course the sum of the obligations outstanding in the past year and the net borrowing (column [5]) of the current year.

Bank. The United States then contributed 88.3 per cent, with 15.3 per cent of the grand total emanating from the Export-Import Bank and as much as 64.7 per cent coming from various private sources such as the Prudential Insurance Company of America.[42] Table 22 summarizes the Financiera's annual operations for the

[42] This summary of the Financiera's participation in foreign borrowing is from its *Informe anual, 1961*, pp. 49–50.

entire period. Among other things it shows that paid interest came to 9.5 per cent of the funds borrowed and used. In part this figure is a relatively high one because it does not take into account total negotiated loans, which included $286,000,000 of unused credits and $62,000,000 of canceled loans. Nevertheless, the interest rate is high. A congenital optimist, undaunted, would undoubtedly point to the satisfactory marginal efficiencies of investment that must have accompanied the use of these borrowed funds.

Aid from abroad should presumably accelerate somewhat with the implementation of La Alianza para el Progreso. At the time of writing the Alliance for Progress was still relatively new, and it was difficult to predict its eventual outcome. Mexicans as a rule have been favorably disposed toward the general purposes of the Alliance. They want economic assistance when it is unattended by outside controls of the Mexican economy and when service charges are not forced to an unduly high percentage of the export proceeds. This implies a general preference for public over private foreign lending, though many Mexican businessmen would not necessarily support this view. There is considerable approval also of several of the reforms required by the program, though again particular groups may be in opposition. Mexico takes great pride in having been the first Latin-American country to experience a major social revolution and in the fact that its land reforms preceded the changes undertaken elsewhere by many years.

Despite the general approval of public assistance and reforms, many Mexicans entertain serious misgivings about the concept and its implementation. First of all, some assert, if it is to be dubbed on alliance let it be so in fact. Let it be what the term implies: a relationship between equals. The failure to control one's destiny is hardly sweetened if interference comes from foreign governments rather than foreign private citizens. The Mexicans, as well as the other Latin Americans, have their particular ideas about politics, economic priorities, the tempo to be pursued in the introduction of reforms, the types of reforms, and like matters, and they would like to preserve their sovereignty and independence in these things. The majority tends to feel, for example, that improved planning and required tax reforms can be introduced only with moderate haste. Further, Mexicans tend to take the alleged altruism in the program with a heavy grain of salt. One of their adages, translated as "nothing for nothing," reflects the scepticism they feel for any apparent giveaways. To some extent this feeling is mollified in the case of the Alliance insofar as assistance takes the form of loans rather than grants, since loans have more of a *quid pro quo* property. All the same, Mexicans recognize that the United States is promoting the Alliance because it expects a political compensation. The vast majority evidently prefers the United States ideology to that of the Communists, but it resents being used as an instrument in the cold war, especially given past encounters with United States power. This in turn reinforces the position that there is not enough of a relation between equals, not enough of a true alliance. Finally, in the Mexican view, the Alliance has moved much too slowly because of the cumbersome United States aid machinery.

The Revolution notwithstanding, Mexico has actually not met all of the requirements for assistance. Perhaps the most glaring illustration of this is given by her failure, until very recently, to engage in any overall planning. To qualify for Alliance aid the Mexican government early in 1962 established an inter-Cabinet commission to be integrated by the President of the Republic, the Secretary of the Treasury, and the Secretariat of the Presidency. Aided by professional economists, this commission has been working to set up three-year and ten-year plans for economic development. The Nacional Financiera has taken similar steps. Except for occasional Export-Import Bank loans, the Financiera had always tended to concentrate on specific projects. Under the influence of the Alliance it has been turning to comprehensive programs, whereby "global loans" obtained from the Agency for International Development, the Inter-American Development Bank, and elsewhere were to be subject to a general supervision by the Financiera.

In sum, post-Revolutionary foreign investments in Mexico are markedly different in quantity, quality, and composition from the foreign investment activities which prevailed before 1910. The Mexican economy has gradually reduced its state of economic dependency, and the Mexican government has increasingly been able to limit, control, and direct foreign investment along the lines of its national objectives.[43] Insofar as Mexico has required external sources of investment funds it has been able to move to nonequity financing, particularly through public agencies. On the basis of the evidence, one can understand the warnings of some Mexican economists against much additional private foreign investment, but it is difficult to accept the view that foreign capital has significantly deterred Mexico's recent economic development. The Mexican authorities have grasped the fundamentals regarding foreign investment—namely, that with sufficient control of aggregates and composition, foreign capital can serve as an important instrument of national economic growth. They may not always have been well advised to require 51 per cent ownership by Mexican nationals, among other reasons because of the many means of evading the requirement; yet this has served as a means of enhancing Mexican control over economic activity and involving private citizens even more in the process of economic growth. Of potentially greater value has been the stress upon the special skills of foreign companies. Thus:

. . . it is expected from the foreign investor not only that he should place his financial resources in the country, but that he should bring in, as well, proper technological knowledge and make it available to Mexican society through the training of technicians and the participation of nationals in executive posts.[44]

This demand forces foreign concerns either to impart skills to Mexican nationals or to hire those who have already been trained. The first helps reduce a major cause of poverty, while the second increases the demand for the graduates of secondary and professional schools. Either is invaluable for Mexican economic development.

Mexico's enhanced economic sovereignty represents yet another triumph of the Revolution.

Summary: The role of the Revolution in Mexico's economic growth. Mexico's history constitutes a significant case study of the

[43] Jorge Castañeda, "Revolution and Foreign Policy: Mexico's Experience," *Political Science Quarterly*, 78 (September, 1963), 391–417.
[44] Banco Nacional de Comercio Exterior, "Foreign Private Investment in Mexico," *Comercio Exterior de México*, 11 (July, 1965), 3.

effects of institutional reform upon economic growth. On balance the Revolution contributed very significantly and in a variety of ways to the country's economic development.[45] The stimuli given the economy by the Revolution include the following:

(1) Mexico rid itself of a highly constraining feudal aristocracy and landholding system. The land reform at least contained the seeds of a more favorable incentive system, and throughout the society the promise of a good life began to replace the old fatalism. The reform further contributed to political stability, as was particularly evidenced during the administration of Cárdenas.

(2) The Revolution greatly enhanced personal freedom, particularly through its reduction of peonage. Freedom's intrinsic value aside, this tended to spur geographic and occupational mobility, the growth of an adequate urban labor supply, and the rise of employees' organizations to protect workers' interests.

(3) The Revolution helped replace status with contract and furthered the possibility of social mobility. Merit rather than the accident of birth now more frequently became the basis of leadership.

(4) The middle class assumed more power. New patterns of consumption and investment arose, and types of wealth other than land became important sources of prestige.

(5) While Díaz had provided a political continuity during his administration, Mexico had generally experienced a long history of frequent political turnover. The Revolution served to introduce a political stability into the system which was based not on dictatorial control but on orderly legal succession. This has surely affected the private sector favorably, particularly in its inducement to invest.

---

[45] For a like statement of the relationships between the several components of the Revolution and Mexico's rapid economic growth see James G. Maddox, "Economic Growth and Revolution in Mexico," *Land Economics*, 3 (August, 1960), 266–278. Maddox does not attempt to argue that the Revolution was a sufficient and necessary condition of growth. His first disclaimer is indisputable, but the effects of institutional restrictions on the underdeveloped areas suggest that Mexico required at least some institutional reform for its economic advancement. For a lengthier treatment of the same subject see William P. Glade, Jr., "Revolution and Economic Development: A Mexican Reprise" in W. P. Glade, Jr., and C. W. Anderson, *The Political Economy of Mexico*, pp. 1–101.

(6) The Revolution ushered in a dynamic progressive government committed to economic growth. Representatives of the middle class, organized labor, and intellectuals have replaced a status quo oligarchy dominated by the landed aristocracy, the church, and the army.

(7) The relatively recent theories of human capital would suggest that the new interest in the development of human resources could only be beneficial for development.

(8) Since the Revolution Mexico has gradually shed its national economic dependency and has increasingly gained control over its economic affairs. It has thus been in a position to gain from foreign contracts at its own terms.

Many of these favorable effects are intangible and as such do not lend themselves well to quantification and measurement. For the most part they are concerned with the human psyche—with human motivations and responses and the desire for freedom, dignity, and respect. Nonetheless, the Revolution freed the masses for participation in the country's economic development.

On the other hand the Revolution initially did little to further agricultural production; in fact, over the short run it hindered agriculture because of an undue reliance on land reform. Many of the social reforms were either too long delayed and/or carried to excess. Then, too, the military struggles of the Revolution lasted until 1920, while political stability did not arrive in Mexico until the beginning of the Cárdenas administration in 1934. Economic growth may thus have been retarded because of the struggles for power and the necessity of completing the Revolution. Finally, the Revolution long could not, or at least did not, profoundly affect the distribution of income and wealth.

Despite these limitations and failures, the following conclusions hold: (a) By 1910 Mexico had experienced some economic dynamism, but a predominantly closed society tended to obstruct further economic development. (b) The institutional structure which Mexico established during the 1910–1940 period provided the framework for her post-1940 economic growth. (c) These two statements suggest a compatibility between greater social equality, which evidently was one of the major accomplishments of the Revolution, and economic growth.

CHAPTER FIVE

Income Distribution and Development

We have already had occasion, in Chapter One, to remark about the poverty of Mexican economic statistics. Yet the figures on such series as population, industrial production, and international trade in certain items are tolerably good compared to the material on income distribution. If one inquires about the latter data he is assured that very little are available and that they represent only the roughest type of estimates. The difficulties are further compounded if one is interested, as this writer happens to be, in changes in income distribution over time, for the data typically yield static pictures.

Under these circumstances one has to look for clues and leads wherever one may discover them. Such hints may appear in data pertaining to each of the following: (a) personal income distribution, (b) functional income distribution, (c) income distribution by economic sectors, (d) income distribution by geographic zones, (e) the behavior of real wages, (f) the concentration of wealth, (g) the composition aggregate demand, and (h) the incidence of saving. For each of these a considerable range of error (assuredly 5 to 10 per cent) may accompany the reported figures. Yet we would once again be well advised to avoid undue criticism, particularly if the several series point to similar results. Mexican policy makers, like those of other underdeveloped areas, must make their decisions on the basis of underdeveloped statistics; they cannot afford the luxury of waiting for highly reliable information. As a matter of fact, such waiting may indeed be in vain,

since the appearance of reliable data may well await the development of a technologically advanced society.

Personal income distribution. When we turn our attention to
this form of income distribution at least one other prefatory remark is necessary, this one concerned with economic theory rather
than with economic statistics. Perhaps the most useful instrument
yet devised for depicting personal income distribution is the
Lorenz curve, but this is ambiguous when two such curves relating to differences in time and/or place are utilized. These curves
can intersect, generally only once but potentially several times.
What sort of generalized description do we then use to indicate
greater or lesser equality? If the second decile has gained at the
expense of the highest decile and each of the remaining ones, as it
presumably did in the United States from 1910 to 1950, then
precisely what has "happened" to income distribution? Since such
contrary movements may occur, it becomes necessary to describe
the relative positions of both those at the top and those at the bottom of the national income ladder. Moreover, there is no standard-
ization regarding the relative sizes of these upper and lower
groups. Do deciles matter, or quintiles? I should personally want
to know about the income distribution within the upper income
group in considerable detail, for this is the more dynamic sector;
in fact, information on the highest decile taken 1 per cent at a
time should be highly desirable, as would data on the highest 15
per cent and 20 per cent. For the lower 80 per cent of the income
recipients, among whom less shifting tends to occur, a distribution
by deciles is probably sufficient. If due attention is thus paid to the
components, it appears legitimate to utilize some average representative datum to depict general changes in income distribution.
Simon Kuznets has at times employed one such simple device, and
I believe effectively. He simply notes any difference between perfect equality and the actual percentage of total income earned by
any quintile or decile of income recipients and then aggregates
these differences, ignoring algebraic signs. We shall employ his
method in this section.

What, then, do the data reveal about personal income distribution in Mexico, primarily during the forties and fifties? Let us
comb the literature for clues.

The broadest approach comes from a Mexican industrialist, who has ventured some views concerning the changes in personal income distribution from 1905 to 1955.[1] According to him, in 1955, 50 per cent of the Mexican population experienced an absolute plane of living that was either equal or inferior to that of the half century previous. Assuming this to be true, and given the considerable increases in per capita income since the turn of the century, this would imply a very severe deterioration in the relative standing of the lower income groups. This judgment is in all likelihood an extreme one. It is of interest because it comes from a representative of the upper income group and because it supports the view that the lowest income groups were relatively worse off in the late 1950's as a result of the economic development.

Few other students of personal income distribution dare go back that far. Miguel Flores Márquez[2] offers no supporting data but expresses the belief that the 1930's witnessed a movement toward greater equality of distribution, presumably at the lower end of the scale. He attributes this to public policies, in particular to the intensified program of land distribution and the government's assistance to labor. Flores Márquez may have confused the distribution of property with the distribution of income; certainly there is not much evidence to support the argument that land acquisition and the plane of living rose for the *ejidatarios* at virtually the same time. Further, he himself points to rising living costs as at least partial offsets to higher money wages. At best the thirties probably represented little more than a slight interruption of the general trend toward a relatively worse position for the lowest income groups. More probably, the relative position of the lower income groups deteriorated continually from 1920 to 1940. Agricultural production declined, sometimes leaving actual starvation as a consequence. The industrial advance was not terribly striking. The cost of living advanced rather sharply in several years, with easily predictable effects upon real wages. We must conclude, on the basis of the available scanty evidence, that most Mexicans were not better off in the absolute sense by 1940 and that

[1] Alfonso Noriega, Jr., "México debe bastarse a sí mismo," quoted by Oscar Lewis, "México desde 1940," *Investigación Económica*, 18 (Second Quarter, 1958), 230.

[2] Miguel Flores Márquez, *La distribución del ingreso en México*, pp. VI-2 and VI-3.

in relative terms the majority was worse off than it had been in 1920.

Several writers have been stirred by a piece by Manuel German Parra which appeared in *Siempre*,[3] a popular magazine of leftist persuasion and considerable reputation. Basing his findings on Nacional Financiera data, German Parra reported that in both 1935 and 1940 the top 1 per cent of all income earners received 40 per cent of the gross national income, already a sizable inequality by any standard. Yet this inequality allegedly sharpened by 1955. During that year, the 100,000 top men of business received 36,300,000,000 pesos, while the remaining 10,100,000 of the economically active population earned considerably less, namely 28,000,000,000 pesos. Translated into percentages, this implies, according to German Parra, that the top 1 per cent received as much as 66 per cent of the national income. His work conflicts with the a priori reasoning regarding the changes within the very top income groups during the course of development (of which more anon). Perhaps more to the point, it is quantitatively and probably qualitatively at variance with the findings of other students. German Parra derives his results from a strange mixture of different income concepts. Given a total national income of 84,000,000,000 pesos he subtracts 9,500,000,000 pesos generated by government purchases, their effects on personal income notwithstanding, and refers to the remaining 74,500,000,000 as incomes to persons. Next he blows up the incomes of the top 1 per cent by adding the business investment of 10,000,000,000 pesos to the 36,300,000,000 pesos which the group "received." The ratio of the resulting 46,300,000,000 to the previously noted 74,500,000,000 then supposedly yields close to two-thirds; actually even this approach results in a percentage of 62. The more legitimate but still inadequate comparison obviously involves the 36,300,000,000 received by the highest 1 per cent and the 84,000,000,000 of gross income, thereby resulting in 43 per cent of the income for the top 1 per cent. Further corrections are of course needed because gross income is not the appropriate concept. While a review of German

[3] Manuel German Parra, "Un programa reaccionario para la Revolución Mexicana," *Siempre*, No. 171 (October 3, 1956), 16–17.

Parra's article is of limited economic value, it does serve as a valuable exercise in public relations and propaganda. The article has affected the thinking not only of laymen in Mexico but also of otherwise responsible United States social scientists, who have quoted it in their work.[4] It evidently does not aid us in our search for information concerning personal income distribution after 1939.

Since 1950 was a census year, the information for that year is relatively good. In the work previously cited Flores Márquez has utilized census data on the incomes of employers and employees in agricultural and nonagricultural pursuits to produce the following breakdown of annual income for 1950.[5]

Gainfully Occupied Persons (thousands)	Incomes of Group (millions of pesos)
1	12,955
2	1,127
5	1,665
10	1,409
23	1,555
77	2,327
150	2,061
401	2,713
3,262	8,987
3,367	3,017
Total 7,298	37,816

In one respect these data tend to overstate the per capita incomes received by the lower income groups. The figures on the gainfully occupied persons exclude an estimated one million workers occupied with the family-run small shops, peasant farms, or other small businesses; their incomes have simply been attributed to the head of the family. The addition of these workers to the total number of gainfully occupied persons yields a total of about

[4] Lewis, "México desde 1940," pp. 227–228; and Robert E. Scott, *Mexican Government in Transition*, p. 90.
[5] Flores Márquez, *La distribución del ingreso en México*, p. V-9, t. 5.

8,300,000. Now we have the top three income groups, totaling eight thousand gainfully occupied persons and constituting slightly less than 0.1 per cent of the economically active population, accounting for about 41 per cent of the national income! The Flores Márquez data also show the top 10 per cent receiving some two-thirds of the national income and the remaining 90 per cent, earning income up to 5,000 pesos (almost $600) a year, receiving the remaining one-third. This is fairly consistent with the distribution reported by Robert Scott,[6] who has also used census data. He concludes that in 1950 virtually 86 per cent of those gainfully employed each received a maximum of 3,600 pesos ($423) a year and that almost half of this group received less than $150 per annum. Lewis' data[7] indicate that some 74 per cent of the families fell into the lowest class category (less than 3,600 pesos), compared with the 86 per cent of the work force indicated by Scott. At the other end of the scale Scott reports only 1.43 per cent of the gainfully occupied persons as receiving a minimum of 1,000 pesos a month ($1,440 a year), while Lewis includes about 3.4 per cent of all families in this highest income group. This information serves as a rather chilling reminder of the degree of poverty still to be found in Mexico after a decade of striking economic growth.

However, according to an official study conducted in 1958 the distribution in 1950 of personal income (which is of course the appropriate concept) was highly skewed but not quite as distorted as the previous sources would indicate (see Table 23). A monthly family income of 800 pesos serves as the point for dividing total personal income, while 300 pesos is the dividing line for the population. Thus the higher 14 per cent and the lower 86 per cent of the income recipients each accounted for 50 per cent of all personal income, with each of the families in the higher income group receiving at least 800 pesos a month. The highest 10 per cent enjoyed a minimum of 1,030 pesos a month and accounted for 42 per cent of the total income, while the highest 5 per cent received a minimum of 1,500 pesos per month and represented 31 per cent of the income. The lower half of the income recipients accounted

6 Scott, *Mexican Government in Transition*, p. 90, n. 10.
7 Lewis, "México desde 1940," p. 229, t. 18.

for only 18 per cent of the income, received a maximum of 300 pesos per family per month, and averaged about 235 pesos per month. The severe inequality of the income distribution indicated by these statistics is perhaps best revealed by Figures 1 and 2.

Ifigenia Navarrete has undoubtedly contributed the most detailed work on personal income distribution in Mexico. She presents data for the upper income level which are very close to Lewis' figures: namely, that 4.8 per cent of the families were to be found in the class of 1,000 pesos a month or better. Further,

TABLE 23. Personal Income Distribution, 1950*

(1)	(2)	(3)	(4)	(5)
			Total Monthly	
		Average	Income	Total
Groups of	Total	Monthly	(Col. [2] ×	Annual
Monthly	Number	Income	Col. [3])	Income
Incomes	of Families	(1950	(thousands	(millions
(1950 pesos)	(thousands)	prices)	of pesos)	of pesos)
0–74	95	74	7,030	84
75–148	493	111	54,723	657
149–222	960	185	177,600	2,131
223–296	1,003	259	259,777	3,117
297–370	526	333	175,158	2,102
371–444	366	407	148,962	1,788
445–518	289	481	139,009	1,668
519–592	237	555	131,535	1,578
593–666	171	629	107,559	1,291
667–740	140	703	98,420	1,181
741–1,110	406	925	375,550	4,507
1,111–1,480	162	1,295	209,790	2,517
1,481–1,850	74	1,665	123,210	1,478
1,851–2,220	47	2,035	95,645	1,148
2,221–2,590	37	2,405	88,985	1,065
2,591–and up	99	5,465	541,048	6,493
Total or average	5,105	536	2,734,001	32,808

* The data are from an official study of income distribution made in 1958.

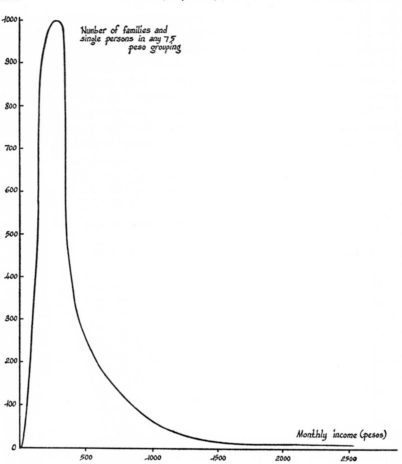

Figure 1. Personal Income Distribution in 1950.

this group enjoyed nearly 40 per cent of all personal income, while the top 10 per cent received almost 50 per cent.[8] This of course represents considerably more inequality than was found in the official study, where, it will be remembered, the shares for the top 5 and 10 per cent appeared as 31 and 42 per cent, respectively.

[8] Ifigenia Martínis de Navarrete, *La distribución del ingreso y el desarrollo económico de México*, p. 83, t. 11, and p. 85, t. 12.

On the other hand she reports somewhat less inequality than do the remaining investigators. While the others had estimated the number of income recipients receiving less than 300 pesos a month to be within the range of 74 to 86 per cent, she reports 49 per cent as receiving such low incomes and accounting for 18.6 per cent of income, a finding which agrees completely with the official study.

The differences in the findings stem from the use of different income concepts, the selection of either families or gainfully employed persons as the unit of study, the varied handling of payments in kind, and the difficulties of determining both corporate profits and the returns of noncorporate enterprises. Of the various sources cited, the official study and Mrs. Navarrete's are of course the most reliable—or the least unreliable. They deal with personal incomes and with incomes of families, they attempt adjustments

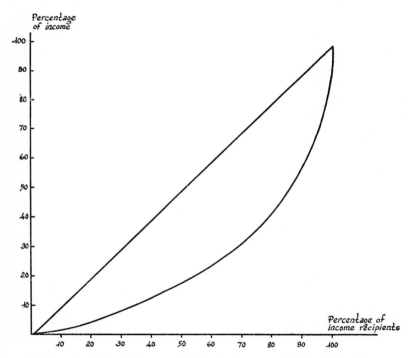

Figure 2. Personal Income Distribution in 1950, as shown by the Lorenz Curve

for payments in kind (*prestaciones*), and so on. On the basis of their combined work it does not seem unreasonable to conclude, in well-rounded fashion, that in 1950 *the top 5 and 10 per cent, respectively, received as much as 35 and 45 per cent of total personal income and that one-eighth of the families accounted for the upper half of the income.*

All this is in static terms, however. It would be valuable indeed to have access to comparable figures for other years in order to determine changes in income distribution. Unfortunately the existing data are again scanty. According to a sample survey undertaken in 1956, 39 per cent of all families outside the Federal District had monthly incomes less than 300 pesos and 61 per cent less than 500 pesos (or $480 per year); almost 10 per cent had monthly incomes exceeding 1000 pesos.[9] Pursuant to this work, another study revealed that 70 per cent of the population had monthly incomes not exceeding 750 pesos and that only about one-quarter to one-fifth experienced sufficient consumption to be able to save.[10] Such data remind us once again of both the poverty and the disparity in the distribution of income, but of course they do not pinpoint the changes that occurred after 1950. Yet, albeit vaguely, they imply little absolute improvement for low income Mexicans during the period. In particular, the fact that 60 per cent of the population outside the Federal District received no more than $480 per year in 1956 can be related to the finding that 50 per cent of the total population received a maximum of $423 a year in 1950 (assuming that changes in the exchange rate adequately reflected changes in purchasing power). Since the Mexican economy developed rather impressively during the intervening years, this also suggests in a very rough way that the relative income position of the lowest 50 or 60 per cent deteriorated to some extent. In addition the inclusion of 1956 data for the Federal District would undoubtedly magnify the inequality reported for that year and would thereby strengthen the impression of a relative worsening for the poorest groups.

[9] Dirección General de Estadística, *Ingresos y egresos de la población de México en el mes de octubre de 1956.*

[10] Benjamin Retchkiman, "Distribución del ingreso," *Revista de Economía,* 21 (August, 1958), 228.

Perhaps the greatest value of Mrs. Navarrete's research lies precisely in her attempt to indicate the changes in personal income distribution over time. For her comparison she has worked up some sample materials for 1957. This procedure evidently does not make the 1957 data strictly comparable with the 1950 distribution since the latter is on census statistics. Yet each of the following items revealed by the comparison (see Table 24) is in keeping both with casual observations and a priori reasoning:

(1) The income recipients in groups I and II and in X(c), especially the poverty-stricken in Group I, actually experienced absolute declines in their personal incomes from 1950 to 1957.

(2) Those in groups III, IV, and V were relatively worse off in 1957, as of course were those in groups I and II. Whereas the lower 50 per cent of the income recipients had received 19.1 per

TABLE 24. Personal Income Distribution in 1950 and 1957, by Deciles*

Decile	1950				1957		
	Average Monthly Income (1957 prices)	Per Cent of Total Income	Per Cent of Accumulated Income		Average Monthly Income (current prices)	Per Cent of Total Income	Per Cent of Accumulated Income
I	247	2.7	2.7		192	1.7	1.7
II	311	3.4	6.1		304	2.7	4.4
III	348	3.8	9.9		350	3.1	7.5
IV	403	4.4	14.3		429	3.8	11.3
V	440	4.8	19.1		485	4.3	15.6
VI	504	5.5	24.6		632	5.6	21.2
VII	641	7.0	31.6		835	7.4	28.6
VIII	788	8.6	40.2		1,128	10.0	38.6
IX	989	10.8	51.0		1,658	14.7	53.3
X (a) (5.2)	1,621	9.2	60.2	(5.1)	2,233	10.1	63.4
(b) (2.4)	2,858	7.5	67.7	(2.6)	5,460	12.6	76.0
(c) (2.4)	12,329	32.3	100.0	(2.3)	11,765	24.0	100.0

* Navarrete, *La distribución del ingreso*, p. 85, t. 11.

cent of the personal incomes in 1950, their cumulative percentage had dropped to 15.6 per cent by 1957.

(3) Not only had the very lowest income groups fallen behind relatively, but so, interestingly enough, had the very highest 2.3 per cent, or 2.4 per cent of the income receivers, Group X(c). In fact its relative decline was sharper than that of the lower 50 per cent, from one-third to just under one-quarter of the total income.

(4) Those who might be characterized as the lower and middle upper class (groups X[a] and X[b]) and as the middle class (groups VIII and IX) were the big gainers, relatively as well as absolutely. Their incomes totaled 36.1 per cent of personal income in 1950 and 47.4 per cent in 1957. Group X(b) alone accounted for 45 per cent of the improvement experienced by the four groups combined.

(5) The Lorenz curves for the two years intersect within Group IX, indicating that in 1957 there was greater equality *within* the upper 20 per cent but less equality between the highest quintile and the remainder of the income receivers than had existed in 1950.

These several points can be summarized in the following array:

Personal Income Received by:	1950(%)	1957(%)
The highest 2.3 or 2.4%	32.3	24.0
The highest 4.8 or 4.9%	39.8	36.6
The highest 10%	49.0	46.7
The highest 20%	59.8	61.4
The highest 30%	68.4	71.4
The lower 50%	19.1	15.6
The lowest 30%	9.9	7.5
The lowest 20%	6.1	4.4

Such expansion of the middle and upper middle income groups is precisely the sort of change one would expect during the course of economic development. Here is the rather notorious, highly vaunted extension of the middle class, which gained relatively at the expense of both the very high and the low income groups.

So much for the behavior of the components. Did income distribution as a whole become more equal over the seven-year interval? The simple method referred to at the beginning of this section provides some clue. According to this procedure, personal inequality became somewhat more intense; the relative losses of the mass more than offset the relative decline of the topmost income group. The changes, in greater detail, were as follows:

Deciles	Departures from Perfect Equality 1950(%)	1957(%)
I	7.3	8.3
II	6.6	7.3
III	6.2	6.9
IV	5.6	6.2
V	5.2	5.7
VI	4.5	4.4
VII	3.0	2.6
VIII	1.4	0.0
IX	0.8	4.7
X (a)	4.0	5.0
(b)	5.1	10.0
(c)	28.9	21.7
Total	78.6	82.8

However, the differences between the results for the two years are minor compared to the possible error in the accumulation of the data. The more modest and conservative conclusion is that income distribution did not alter materially, but may have become somewhat more unequal, from 1950 to 1957.

The most distressing aspect of these developments is the absolute decline in the real incomes of the lowest two deciles. Relative income changes may well be the stuff economic development is made of; in some cases they may further change and in others constitute the cost of growth. One would hope, however, that at the very least no low income families would be worse off as a result of growth. One might further express the value judgment that an alteration in income distribution is tolerable only insofar as it provides some minimum improvement in the planes of living of lower income families.

To give formal expression to the problem of deterioration, or insufficient advances, in absolute levels of income, let us set up what might be deemed a desirability index of altered distribution.

The index yields the most satisfactory result when it assumes the value of one. In symbols,

$$d = \frac{h + s}{m}, \tag{1}$$

where h represents the percentage of the total income lost by the highest income group, s the relative loss experienced by the low income groups *despite the constancy or designated improvement of their planes of living*, and m the percentage of total income gained by the middle income groups (VI through X[b] in Table 24). Since the algebraic signs of these variables do not alter, they can be ignored. In the Mexican economy from 1950 to 1957, d would have assumed a value of 1 if h and m not only equaled 8.3 per cent and 11.8 per cent, respectively, as they did, but s made up the difference while the planes of living of the low income groups did not fall. The actual changes, however, did represent a case of either deterioration or insufficient improvement for the low income groups, and as such requires a more general formulation.

Let f reflect the decline in real incomes for any particular decile (or other grouping) at the lower end of the scale. Then:

$$d = \frac{h + s - (f_1 + f_2 + f_3 + \ldots)}{m} \tag{2}$$

An f can be taken as the difference between the percentage of total personal income the families in a particular decile would have received if they had managed some minimum improvement (no less than 0.0 per cent a year) and the percentage of income they actually received. To determine an f for any particular decile, let i represent the agreed upon annual rate of improvement in real income per family (at least zero), Y_t the total incomes received in some given year, y_0 the average real income per family for a decile in a base year, y_t the average real income per family for a decile in some later year, and p the number of families in each decile. Then for any decile in the lower income group:

$$f_j = 100 \left[\frac{y_0 (1 + i)^n \cdot p_t}{Y_t + y_0 (1 + i)^n \cdot p_t - y_t p_t} - \frac{y_t p_t}{Y_t} \right], \tag{3}$$

where the first term within the brackets expresses the potential share of the decile if some given i is achieved, while the second term indicates the actual share. If $f_j \leq 0$, it can be neglected in equation (2).

The denominator in the first term of equation (3) is troublesome. If the families within a given decile could have improved their lot, would this have resulted in a simple net addition to total income received? On the one hand it can be argued that the benefits accruing to this group may have come merely at the expense of other groups and on the other, that their gains would have directly and indirectly stimulated other segments of the economy through interactions of supply and demand. Given the low income position of the families within the decile as well as the high incidence of external economies in developing countries, the second alternative, that of a still higher $(Y_t - y_t p_t)$, seems more likely. The denominator is probably understated, though it is most difficult to judge by how much. As this is done, f_j in equation (3) is decreased wantonly, and the desirability of the changed income distribution, d, is thereby overstated. Some offset to this likely bias seems justified. Since f_j becomes larger when i, the rate of proposed improvement, increases, permit i to exceed zero. This not only counters the possible understatement of f_j but is consistent with the position that a developing economy assist its poorest elements. Thereby assume, for example, that i equals 0.01. For any decile:

$$f_j = 100 \left[\frac{(1.01)^n \cdot y_o \, p_t}{Y_t + (1.01)^n y_o p_t - y_t p_t} - \frac{y_t p_t}{Y_t} \right]. \qquad (4)$$

It is now possible to estimate the desirability index for the changes in income distribution that occurred between 1950 and 1957, beginning with the computations of the f's. Some simplifications are not out of order. Since p is a constant whose magnitude does not greatly affect the results, let p equal 1. This sets up a miniature economy of ten families with the same income distribution that prevailed in Mexico in 1957. Further, it does not matter if monthly income is used to represent the total income. This datum can be readily computed from the y_t and the $\dfrac{y_t}{Y_t}$ for any given decile (192 pesos per month and 1.7 per cent, respectively, for Group I); it approximates 11,290 pesos per month for the tiny, Mexican-like economy. Then, according to equation (4):

$f_1 = 0.6\%$
$f_2 = 0.1\%$
$f_3 = 0.1\%$
$f_4 = -0.1\%$.

The finding for f_4 can be ignored, whereupon,

$f_1 + f_2 + f_3 = 0.6\% + 0.1\% + 0.1\% = 0.8\%$.

Substitution within the basic equation (2) for the desirability index then yields:

$$d = \frac{8.3\% + 3.5\% - 0.8\%}{11.8\%} = 0.93.$$

Thus, under the assumption of an improvement rate of 1 per cent, most of the changes in income distribution during the period were potentially beneficial for the economy's growth.[11] These results are not surprising considering the years covered. Mexican economists do not believe that there was a marked swing toward income inequality during the 1950's, even though many have registered disappointment that there was no converse movement toward greater equality. On the other hand if the families within the lowest deciles had actually experienced an improvement of 1 per cent a year in their planes of living, the values of f_1, f_2, and f_3 suggest that the growth rate for the economy could have risen by as much as 1 per cent a year.

Thus far we have little noted the changes in income distribution that occurred during the 1940's. Mexican economists are convinced that the movement toward greater income inequality which probably occurred during the twenties and thirties accelerated in the forties as the economy spurted ahead. However, their conviction is based upon information concerned not with household incomes, which is apparently unavailable, but rather with functional income distribution. Let us therefore turn to the latter subject.

Functional income distribution. During the 1940's increases in the demand for commodities, rising price levels, and the expansion of labor services all helped turn Mexico's income distribution against the lower income groups by directing real income from wage earners to profit recipients. Differences in the findings in

[11] It is evident that other conditions, particularly a high propensity to save on the part of the high income receivers, must be met if an enhanced inequality is to promote growth. See the discussion in chapters 6 and 11.

this area hinge much more around the quantification of the change rather than the direction which it took. The disagreements about the extent of the changes in turn stem largely from the difficulties of handling the categories of mixed incomes and imputed earnings of the self-employed. These returns are rather heterogeneous, including as they do the incomes of artisans, *ejidatarios*, small landowners, vendors of various sorts, and the owners of private businesses. Were it not for their earnings, comprising about one-third of the national income in 1940 and one-quarter in 1955, it would also be possible to know more the nature of distribution by size. Still another major source of disparity among the several findings lies in the difficulty of estimating profits in trade and commerce, where tangible production cannot provide a check.

Scott indicates that from 1939 to 1950 real incomes rose for the 14 per cent of the Mexicans who obtained their income primarily from capital and salaries, while they actually fell for the remaining 86 per cent.[12] Aubrey reports profits, rents, and interest rising from 34.3 per cent of national income in 1939 to 52.6 per cent in 1952 and, by the same token, all other incomes including the small entrepreneurial declining from 65.7 per cent to 47.5 per cent during that time.[13] The Economic Commission for Latin America notes some decline in "wages and other wage earning income" during the nine-year period beginning in 1945, from 52 per cent in that year to 49 per cent in 1953.[14] The major sources of substantial agreements are not difficult to locate. Most studies of changes in functional income distribution after 1939 evidently rely on the work of the combined Mexican Working Party for the years through 1950[15] and on Nacional Financiera estimates for the ensuing years. Table 25 draws from each of these sources, while Table 26, covering the fifties, utilizes the work of the Financiera.

[12] Scott, *Mexican Government in Transition*, pp. 90–91.

[13] Henry G. Aubrey, "Structure and Balance in Rapid Economic Growth: The Example of Mexico," *Political Science Quarterly*, 69 (December, 1954), 522.

[14] United Nations, Economic Commission for Latin America, *Economic Survey of Latin America, 1953*, p. 19, t. 15.

[15] The Combined Mexican Working Party, *The Economic Development of Mexico*, esp. p. 178, t. 4.

TABLE 25. Functional Income Distribution, 1939 and Following*

Year	(1) Wages and Salaries (%)	(2) Profits (%)	(3) Rents and Interest (%)	(4) Property Incomes (Col. [2] + Col. [3]) (%)	(5) Mixed Incomes plus Imputed Incomes of Self- Employed (%)
1939	30.5	26.2	8.3	34.5	35.0
1940	29.1	28.6	8.1	36.7	34.2
1941	27.9	30.7	7.8	38.5	33.6
1942	26.5	33.0	7.5	40.5	33.0
1943	25.0	35.3	7.2	42.5	32.5
1944	23.7	37.6	6.9	44.5	31.8
1945	22.6	41.3	6.7	48.0	29.4
1946	21.5	45.1	6.4	51.5	27.0
1947	22.0	44.3	6.5	50.8	27.2
1948	22.9	42.9	6.5	49.4	27.7
1949	23.7	41.5	6.7	48.2	28.1
1950	23.8	41.4	6.0	47.4	28.8
1951	25.0	42.0	6.4	48.4	26.6
1952	27.0	44.0	6.4	50.4	22.6
1953	32.0	38.0	6.4	44.4	23.6
1954	29.0	39.0	6.4	45.4	25.6
1955	26.0	42.5	...	...	...
1956	...	39.0	...	...	...
1957	...	38.0	...	...	...
1958	...	37.5	...	...	...
1959	...	36.5	...	...	...

* The source of the 1939–1954 data is Adolfo López Romero, "Desarrollo económico de México (1934–1959)," *El Trimestre Económico*, 29 (January–March, 1962), 47, t. 12. The few figures cited for the years 1955 through 1959 are from successive issues of the Nacional Financiera's Annual Reports. The Nacional Financiera apparently regards these data as so rough that it cites no statistics as such but merely employs graphs to reveal the broad outlines of changes in functional income distribution.

TABLE 26. Participation of the Factors of Production
in the National Income, 1950–1960*

Year	Labor (%)	Capital (%)	Mixed (%)
1950	23.8	47.4	28.8
1951	22.4	48.3	29.3
1952	22.3	48.3	29.4
1953	25.5	46.5	28.0
1954	28.5	44.5	27.0
1955	26.4	45.8	27.8
1956	25.9	46.1	28.0
1957	27.8	44.9	27.3
1958	29.9	43.6	26.5
1959	30.8	43.0	26.2
1960	31.4	42.6	26.0

* Juan Delgado Navarro, *Desarrollo económico y justicia social en México*, pp. 160, 220, and 256.

Table 25 indicates that the percentage of wages, salaries, and their supplements to net domestic product at factor cost declined steadily from 30.5 per cent in 1939 to 21.5 per cent in 1946. Labor's share then rose again, so that by the mid-fifties wages and salaries had almost recovered their relative position of 1939. Table 26 suggests a recovery somewhat later, perhaps by the end of the decade. By far the most striking picture is the one presented by profits computed as a share of net domestic product at factor cost. They rose continuously from an already impressive 26.2 per cent in 1939 to a remarkably high 45.1 per cent in 1946, dipped steadily to 41.4 per cent in 1950 and then, accompanied by cyclical oscillations, declined to about 37 per cent by the end of the fifties— still considerably higher than in 1939. Profits also managed to gain at the expense of rent and interest, which, except for fractional improvements in the late forties and early fifties, fell from a combined 8.3 per cent of national income in 1939 to some 6.4 per cent in 1952. The eventual recovery of labor's prewar position and the increased property share were both made possible by a decline in the ratio of mixed income to national income. A consistent downward trend in the mixed income share is of course to be expected as an economy expands and the economically active population increasingly takes on the role of employer or employee.

Some dissenting voices have been raised against the Working Party data, widely used though they may be. Working with Banco de México–Nacional Financiera revisions, Mrs. Navarrete has argued that the usually accepted figures on functional income distribution vastly overstate the profits share in 1950 and, presumably, in proximate years. The percentage of profits to income should be not 41.4 per cent, but 26.7 per cent! The statistics, she asserts, should appear as follows:[16]

Type of Share	Per Cent of National Income 1940		1950	
Total wages and salaries		29.7		29.6
Profits	27.0		26.7	
Rents	6.7		5.9	
Interest	1.5		1.1	
Total property income		35.2		33.7
Net agricultural income	20.7		26.1	
Mixed non-agricultural income	14.7		10.4	
Total mixed income		35.4		36.5
		100.3		99.8

These revised data in turn do not seem valid in every respect. It is now felt, for example, that the Central Bank underestimated the profits emanating from commerce. In addition, the impressive gains recorded for agriculture in the revisions seem extreme given the comparative growth rates of other sectors of the economy after 1940. The truth assuredly lies somewhere between the older and the revised data, perhaps somewhat closer to the more recent estimates. However, there is no reason to suppose that the older, unrevised data err in reporting the directions of change, particularly the rise in the profits during the war and the consequent trailing off until 1950 and beyond. The older data also have the advantage

[16] Navarrete, *La distribución del ingreso*, pp. 56–57, t. 4.

of annual coverage, and, willy-nilly, one is compelled to use them in analyzing functional income distribution.

In terms of composition the behavior of the profit share during the forties is rather well accounted for by the profits received in commercial activities (see Table 27). As profit income rose steadily through 1946, commercial profit income behaved accordingly. The latter experienced its strongest increases in 1945 and 1946, the years in which total profit income also expanded the most sharply. Thereafter, through 1950, the two series declined together moderately. Commercial profits as a percentage of total profits rather than national income continued to climb for three additional years, 1947 through 1949. For the entire decade commercial profits made up an extraordinarily high percentage of both total income and total profits, insofar as the statistics are valid. Tentatively it is possible to conclude that profits in the commercial sector accounted very significantly for changes in the over-all profits share.

TABLE 27. Total Profits and Profits in Commerce, 1939–1950*

Year	Profits as a Per Cent of National Income	Commercial Profits As a Per Cent of National Income	As a Per Cent of Total Profits
1939	26.2	13.9	53.1
1940	28.6	15.4	53.8
1941	30.7	16.9	55.0
1942	33.0	18.4	55.7
1943	35.3	19.9	56.4
1944	37.6	21.4	56.9
1945	41.3	24.2	58.6
1946	45.1	27.0	59.9
1947	44.3	26.5	59.8
1948	42.9	25.9	60.4
1949	41.5	25.4	61.2
1950	41.4	24.7	59.7

* López Romero, *Desarrollo económico de México*, p. 47, t. 12, and p. 52, t. 16.

The propositions about commerce have served to bring sectoral income distribution into the discussion. We next consider the sectoral aspects more systematically, with intercountry comparisons the first item on the agenda.

Intersectional inequality of income distribution. According to world data on the distribution of income by sectors, intersectoral inequalities are most skewed in the poorest countries, with a tendency toward greater inequality of personal income distribution as a consequence. A way of calling attention to this is to deal with four sectors: namely, agriculture, manufacturing, transportation and commerce, and other services. For each sector one can calculate the ratios of the labor force and income, respectively, to the total force and the national income, note the differences between these two types of shares, and sum all differences disregarding signs. Letting the poorest countries represent Group I, the figures that emerge from this procedure are as follows:[17]

I	II	III	IV	V	VI	VII
27.8	30.5	28.2	43.2	22.3	13.9	17.7

These suggest that the typical development pattern may be not only that of increasing sectoral equality over the long run, but some intervening mounting inequality as well. Further, the poorest countries are relatively worse off in agriculture. Over the very long run, income per worker in agriculture actually tends to rise relative to the income per worker in nonagricultural pursuits, though still remaining lower in the currently advanced countries. Yet insofar as cross-sectional differences imply anything about the secular developments, the data again suggest an initial movement toward greater inequality and then a reversal.

Another procedure for measuring intersectoral income inequality consists of dividing the ratio of any sectoral income to total income by the ratio of the sector's labor force to whole labor force. This gives us an index of the value of the average product per worker for the sector in question. It is to be emphasized that the index concerns values—that it need not at all reflect changes in

[17] For these and the following data on world sectoral incomes see Simon Kuznets, *Six Lectures on Economic Growth*, pp. 43–49 and 54–55, esp. pp. 45–47, t. 5.

physical productivity. As such it constitutes a useful instrument for comparing returns among the several economic sectors.

In the case of agriculture, this measure yields the following data for groups of countries, again beginning with the poorest:

	I	II	III	IV	V	VI	VII
Income share	54.6	42.5	35.4	30.1	19.2	17.2	13.1
Labor share	61.2	57.5	49.7	51.1	27.9	23.4	14.4
$\frac{\text{Income share}}{\text{Labor share}}$	0.89	0.79	0.75	0.59	0.75	0.85	0.92

Once similar computations are performed for manufacturing and total services and the productivity measure for agriculture is compared with those for the other two sectors, that is

$$\frac{P_a}{P_{(m+s)}},$$

the results again demonstrate agriculture's backwardness among the poorer nations. The array now takes the following form:

I	II	III	IV	V	VI	VII
0.76	0.65	0.61	0.45	0.70	0.81	0.95

The productivity measure for manufacturing exhibits little modification and generally remains in the neighborhood of 1 for the poor and the rich countries. The income and labor shares of this sector both tend to expand in the wealthier economies, and apparently they may do so at approximately equal rates. The distribution in this instance:

	I	II	III	IV	V	VI	VII
Income share	13.7	17.8	24.3	24.2	29.2	41.5	38.1
Labor share	15.1	16.4	22.0	20.7	30.3	34.8	40.3
$\frac{\text{Income share}}{\text{Labor share}}$	1.18	0.97	1.18	1.24	0.95	1.11	1.02

The figures for services cover several economic activities—namely, transportation, commerce, the professions, and domestic services. As a group these several elements perform relatively well in the low income countries. The "productivity" index is almost 1.4 for the Group I nations; then it declines but nevertheless remains above 1 in the richest communities. The decline is particularly characteristic of commerce and services other than transportation and communications. Since commerce takes on special significance for Mexico, let us note its behavior for the various groups of countries:

	I	II	III	IV	V	VI	VII
Income share	14.4	12.1	13.5	16.7	14.3	12.7	14.1
Labor share	5.8	6.1	8.2	8.0	11.5	11.4	15.1
Income share / Labor share	2.5	2.0	1.6	2.1	1.2	1.1	0.93

While Mexico has generally exhibited the intersectoral inequalities characteristic of the rest of the world, the disparity between its manufacturing and commerce on the one hand and its agriculture on the other has been even more marked. According to Rodrigo Vidal the following sectoral ratios prevailed in 1950:[18]

Activity	(1) Per Cent of National Income	(2) Per Cent of Labor Force	(3) (Col. [1] ÷ Col. [2])
Commerce	30.9	8.3	3.72
Transportation	4.3	2.5	1.72
Industry	25.1	15.9	1.58
Miscellaneous	6.0	4.0	1.36
Services (including government)	14.0	10.6	1.33
Agriculture	19.6	58.0	0.34

The ratios for industry and especially commerce are evidently higher, and the ratio for agriculture lower, than elsewhere in the world. The relevant group to consider is the one labeled II, which pertains to countries with per capita incomes averaging $200 per year. While Mexico experienced ratios of 3.72, 1.58, and 0.34 in commerce, manufacturing, and agriculture, respectively, the comparative coefficients for the Group II countries were 2.0, 0.97, and

[18] Rodrigo V. Vidal, "La estructura del ingreso y su composición en consuma y ahorro," in *La intervención del estado en la economía*, p. 133, t. 1.

0.79. Vidal has also performed the rather interesting experiment of applying the Lorenz curve to intersectoral income differences by placing the percentage of the total labor force of a sector on the horizontal axis and the percentage of total income on the vertical one. The resulting curve of course exhibits several discontinuities as well as a very sharp bulge for the low income sector, agriculture. It is strikingly similar to the Lorenz curve for personal income distribution in Mexico in 1950.[19] As such, it demonstrates the value of utilizing intersectoral distribution as a rough estimate of personal distribution.

Support of Vidal's findings comes from other Mexican economists. Flores Márquez[20] presents data from which ratios can readily be computed. His productivity index for agriculture is 20% of income/54.5% of the work force, or 0.37, while his ratio for nonagricultural pursuits comes to 80.0%/45.5%, or 1.76. Retchkiman names no date but also reports agriculture as accounting for only 19 per cent of the national income and yet comprising 55 per cent of the work force;[21] this results in a ratio of 0.36(+) in agriculture and 1.8 in all other sectors. In turn these signify $\dfrac{P_a}{P_{(m+s)}}$ ratios of 0.21 or 0.20 for Mexico, whereas Kuznets reports a comparative figure of 0.65 for the Group II countries. Mrs. Navarrete's productivity index for commerce is 2.75 instead of the 3.72 offered by Vidal, while that for agriculture appears in the neighborhood of 0.4 rather than 0.33 and manufacturing yields a relatively high return.[22] Nevertheless, her several sectors may be ranked in the same order as Vidal's.

These data bring us face to face with the problem of norms. Mexico's departure from the average could simply have been the consequence of pronounced progress in nonagricultural activities. In part this appears to be the case. In manufacturing especially, the Mexican productivity index was significantly higher than the average for the Group II countries. Otherwise the performances seem less attractive. Mexican commerce enjoyed nearly

[19] *Ibid.*, p. 35, fig. 1.
[20] Flores Márquez, *La distribución del ingreso en México*, p. V-9, t. 5.
[21] Retchkiman, "Distribución del ingreso," p. 225.
[22] See Table 29.

31 per cent of the national income in the course of employing
8.3 per cent of the labor force, while the other Group II countries
realized a much smaller percentage of national income, 12 per
cent, with a slightly smaller percentage of the work force, 6 per
cent. This feature of Mexican economic development appears as
deplorable here as in the context of functional income distribution.
For the rest we must simply conclude that low productivity and
relatively weak bargaining power have plagued Mexican agriculture. In 1950 Mexico devoted as large a percentage of the work
force to agriculture as the Group II countries but realized a much
smaller share of the national income from it. These data do point,
clearly and definitely, to an unbalanced picture.

Yet many economists have lauded Mexico's "balanced" economic development.[23] By this they generally mean that the various
sectors advanced at not terribly unequal rates and particularly that
agriculture managed to keep up with the over-all pace of development. As a group they present a picture of agriculture on the
move. One of them is Aubrey.[24] Another is Edmundo Flores, who
first notes the burdens borne by agriculture in industrialization
and then discusses agriculture's progress. He explains the latter
in terms of more extensive and intensive cultivation, higher export prices, and the reductions in the percentage of the work force
engaged in agriculture, which added to the consumption of food
on the farms.[25] Antonio Carillo Flores, a former ambassador to the
United States, concentrates on agriculture's place in international
trade. In 1939, he points out, agricultural products accounted for
only 28 per cent of all exports, while in the late fifties it was responsible for 55 per cent (mining having dropped from 65 per cent
to 29 per cent during the interval). Mexico was thereby able to
import capital goods for agriculture and the other sectors instead
of exhausting her foreign reserves for food; she in fact became
virtually self-sufficient in food consumption.[26] These comments
help reconcile the data showing low agriculture productivity with

[23] See chapter 2, Mexico's diversified economic growth.
[24] Aubrey, "Structure and Balance in Rapid Economic Growth," pp. 517–540.
[25] Edmundo Flores, "The Significance of Land-Use Changes in the Economic
Development of Mexico," *Land Economics*, 35 (May, 1959), 123.
[26] Antonio Carillo Flores, "Mexico Forges Ahead," *Foreign Affairs*, 36
(April, 1958), 499 and 494.

those indicating fairly rapid advances in the sector. Specific activities within agriculture tended to prosper while the remainder stagnated. The several devaluations especially encouraged exports as well as import substitution, but they altered income distribution considerably in the process.[27] The advance of manufacturing similarly stimulated particular products; for example, by the end of the fifties raw materials for industry comprised 40 per cent of agricultural output.[28] Yet some ten million out of nineteen million persons in agriculture remained virtually untouched by modern techniques.[29] There can be little question about the inequality of income and productivity within the agricultural sector itself.

Thus far this section has been concerned primarily with 1950 data and rather little with changes in intersectoral inequalities over time. The latter now calls for some examination. The availability of figures for 1940, and even for 1929, is indicative of the relatively superior statistics in this field.

Mexico in 1929 and in 1940 would have fitted into the upper ranges of the Group I category. How, then, did the Mexican economy behave as it passed from Group I to Group II status? While the data for 1929 are not strictly comparable with those of the later years, they yield some worth-while insights and they are strikingly in accord with the findings for other years (see Table 28). The 1929 index for agriculture is as low, and the index for manufacturing as high, as in the later Mexican data. The index for commerce is fairly similar to that of the poor countries in Group I; this sector had as yet not surged forward in Mexico. The returns in mining were quite spectacular, as was to be expected, and those in other services were surprisingly high relative both to the experiences of other countries and to Mexico's later situation. Total services seem in 1929 to have accounted for about one-half of Mexico's national income, with only one-third accruing to the primary pursuits and one-sixth to secondary activities, including mining and petroleum.[30] In sum, the major changes that were to occur in the productivity indices in the following two decades

[27] UNESCO, *External Disequilibrium in the Economic Development of Latin America: The Case of Mexico*, p. 46.

[28] Carillo Flores, "Mexico Forges Ahead," pp. 492–493.

[29] Scott, *Mexican Government in Transition*, p. 54.

[30] *Ibid.*

TABLE 28. Income per Gainfully Employed Person, by Sectors, 1929*

Sector	(1) Annual Income per Gainfully Employed Person	(2) (Col. [1] Divided by the national average)
Extractive	1,503	3.81
Nonagricultural	952	2.41
Commerce	945	2.39
Processing	744	1.88
National average	395	1.00
Agriculture	157	0.40

* Column (1) is based on Federico Bach, "The Distribution of Wealth in Mexico," *Annals*, no. 208 (March, 1940), 76.

were to involve a rise in commerce and a decline in other services and mining.

Between 1940 and 1950 the index for manufacturing improved slightly (see Table 29). This was in contrast to the differences between the Group I and Group II countries, assuming again that differences among countries are at all indicative of trends experienced by particular countries. Transportation and communication proved unexpectedly weaker. Productivity in other services declined relatively, as anticipated. Instead of diminishing in relative importance, commerce actually improved somewhat from 1940 to 1950. The vehicle for this was apparently a fall in the share of the labor force rather than a rise in the national income share. (In Retchkiman's hands commerce also improved relatively, but the share in the labor force remained about 9 per cent from 1940 to 1955 while the income share rose somewhat from 28.8 per cent to 29.6 per cent.)[31] The behavior of the agricultural productivity index introduces an element of surprise in that it improved somewhat from a very low base. Here is another reason for the claim of balanced development. Mexican agriculture tended to keep pace marginally while still remaining in an extremely inferior position in terms of averages. As was to be expected, much of the improvement assumed the form of a reduction in the labor share.

[31] Retchkiman, "Distribución del ingreso," p. 225.

TABLE 29. Labor Productivity in Various Sectors, for Selected Years*

Activity	1940	1950	1957
Petroleum	$\dfrac{1.7}{0.3} = 5.67$	$\dfrac{2.9}{0.3} = 9.67$	$\dfrac{3.7}{0.4} = 9.25$
Minerals	$\dfrac{4.4}{1.5} = 2.93$	$\dfrac{3.2}{0.9} = 3.56$	$\dfrac{2.4}{0.8} = 3.00$
Electric energy	$\dfrac{0.6}{0.1} = 6.00$	$\dfrac{0.9}{0.3} = 3.00$	$\dfrac{1.2}{0.3} = 4.00$
Commerce	$\dfrac{25.1}{9.3} = 2.70$	$\dfrac{22.0}{8.0} = 2.75$	$\dfrac{19.5}{8.7} = 2.24$
Banking and insurance	$\dfrac{1.3}{0.2} = 6.50$	$\dfrac{0.7}{0.3} = 2.33$	$\dfrac{0.8}{0.4} = 2.00$
Communication and transportation	$\dfrac{5.8}{2.5} = 2.32$	$\dfrac{5.1}{2.6} = 1.96$	$\dfrac{4.9}{3.5} = 1.40$
Manufacturing	$\dfrac{16.4}{9.0} = 1.82$	$\dfrac{22.2}{11.7} = 1.90$	$\dfrac{22.2}{12.1} = 1.83$
Construction	$\dfrac{1.8}{1.8} = 1.00$	$\dfrac{3.3}{2.7} = 1.22$	$\dfrac{5.0}{3.2} = 1.56$
Private services	$\dfrac{15.4}{6.6} = 2.33$	$\dfrac{12.6}{11.5} = 1.10$	$\dfrac{14.1}{13.6} = 1.04$
Government	$\dfrac{7.0}{3.0} = 2.12$	$\dfrac{3.3}{3.4} = 0.97$	$\dfrac{3.3}{3.5} = 0.94$
Agriculture	$\dfrac{20.5}{65.4} = 0.31$	$\dfrac{23.8}{58.3} = 0.41$	$\dfrac{22.9}{53.6} = 0.43$

* Navarrete, *La distribución del ingreso*, p. 51, t. 3.

The developments after 1950 support the conclusions, reached in the discussion of personal income distribution, that there were no major shifts in the division of income during the period. The relative declines in commerce, minerals, and communication and transportation were fairly sharp; manufacturing fell off somewhat; and electric energy, construction, and agriculture picked

TABLE 30. Labor Productivity for Various Sectors, 1960*

Activity	(1) Share of GNP	(2) Labor Share	(3) (Col. [1] ÷ Col. [2])
Commerce	20.9	9	2.32
Manufacturing	25.6	13	1.97
Agriculture	20.4	53	0.39
Others	33.1	25	1.32

* Columns (1) and (2) are based upon Nacional Financiera, "Mexican Economy: Selected Indicators, 1961," p. 1.

up to some extent. But there were few significant changes. Less detailed Nacional Financiera data for 1960 (Table 30) suggest even fewer alterations in intersectoral inequalities for the whole decade.

In sum, every shred of evidence points to a highly unequal, and probably inequitable, division of income between commerce and agriculture, to say nothing of marked disparities within agriculture. One is thus surely tempted to recommend increased taxation of commercial transactions and commercial incomes in order to defray the costs of raising agricultural production through the usual means of increased capital formation and the dissemination of technological knowledge. To designate a sector in the Mexican economy more in need of official help than subsistence agriculture would indeed be difficult. Here, certainly, is an instance of compatibility between greater equality and more rapid economic growth. The case for assisting agriculture becomes even more compelling as soon as one questions the normative value of the other countries' performances. The relative neglect of agriculture has characterized most poor countries; if Mexican agriculture emerges as relatively weak even by these limited standards, it must assuredly have received short shrift.

This conclusion is further supported by the historical record.[32] Not only have urban dwellers possessed superior economic bargaining power, but officialdom has tended to intensify the differ-

[32] See Flores, "Mexico Forges Ahead," p. 122.

ences already in existence. The government has followed policies of relatively low food prices and heavy duties on agricultural exports. In its expenditure on public education and public works it has similarly favored the urbanites. The economic imbalance between town and village has in turn led to political imbalance.[33] In a country where the government has been pervasive in its influence on the economy, such a political development can be devastating for an underprivileged sector. True, the authorities have not permitted agriculture as a whole to stagnate; in fact they have assisted it considerably. Yet they have not acted with sufficient force to preclude exceedingly serious inequities.

The distribution of income by regions. A consideration of this fourth type of distribution further tightens the evidence regarding the backwardness of some sections of agriculture.

The following is a breakdown of the geographic income distribution in 1956, with the monthly income per family in each zone compared to the average for the whole Mexican Republic, that of 693 pesos per month.[34]

Groups of States	Monthly Income Per Family	
	Pesos	Ratio to Republic
Federal District	1,282	1.85
North Pacific	1,189	1.72
Gulf of Mexico	689	0.99
North	675	0.97
Center	464	0.67
South Pacific	447	0.65

Four zones depart significantly from the average. As anticipated, the Federal District, which includes Mexico City, occupied the highest position,[35] while the north Pacific area, which is known for its ex-

---

[33] Scott, *Mexican Government in Transition*, pp. 53–54.

[34] Navarrete, "La distribución del ingreso," p. 72, t. 6. Also see Dirección General de Estadística, Departamento de Muestro, *Ingresos y egresos de la población de México* (1958), p. 73.

[35] Yet in 1954 the income of more than 25 per cent of the families in the Federal District was less than 300 pesos per month (Scott, *Mexican Government in Transition*, p. 52), which was far below even the South Pacific area average; while in 1950, 72 per cent had incomes less than 600 pesos per month. The

tensive, relatively modernized agricultural sector, emerged a close second. At the other extreme lay the center and south Pacific areas, which have remained tied to traditional agriculture. In 1956 the family incomes in these zones approximated one-third of those in Mexico City, and per capita incomes came to less than $100 per year. Yet these two zones accounted for about 50 per cent of the population. On the other hand most of the one million persons in the higher income classes lived either near the industrial centers of the Federal District or in the northern sections where agriculture has been export directed.[36]

The use of average minimum daily money wages in agriculture by zones yields similar results.[37] The rates are for 1938–1939 and 1948–1949, and they take on the following magnitudes:

Zone	Pesos 1938–1939	1948–1949	Percentage Increase
North Pacific	1.69	3.93	132.54
Gulf of Mexico	1.82	2.80	55.15
North	1.26	2.35	86.51
Center	1.18	2.24	89.93
South Pacific	1.19	2.21	85.71

Compared to the previous data, the Gulf of Mexico zone registers a relatively high figure for 1938–1939, and the North appears a trifle on the low side for both periods. Yet the general outlines are evidently similar. The data do not reveal any close relationship between levels of achievement and rates of improvement. This lack of correlation between levels and change has apparently persisted in more recent years (see Table 31).

That the interregional differences in incomes and minimum wages are no greater is the result of adjustments dear to orthodox economics. Probably pushed more than pulled, Mexican workers

---

latter datum is from Jorge Espinosa de los Reyes, "La distribución del ingreso nacional," in Universidad Nacional Autónoma de México, *Problemas del desarrollo económico de México*, pp. 169–170.

[36] Dirección General de Estadística, *Compendio estadístico, 1960*, pp. 13–14.

[37] D. G. López Rosado and J. F. Noyola Vázquez, "Los salarios reales en México, 1939–1950," *El Trimestre Económico*, 18 (April–July, 1951), 201, t. 1.

TABLE 31. Comparative Growth Rates of the Various Zones, 1955–1960*

Zone	Gross Income from Sales 1955, Compared to Total (%)	Variation 1955–1960 (%)	Sales per Inhabitant, 1960 (pesos)
Northwest	11.8	75.9	1,956
North	4.3	97.0	892
Northeast	13.2	115.8	1,987
North Central	2.4	55.0	428
Pacific	5.8	125.9	854
Bajio	3.9	112.8	444
Center	4.9	127.1	415
Federal District	44.0	107.1	3,934
Gulf	5.2	103.2	690
Yucatan Peninsula	1.3	148.1	810
South	3.2	64.7	262
Mexican Republic (pesos)	21,006,010	...	1,228

* Banco Nacional de México, *Review of the Economic Situation of Mexico*, 38 (April, 1962), p. 11.

have responded to existing differentials by shifting in rather considerable numbers from the high density, low income areas to those more attractive economically. The latter have consisted essentially of the northern border, the seven largest cities in central Mexico, and the territory of Quintana Roo at the very eastern tip of Mexico. The percentage of the total population in these main areas of attraction rose from only 11 in 1900 to 30.5 in 1950, while four principal areas of demographic pressures experienced declines from 61 per cent to 45.4 per cent during this half century.[38]

These movements have of course served to lessen differentials in labor productivity and real incomes. Seemingly, the higher and more rapidly shifting production functions in the growth sectors have encouraged mobility, which in turn has resulted in move-

[38] UNESCO, Economic Commission for Latin America, *Recent Events and Trends in Mexico*, pp. 3–5.

ments down the production functions for the growing industries and movements up the productivity schedules in the lagging sectors. As a consequence, real wage income within the expanding occupations has of course been restrained from rising significantly. This sort of response to regional differences is generally adjudged beneficial for development. It reflects the structural changes that must necessarily accompany economic advancement, and it has served to raise the real incomes of many of the migrants.

If this were a once-for-all development—that is, if the advanced sectors absorbed the migrants, real wages were temporarily constrained, and further growth restored the advances in productivity and real income—then mobility would be most desirable. This has not, however, been the case. Because of the population growth in the areas of emigration, the migrants have continued to pour in. Between 1950 and 1960 the rural population advanced at an annual rate of 1.5 per cent while natural increases and migration combined to yield an expansion of 4.8 per cent in the urban areas.[39] These developments placed long term constraints upon advances in real wages, but the unfavorable effects of a growing population and migration have not been confined to that portion of the labor force fortunate enough to have jobs. Many of the migrants simply transfer their poverty from the countryside to the city, and, in fact, may even suffer some deterioration in their plane of living. Some, for example, construct primitive shelters on or near garbage dumps and seek survival in such an atmosphere. Needless to say, this gives rise to a health record that is probably the poorest in the entire country. Further, the authorities must offer some additional public services to the migrants. This forces resources into the production of the capital goods with the highest capital-output ratios or the lowest immediate returns—in effect, urbanization with little development. Once again, if the phenomenon were temporary the situation would not be serious, particularly since this investment would continue to bear fruit over a long period. But it has degenerated into a vicious circle. The more effective the provision of urban services, the greater the migration from the countryside,

[39] Marianne Gellner, "Mexico: New Frontiers of Progress," *World Today*, 20 (December, 1964), 527.

with the continuing natural population growth yielding a process without a foreseeable end.[40]

Since the internal migrations will continue, considerable value should lie in the industrialization of regions removed from the capital city and from other urban centers.[41] This may initially occasion high costs because of the existing facilities and markets in the presently more concentrated areas. Even this disadvantage is not clear, however. As appears to be true of Mexico City, many diseconomies, such as those relating to transportation, may have already appeared in the more established regions. Then, too, the growth of Mexico City has partially been of the hothouse variety, since the government has provided subsidies to both households and firms in the area.[42] In the longer run the opportunity costs of building up new urban centers should be reasonably low. Sociological criteria further point to the development of new centers. Economic growth in much of Mexico still awaits alterations of the traditional fatalistic views toward change. To aim for more urbanization in these regions is to touch the surrounding villages with modernization and to help reduce the regional inequalities discussed in this section. It is clear that such a reduction is essential, if for no other reason than because of the harm the differentials inflict upon the more advanced areas.

The behavior of real wages. While some data for the decade of the thirties show that the price increases left many members of the labor force no better off than they had been in the beginning of the period, the relatively reliable work on wage incomes begins with the year 1939. D. G. López Rosado and J. F. Noyola Vázquez have examined the forces playing upon real wages from 1939 to 1949 and have classified them as contributing to or detracting from the real incomes received. Any increase in daily wages in a given pursuit would obviously be one of the positive factors. The following array indicates the extent to which daily money wages

---

[40] See UNESCO, *Seminar on Urbanization Problems in Latin America*, pp. 83 ff. for a discussion of these issues.

[41] *Ibid.*, pp. 85–87.

[42] Richard Bird, "The Economy of the Mexican Federal District," *Inter-American Economic Affairs*, 17 (Autumn, 1963), 50–51.

rose for different activities during the decade in question.[43] In addition, annual wage incomes increased in value because of additions

Activity	Daily Wage (pesos)		Per Cent Increase
	1939	1948 or 1949	
National railways	5.64	16.50	192.5
Petroleum	11.81	33.50	183.7
Average of 24 industries	3.46	9.04	161.3
Government workers	4.20	9.13	117.4
Average agricultural income	1.31	2.40	83.2

in the number of hours and days worked, more workers per family, and various social services, such as medical care. Finally, occupational mobility contributed to higher productivity and declining disguised unemployment in the economy as a whole.

In opposition to these the writers mention only a single counterforce, but one powerful enough to offset all of the others. This was the inflation factor. According to their estimates the general price level tripled during the 1940's, and this 200 per cent increase exceeded the improvement in money wages per worker which occurred in the most favored of sectors. Purchasing power per worker thereby decreased in almost every occupation from 1939 to 1949: in industry, by 7 per cent (until 1947); for federal public employees, by 35 per cent; in the cities, by 39 per cent; and for agricultural workers, by 46 per cent.[44] Simultaneously, most industries experienced increases in productivity. Combined with the decline in real wage rates, this yielded the additional profits we have already noted. Here was a situation which surpassed W. Arthur Lewis' prescriptions in his well-known article on profits and wage rates. In effect, not only did the productivity curve shift upward while the real wage function remained perfectly elastic, but the latter shifted downward over time.

In the face of the declining relative shares and the falling real wages that occurred in specific activities during the 1940's, absolute real aggregate wage income nevertheless tended to hold its own. The Economic Commission for Latin America has found no

[43] López Rosado and Noyola Vázquez, "Los salarios reales en México," p. 201 and p. 204, t. 3.
[44] *Ibid.*, pp. 205–206.

marked change in average real labor income from 1945 through 1953. For example, the average income in constant dollars was 296 and 273 in 1945 and 1946, respectively, and 316 and 291 in the years 1951–1952.[45] Sturmthal notes that weighted average real wage income actually increased by about 10 to 12 per cent from 1940 to 1950. This increase in average real wages together with the worsening terms of trade for specific wage earners can be explained partially by differences in the handling of fringe benefits but much more importantly by the movement of workers into higher paying occupations, especially from agriculture to nonagricultural employment.[46] Apparently, as the complete story of the 1940's is pieced together, labor's over-all relative share tended to decline, labor's absolute gains were due primarily to labor mobility, and nonmobile wage earners bore the major brunt of inflation by foregoing advances in their real wages.

Table 32 carries the developments into the decade of the fifties and focuses first upon manufacturing (columns [1] and [2]). While this sector is a favored one, the data serve to suggest the considerable improvement which took place during the fifties. The year 1952 represents the low water mark for real wages in manufacturing for the 1939–1958 period. Real wages declined almost monotonically from 1940 to 1952 and then generally climbed until 1958. At that time they had still failed to recover their 1939 or 1940 position. In the meantime labor productivity in manufacturing rose rather uniformly over the two decades, yielding an index number of 180 for 1957–1958. The productivity index was thus nearly twice the wage index at the close of the period. The implications for property incomes are evident.

Columns (3) and (4) extend the data beyond manufacturing to embrace petroleum, minerals, and railroads as well. During World War II commodity prices forged ahead of money wages as the latter struggled vainly to close the gap. This they finally managed to accomplish by 1949, only to have the Korean war give fresh impetus to the rise in prices. Beginning in 1955, money wages

45 Economic Commission for Latin America, *Economic Survey of Latin America, 1956*, p. 25, t. 12.

46 Adolf Sturmthal, "Economic Development, Income Distribution, and Capital Formation in Mexico," *Journal of Political Economy*, 63 (June, 1955), 187–190.

156 — Growth, Equality, and the Mexican Experience

TABLE 32. Indices of Wage, Productivity, and Wholesale Prices, 1939–1958 (1939 = 100)*

	(1)	(2)	(3)	(4)
	In Manufacturing		In Manufacturing and Added Activities	
Years	Real Wages	Productivity	Average Money Wage	Wholesale Prices
1939	100.0	100.0	100.0	100.0
1940	103.2	99.4	103.9	104.0
1941	103.0	104.8	105.3	109.3
1942	95.2	109.9	111.9	120.6
1943	91.4	108.6	133.1	145.7
1944	83.2	110.2	154.6	178.5
1945	87.6	115.8	179.9	198.7
1946	85.7	112.0	210.7	222.7
1947	82.1	111.4	236.6	242.3
1948	82.7	117.3	258.6	260.0
1949	90.0	126.0	289.3	284.8
1950	88.8	137.2	298.5	311.2
1951	85.7	150.5	352.5	386.0
1952	79.6	149.9	360.1	400.0
1953	85.1	152.8	366.7	392.5
1954	89.2	172.8	399.1	429.4
1955	91.4	175.5	464.5	487.9
1956	90.6	174.6	505.6	510.5
1957	92.1	181.6	533.5	532.7
1958	93.9	178.7	571.8	556.3

* Secretaría de Economía, *Memoria, 1958.* Column (1) is taken from p. 135, column (2) is from p. 154, and columns (3) and (4) are from p. 173.

began to move upward more vigorously than prices and finally managed to match the price index again in 1957–1958. For most of the years, however, inflation corroded the value of money wages, reduced real wages for employers, and performed its familiar role of heightening income inequality.

Table 33 indicates the improvements in real wages that have accrued to workers in more recent years. Once again the year

TABLE 33. Indices of Money Wages, Cost of Living, and Real Wages,
1948–1964 (1958 = 100)*

Year	Money Wages	Cost of Living	Real Wages
1948	44	47	93.6
1949	47	50	94.0
1950	52	52	100.0
1951	57	59	96.6
1952	60	68	88.2
1953	64	66	97.0
1954	70	70	100.0
1955	80	81	98.8
1956	87	84	103.6
1957	92	89	103.4
1958	100	100	100.0
1959	111	102	108.8
1960	122	108	113.0
1961	128	109	117.4
1962	139	110	126.4
1963	163	111	146.8
1964	179	114	157.0

* International Monetary Fund, *International Financial Statistics: 1965/1966 Supplement*, p. 167.

1952 represents the low point. Thereupon real wage rates rose moderately through 1958 and then advanced quite sharply from 1959 through 1964, when the pace of inflation slackened.

The concentration of wealth. This is an aspect of distribution which has not received much scholarly attention in Mexico. It also happens to be one fraught with considerable emotion, since many of the larger firms have not been owned by Mexican nationals.

Some of the few known facts are as follows. The four hundred largest companies in Mexico have in recent years accounted for about 17 or 18 per cent of the GNP.[47] In 1951, 10 per cent of the entrepreneurs, with annual incomes of more than 100,000 pesos,

[47] According to an informant.

realized 70 per cent of all sales.[48] Finance has witnessed the creation of empires—the Big Nine, no less—which have had the wherewithal to venture into vast and diversified projects.[49] An exceedingly high degree of monopolization has been detected in commerce. Within this sector small business has accounted for 4 per cent of the value added, 16 per cent has gone to the labor employed by the larger firms, and as much as 80 per cent has accrued to capital. Here is a major explanation of the high "productivity index" in commercial activities. The answer lies not as much in superior technical efficiency as in the high commodity prices made possible by the market structure within the sector.[50] Manufacturing performs as expected. Two students of the degree of concentration in this sector have judged only seven industries out of nineteen, most of them in textiles and food products, to be reasonably competitive (see Table 34). Interestingly, the term they employ to describe competition is "libre," or free.

The implications of concentration for growth, and also equality for that matter, are not crystal-clear. Of the nineteen listed under manufacturing, the five most rapidly growing industries are oligopolistic, while four of the five most sluggish ones are fairly competitive. A more important determinant of an industry's growth rate could well be the type of product manufactured. The producers' goods and consumers' durable industries performed considerably better than the staples, though preserved foods and beer provide some exceptions even to this generalization. In any event, given the size of the market, the technological requirements, and economies of scale, most manufacturing firms simply cannot tolerate highly competitive market structures. Further, the effects of concentration in manufacturing upon income are not necessarily unfortunate. This has been the sector of relatively high labor productivity and correspondingly high wage rates, and its expansion has provided the major avenue for labor's shift to better-pay-

[48] Jorge López Rosado, *El productor marginal y la distribución del ingreso nacional*, p. 5.

[49] Frank R. Brandenburg, "A Contribution to the Theory of Entrepreneurship and Economic Development: The Case of Mexico," *Inter-American Economic Affairs*, 16 (Winter, 1962), 21–23.

[50] Sturmthal, "Economic Development, Income Distribution, and Capital Formation in Mexico," p. 198, t. 5.

TABLE 34. Market Structure and Volume of Production, 1947–1949, for Selected Manufacturing Industries (1939 = 100)*

Industry	Market Structure	Volume Index		
		1947	1948	1949
General		136.7	143.7	164.2
Preserved food	Oligopoly	343.6	362.5	309.2
Iron and steel	Oligopoly	275.3	239.1	306.2
Beer	Oligopoly	210.9	223.3	250.1
Plane glass	Oligopoly	209.8	286.2	205.0
Linoleum and oilcloth	Oligopoly	190.8	207.1	193.1
Cement	Competition	163.3	189.4	180.2
Sugar	Monopoly	162.6	188.3	178.6
Cotton goods	Competition	146.5	157.5	162.7
Woolen goods	Competition	102.6	95.2	165.0
Alcohol	Monopoly	213.7	160.3	154.6
Paper	Oligopoly	121.6	131.3	136.4
Cigars and cigarettes	Monopoly	120.2	124.1	134.8
Matches	Monopoly	121.1	123.2	118.7
Soap	Oligopoly	90.7	106.0	119.8
Artificial silks	Competition	60.8	89.7	104.9
Wheat mills	Competition	95.8	97.3	98.6
Vegetable oils	Competition	71.2	67.4	97.3
Hats	Competition	48.6	55.9	62.1
Footwear	Oligopoly	48.1	56.6	57.2

* This table is based upon four articles which appeared in *Revista de Economía*, Vol. 17 (1954). The information regarding market structure is from Emilio Mújica Montoya, "Repercusiones de las características generales de la industria en los precios" (September–October), p. 284, and from Edmundo Moyo Porrás, "Repercusiones de las características generales de la industria en el comercio exterior" (November), p. 294. The production indexes are taken from Vicente Riós G., "Tendencia de la industria en México" (November, 1954), pp. 301 and 304, and from Julio López Hurtado, "Repercusiones de las características generales de la industria en la capacidad productiva" (November, 1954), pp. 305.

ing occupations. The wage earner as consumer can of course be injured by the resulting high prices. However, the state has established plants in a variety of basic industries. Further, let us recall that foreign trade is one of the best antitrust programs ever conceived. If it so wishes the Mexican government can protect the consumer considerably both by charging lower prices for its commodities and by limiting the price differentials it permits its protected industries. Given all these circumstances, concentration in manufacturing need not be one of the major sources of official concern. Nevertheless, it is incumbent upon the government to prevent the giant firms from receiving artificial advantages, such as discriminatory patent and credit arrangements. The Nacional Financiera, for example, can play an important role in directing sufficient funds to small business.

In the case of commerce, the several propositions concerning economies of scale, relatively high wages, and foreign competition do not apply with equal vigor. The authorities ought to find it highly rewarding to delve into the monopolization in this sector and to devise mechanisms for introducing more competitive results.

CHAPTER SIX

Income Distribution, Consumption, and Saving

The extent and composition of aggregate demand. The behavior of the components and subcomponents of total demand should yield further evidence of the degree of equality of income distribution; one need bear in mind only luxury consumer goods and staples and the investment each type requires.

A review of the performance of aggregate demand should serve other purposes as well. For one thing it acts as a reminder of the value of markets in economic development. A deficiency in aggregate demand is a major, and sometimes neglected, cause of underdevelopment, whereas improvements in markets are an integral part of the development process. Secondly, a discussion of demand yields insights into the timing of the advances of its several components, and the behavior of the components should in turn be correlated with changes in the distribution of income. Just as one would expect income distribution to become more unequal during the early phases of economic development, so economic advance is initially consistent with lagged increases in mass consumption; most economists in fact view this as the heart of the development process. Thus the developing economies may at first find their markets in the mutual stimuli of producers' goods industries, the activities of the government, the effective demands of foreigners, and the specialized needs of wealthy domestic consumers. Then, as a nation seeks industrialization and perhaps wishes also to lessen its dependency on foreign markets, it tends to turn increasingly toward mass consumer goods and the accompanying productive apparatus.

It is a relatively easy matter to correlate Mexico's economic progress with these several developments in aggregate demand. During the early twenties a particularized demand invigorated the economy. As the affluent flocked to the center in search of economic security they thereby instituted a tremendous boom in Mexico City and in the adjoining areas.[1] Governmental expenditures featured the economic expansion under Cárdenas in the 1930's. During his administration additional export earnings began to add further zest to Mexico's growth. These assumed major significance during World War II, the Korean war, and in 1955; in 1950 exports made up 11 per cent of the GNP.[2] The demand for consumer durables, when not satisfied by imports, contributed to activity. (To some extent consumer durables are of value even when imported because of their effects on incentives, but the opportunity costs must be exceedingly high.) Producers' goods industries frequently provided markets for each other, as in the demand created for coke through the expansion of iron and steel industry. More generally, from 1939 to 1949 Mexico's industrial output expanded 70 per cent, but its productive capacity in manufacturing approximately quadrupled, ". . . a natural tendency in a rapidly developing economy in which the rise in demand is fast and the most serious obstacle to progress is rather the inadequacy of existing equipment in relation to requirements."[3] The capital goods industries often took on new forms, since about 20 per cent of the gross private investment from 1939 to 1949 was designed to produce goods previously not turned out in Mexico. Encouraged by the government, Mexican industry introduced new products in such lines as meat packing, electrical equipment, chemicals, and artificial silk. Exceedingly difficult though it may be to render judgments about quality (the only widely suggested measure involves the use of price increases, *ceteris paribus*), Mexican products appear to have improved in this respect. Firms became exceedingly

[1] Edmundo Flores, "The Significance of Land-Use Changes in the Economic Development of Mexico," *Land Economics*, 35 (May, 1959), 115–124 *passim*.

[2] The Combined Mexican Working Party, *The Economic Development of Mexico*, p. 114.

[3] UNESCO, Economic Commission for Latin America, *Recent Events and Trends in Mexico*, p. 11. The Nacional Financiera financed much of this production of capital goods (*ibid.*, p. 12).

conscious of such matters as technology, productivity, and education; and the role played by technicians in the management of industry continually increased.[4]

By the same token the period after 1939 was characterized by a lagging rate of increase in mass consumption. The totals for consumption as such do not look particularly bad. For example, from 1945 through 1955 aggregate demand and gross investment (private plus public) grew at annual rates of 5.7 per cent while private consumption grew at a rate of 5.5 per cent.[5] (See Table 35 for additional data.) Also, some of the staples performed quite well. In the two important cases of corn and beans, production increased more rapidly than the population from 1939 through 1952. During the 1945–1955 interval, however, the consumption by the recipients of property incomes increased about 60 per cent faster than for the remaining groups. Real per capita consumption may actually have decreased from 1946 to 1949; and there is little doubt about the per capita decline in 1952, when total consumption apparently dropped.[6] The 1952 reduction was so severe, and the forces of recovery so weak, that per capita consumption had barely recovered its 1951 level by 1955. For the decade 1945–1955 the per capita consumption of foodstuffs increased only 13 per cent, while that of other consumption goods grew 55 per cent.[7] Capital goods production increased 156 per cent compared to the 57 per cent rise in the production of consumer goods over the same ten-year interval.[8] Since the rise in total consumption almost matched the growth of producers goods, this calls attention to the expansion in services during the period. One can rather safely conclude that the well-to-do profited from this particular develop-

[4] *Ibid.*, pp. 9, 12.

[5] UNESCO, *External Disequilibrium in the Economic Development of Latin America: The Case of Mexico*, p. 12, t. I-1.

[6] Henry G. Aubrey, "Structure and Balance in Rapid Economic Growth: The Example of Mexico," *Political Science Quarterly*, 69 (December, 1954), 523–524.

[7] UNESCO, *External Disequilibrium*, pp. 26–31. Since the figures embrace inventory changes, they overstate the consumption enjoyed by the wealthy groups to that extent.

[8] Alberto Baltra, "La reforma agraria y el progreso económico," *Revista de Economía*, 23 (January, 1960), 6.

TABLE 35. Annual Rates of Increase for Selected
Components of Aggregate Demand, 1940–1958*

Years	Public Investment	Private Investment	Con- sumption	Total Domestic Demand
1940–1958	6.8	8.2	6.3	6.4
1942–1946	13.5	18.4	6.4	7.6
1947–1950	7.8	−4.8	4.6	3.9
1952–1958	1.9	2.7	5.0	4.7

* Víctor L. Urquidi, "La inflación en México," p. 28, t. 7.

ment. Needless to say, this in turn reflected the changes in income distribution that occurred at the time.

As long as other components of demand continued strong, the economy—and presumably the underlying social structure—could tolerate these weaknesses in consumption demand. From 1945 to 1955 external income, including tourist income, was still expanding at an average rate of 6.8 per cent per year.[9] Yet Mexico was not very deep into the 1950's before accumulating evidence indicated that continued progress at previous growth rates depended on structural changes in demand. The recession accompanying the termination of the Korean war dramatically raised the question of whether the past composition of demand had served its purpose and was becoming antiquated. In the late fifties and very early sixties Mexico certainly did not enjoy the glittering and spectacular growth records which she reported to the rest of the world from 1939 through 1951. By 1961–1962 many Mexican economists expressed the fear that the country's vaunted growth was in the process of slowing down considerably unless the government adopted appropriate countermeasures. The probable alternative to a vigorous public policy to reduce the obstacles to growth was stagnation, in the sense of lower growth rates. As will be noted in many remaining sections of this work, various reforms were instituted in the early sixties, and, coincidently, the Mexican economy began to recover its previous growth rates. What had then seemed

[9] UNESCO, *External Disequilibrium*, p. 12, t. I-1.

to be a trend can now be interpreted as a relatively long cyclical slowdown. But for several years the Mexican economy undoubtedly appeared to be in a precarious position.

One of Mexico's severest problems with demand arose in the very sector that sustained her prosperity in the more successful years. From 1940 through 1955 the foreign demand for Mexico's goods and services, again including tourist expenditures, had expanded at a more rapid rate than aggregate demand. By 1956–1958, however, its annual average rate of increase diminished to 1.1 per cent.[10] For goods alone export proceeds stagnated in 1958 and 1959 and then advanced 2.8 per cent and 6.5 per cent respectively, in 1960 and 1961.[11] Behind these developments may be found persistent terms of trade problems and cyclical changes in the volume of exports. The latter increased at an average annual rate of more than 3 per cent from 1940 through 1958.[12] but stagnated during 1956–1960 (see Table 36). The commodity terms of trade, based on 1950 indices, rose fairly steadily from 46 in 1939 and 75 in 1940 to 112 in 1948, fluctuated during the next three or four years,[13] and then, except for 1955, began a downward march which reached the mid-seventies over the period 1958–1961. The terms thus did not suffer long run deterioration but rather returned to World War II levels. However, combined with the behavior of the volume of exports, this was sufficient to interfere with Mexico's growth, particularly after 1955. During the entire decade of the fifties the value of Mexican exports of course corresponded rather closely to United States cyclical changes. To use the familiar analogy, by 1958 Western Europe might murmur "bless you" sympathetically when the United States suffered from a cold, but Mexico, like many other nations, still could not resist the pneumonia.

As the contribution from foreign trade declined, governmental expenditures once again attained a greater relative prominence. Yet there were limits to their expansion, given the inadequacy of tax revenues and the threat of serious inflation in the event of

[10] Urquidi, "La inflación en México," p. 28, t. 7.
[11] Banco Nacional de Comercio Exterior, *Comercio Exterior de México*, 8 (March, 1962), 2, t. 1, and 9 (March, 1963), 2, t. 1.
[12] Urquidi, "La inflación en México," 31, t. 8.
[13] *Ibid.*, p. A-15, t. A-14.

TABLE 36. Selected Indices of International Trade, 1951–1961*

Year	(1) Index of Value of Exports	(2) Index of Volume of Exports	(3) Index of Export Prices	(4) Index of Import Prices	(5) Unit Terms of Trade $\dfrac{(\text{Col. } [3]}{\text{Col. } [4]} \cdot 100$
			(1950 = 100)		
1951	118	98	131	115	114
1952	126	103	129	119	108
1953	113	115	113	119	95
1954	158	117	145	153	95
1955	215	141	164	168	98
1956	215	137	173	182	95
1957	188	131	162	188	86
1958	189	142	145	194	75
1959	192	152	152	199	76
1960	196	146	165	220	75
1961	214	160	180	232	78

* Columns (1), (2), and (3) are taken from Secretaría de Industria y Comercio, *Anuario estadístico de los Estados Unidos Mexicanos, 1960–1961*, p. 558, t. 14.6; column (4) is from *ibid.*, p. 557, t. 14.4.

further unbalancing of the budget. Luxury goods had obvious limits as a sustaining force. Poor capital-labor proportions discouraged investment, as was exemplified by the use of labor rather than steam shovels for excavation work in Mexico City as late as the 1960's. If the *patrón* could hire a worker for some 400 pesos for a 48-hour week (about $.67 per hour), he apparently had little incentive to invest in a technically advanced mode of production.

The refuge, then, seems to have lain in great part in a rising demand for wage goods. However, how does one demonstrate this aside from pointing to less easily remedied weaknesses in the other major components of aggregate demand? Certainly not by concentrating on propensities to consume. These ratios were already on the fairly high side, and one can hardly argue for higher propensities as such as vehicles for development. The point of course is that mass consumption demand was not *expanding* at a sufficiently rapid rate. This weakened aggregate demand directly. Further, through a rough application of the capital stock adjustment principle,[14] this retarded rate of advance appears to have had serious implications for some capital formation, irrespective of whether the capital goods were imported or produced at home.

Economic theory as well as popular opinion points to the value of studying excess capacities in order to highlight the weak demand for the necessitous goods. Excess capacity, however, is a notoriously difficult concept to cope with. The definitions are not precise and in fact tend to vary from industry to industry. They may embrace normal shifts or around-the-clock production; they may take into account rising unit costs or then again they may not; and so on. As usual, the data are fairly difficult to procure. Further, assuming adequate measurement and the reliability of the data, the relationships between excess capacity and insufficient demand are not easily demonstrable. Consider, for example, the following statistics on the utilization of blast furnace and cement capacities for the years 1949–1952.[15]

Year	Per Cent of Blast Furnace Capacity	Per Cent of Cement Capacity
1949	49	66
1950	54	70
1951	60	74
1952	70	78

These industries suffered excess capacity primarily because of supply shortages. Iron and steel especially experienced bottlenecks in the production and transportation of fuel. Although coke was stimulated by the demands from iron and steel, it was persistently in short supply because of coal shortages, poor operating and maintenance practices in coke production, the lack of a coordinated railroad system, and the absence of storage facilities at the blast furnaces. Materials other than coke were also frequently late in

---

[14] R. C. O. Matthews, *The Business Cycle*, pp. 40–43.
[15] Aubrey, "Structure and Balance in Rapid Economic Growth," pp. 536-537.

arriving.[16] Essentially iron and steel required a better coordination of industrial activity.

Nevertheless, the available evidence indicates that in the early 1950's limitations in consumer demand were already creating excess capacity and retarding the growth of Mexico's economy. Sugar, for example, suffered from insufficient demand. The statistics on leather footwear, admittedly poor even for an underdeveloped country, showed that production in 1946 exceeded that of 1951 or 1952. In the boom year of 1951 textiles operated at an estimated 47 per cent of capacity,[17] with cotton goods responsible for much of the poor performance. In 1953, 27,000,000 Mexicans consumed less cotton cloth than had 19,000,000 15 years earlier. Subsequently synthetics affected cotton sales in the urban areas, but rural consumers could not take up the slack because fourteen million of them did not possess sufficient purchasing power. In the process cotton textiles became an exceedingly inefficient industry. So antiquated was its equipment that 85 per cent of the spindles and 95 per cent of the looms were adjudged to be out of date. The defects in maintenance, the low quality of the yarn, the inadequate organization and poor working methods, the overabundance of labor together with its resistance to technological change, and the high degree of tariff protection all further betrayed the sickness of cotton.[18] The industry thus serves as a most interesting illustration of the relations between the demand for an industry's product and its improvements in productivity. Cotton history also supports Mosk's conclusion that rapid industrial growth in Mexico during the fifties awaited rising incomes and productivities in agriculture and the consequent strengthening of domestic markets.

A rewarding study of excess capacity in Mexican industry appeared as early as 1954.[19] The investigator divided the manufac-

[16] Combined Mexican Working Party, *Economic Development of Mexico*, pp. 70–71.

[17] Aubrey, "Structure and Balance in Rapid Economic Growth," p. 540.

[18] See United Nations, Economic Commission for Latin America, *Labor Productivity of the Cotton Textile Industry in Five Latin American Countries, passim.*

[19] Vicente Ríos G., "Tendencia de la industria en México," *Revista de Economía,* 17 (November, 1954), 302–304.

turing sector into three classes: (a) the "basic" industries of iron and steel, cement, linoleum, paper, glass, and so on; (b) the "vital" industries, made up of such necessitous goods as wheat, preserved foods, sugar, vegetable oils, textiles, hats, footwear, soap, and alcohol; and (c) the "secondary" industries, such as beer, matches, cigars, and cigarettes. The first group is not of major concern at this point. It operated in the range of 50 per cent to 75 per cent of capacity, but, as mentioned above, its problems were essentially those of supply, having to do with such matters as insufficiencies in raw materials arising from import difficulties and inadequacies of marketing. The "vital," or necessitous, group tended to operate from less than 50 per cent to about 75 per cent of capacity. It also was hampered by raw materials shortages, but underconsumption represented the major problem of this group. The "secondary" industries operated within the range of 40 per cent to 60 per cent of capacity. Their growth was relatively satisfactory, however, and their modernization was an important factor in accounting for their idle capacity.

During 1956–1958 the producers' goods industries continued to make rapid headway, advancing 6 per cent even in 1958 (see Table 37). The consumption goods industries, on the other hand, stagnated. In 1957 the production of soft goods remained quite stationary, while the demand for durables exhibited little added strength. The production of automobile tires, beer, and vegetable oils made almost no progress; tobacco expanded a bare 1.2 per cent; cotton goods moved up as much as 4 per cent only to be more than countered by a decrease in artificial fiber textiles of 14 per cent; and tinned foodstuffs declined by 7.6 per cent.[20] The year 1958 differed only in some of the details. This time durables such as automobile tires and electrical appliances showed "fairly substantial increases," while the food-preserving industry climbed 8 per cent and cigarettes 3.4 per cent. But cottons remained about level, and rayons and brewing each declined approximately 10 per cent.[21] Beds and footwear also did not perform well during these years.

According to two informants who occupied official capacities, about one-quarter of the industries suffered from excess capacity

[20] United Nations, Economic Commission for Latin America, *Economic Survey of Latin America, 1957*, pp. 215 and 219.
[21] *Ibid., 1958*, p. 144.

TABLE 37. Indices of Manufacturing Production, 1956–1958
(1955 = 100)*

Category	1956	1957	1958
Total manufactured goods	107.8	115.4	119.1
Consumption goods	101.7	100.8	101.4
Production goods	111.6	124.1	131.9
Cement	109.1	120.8	119.7
Pig iron	124.3	130.8	151.1
Steel	128.5	151.8	161.3
Rolled products	121.1	150.1	156.8
Sulphuric acid	125.5	143.5	157.9
Caustic soda	109.0	144.1	171.2

* United Nations, Economic Commission for Latin America, *Economic Survey of Latin America, 1958*, p. 144, t. 140. The 1958 figures are provisional.

in the early sixties. As one of them phrased it, 50 per cent of the industries experienced excess capacity about 50 per cent of the time. For the most part the troubled industries again dealt in soft consumer goods such as flour, matches, woolens, cottons, henequens, and soaps and detergents. Car batteries and iron and steel also found themselves in difficulty, but the durable "middle class" consumer goods (especially household appliances) and the producers' goods industries generally performed well. Possibly because the informants were speaking to an outsider, both were hopeful about the future developments in the wage goods industries and the economy as a whole. Final demand, one of them felt, was about two or three years behind installed capacity; if no new installations were added during the next three years, demand would catch up. Negative multiplier effects of course render this view rather difficult to accept, to say nothing of the consequences of marking time for three years. Both believed that the Free Trade Zone would eventually provide a significant basis for expanding markets, particularly in the automobile industry.

It was not necessary to contact government officials to sense the vast concern over the performance of the Mexican economy in 1961. During the year the GNP advanced at a rate of 3.5 per cent, a trifle more than the percentage growth in population. This occurred despite the very creditable increase of 6.5 per cent in exports, 8 per cent in steel, and 7 per cent in chemicals, as well as even more pronounced growth rates in petroleum and electricity (see Table 38). It occurred also despite a 20 per cent increase in public investment. The implication for the remaining sectors, and for the welfare of the low income groups, are evident.

The following quotation, lengthy though it may perhaps be, serves to summarize these basic points. Not only does it emanate from a large banking institution, normally expected to be fairly conservative, but it appears in a North American edition, normally expected to be fairly circumspect. The more conventional bankers' point of view appears only at the end of the passage.

. . . Mexico's economy in 1961 was maintained at a level of virtual stagnation.

In effect, the Bank of Mexico reported that Mexico's real gross national product increased by 3.5% during the year. If the average rate of population growth observed in the last decade is projected for 1961 on

TABLE 38. GNP by Sectors, 1960–1962*

	Per Cent of GNP		(1950 prices) Growth Rates (%)		
Activity	1960	1961	1960/1959	1961/1960	1962/1961
GNP	100.0	100.0	5.7	3.5	4.2
Petroleum	4.5	5.0	6.5	15.0	1.4
Electricity	1.3	1.4	9.8	9.5	6.5
Manufacturing	25.6	25.8	8.6	3.5	5.2
Construction	3.5	3.4	12.7	1.0	4.8
Transportation and communication	5.3	5.1	8.2	0.5	−0.3
Commerce	20.9	20.8	6.0	3.0	4.2
Agriculture, livestock, fisheries, and forest products	20.4	20.3	0.4	3.0	5.0
Minerals	2.2	2.0	2.7	−3.0	−0.4
Others	16.3	16.2	5.4	3.5	4.2

* Nacional Financiera, *El Mercado de Valores*, 22 (March 5, 1962), 119, and 23 (March 4, 1963), 113.

the basis of the 1960 population census, real per capita income is shown to have remained at approximately the same level as the year before. Given the extremely unequal distribution of income in Mexico, a period of stagnation in per capita income most certainly signifies a substantial deterioration in the income of the population groups that are the least well off economically, thus aggravating their situation. This last-mentioned circumstance is particularly demonstrated by the fact that agricultural production increased at a slower pace than the population (by only 3%) while imports of foodstuffs and beverages decreased by 16.5% and exports of the commodity group expanded by 7%. It is therefore logical to assume that there was a decline in the domestic supply of foodstuffs, (despite a 15% increase in wheat production and increments in the output of corn and beans in comparison with the previous year)—a decline that primarily affects the low-income groups. Further proof of the aggravation of the situation is had in the level of production of consumer goods of industrial origin, which rose by only 2.5%, implying a decrease in per capita consumption of those items.

In explaining the economic stagnation it is hardly necessary to emphasize that several factors worked together in bringing it about. However, certain of these are of preponderant importance. One fact, for example, is that expanding government investment could not compensate for the slow development in the private investment field. (Private investments decreased, particularly during the first half of the year.) In like manner, the improvement in Mexico's trade balance helped lessen the balance of payments pressures deriving largely from short-term capital flight, but was unable to prevent a decrease of some 200 million dollars in the Bank of Mexico's net international reserves. Foreign direct investments increased by 14.6 million dollars, but foreign exchange outgo representing returns on those investments exceeded the total amount of new investments and reinvestments by more than 30 million dollars.

According to widely-held opinion, had it not been for the noteworthy increase in public expenditure in 1961, the economic stagnation would have turned into an outright recession. The unfavorable forces that were influencing the country's economy and in large measure conditioned the government's economic policy held back the increase in ordinary liquid revenues to a scant 4%, while budgetary expenditures expanded by almost 10% and authorized public investment rose by 20%. In any event, this public expenditure policy would not have been able to compensate for the sluggish development of private economic activity. The results achieved can be attributed in greater degree to the large private and public investment programs conducted in previous years than to those effected during the year under review.[22]

The growth rate in excess of 4 per cent in the following year, 1962, represented a moderate improvement, though it was of course below Mexico's long run achievement. Some of the key activities, such as construction and manufacturing taken as a whole, performed reasonably well. Agriculture, however, again lagged behind the national average.

Facts of this sort demanded an explanation. This assumed two main forms, in a fashion reminiscent of orthodox business cycle analysis. One group emphasized supply and cost difficulties, while the other focused on problems of aggregate demand. The first group, reflecting primarily the banking and commercial interests, began its account with subjective factors—that is, by calling attention to the lack of confidence on the part of the business community. The fears and pessimism, it argued, stemmed at least in part from the behavior of the national government. To mollify the lower income groups the public sector had taken over a number of industries, such as the distribution of motion pictures and electricity, and although it had offered sufficient compensation it had often tightened its regulation beforehand. Uncertainty was thereby created. There was little point in planning for expansion and in undertaking investment if the government might assume ownership of an industry on short notice. Finally, President López Mateos had very early in his administration made a remark which was designed to placate the more progressive elements but which was unfortunate in terms of both the interpretation and the attending publicity. He asserted that his government was of the Left within the framework of the Constitution.[23] With respect to public ownership the Mexican Constitution does not happen to be

[22] Banco Nacional de Comercio Exterior, "The Mexican Economy in 1961," *Comercio Exterior de México*, 8 (April, 1962), 2 ff.

[23] Because of the trends in the distribution of income and wealth, the government ". . . attempted to counteract this development by presenting itself as not only continuing the Revolution but giving it a new and radical turn." The quotation is from I. A. Langnas, "Mexico Today, Aspects of Progress Since the Revolution," *World Today*, 17 (April, 1961), 162.

a terribly revolutionary document, but the President's qualifying phrase received scant notice relative to his alleged gaucherie.

Despite these grievances against the administration, this more conservative group recognized investment in infrastructure as a proper public function. Further, it has had only minor fears of devaluation and virtually no fears at all of eventual communism in Mexico. Events in the remainder of Latin America, however, have been unsettling. The fear of communism abroad has reduced commercial intercourse with other nations and has generally impaired confidence. The market has registered this in the forms of capital flights,[24] reductions in the supply of investment funds, and higher credit costs. Insofar as funds remained in Mexico, they were placed with nonbanking financial institutions at interest rates of 10 per cent. These agencies in turn lent at 16 per cent to 18 per cent, which of course meant that firms could afford to borrow for only the most profitable ventures. This also involved the commercial banks in an unfortunate side effect: legally prevented from charging more than 12 per cent for a loan, they were driven into government securities for their investments. It is interesting also to note that labor unions were not held responsible for the cost push; one could hardly fly so in the face of the evidence. In any event, since the difficulties arose on the monetary side and not because of inadequacies of aggregate demand, the remedy consisted of introducing more money into the economy and, as a consequence, reducing interest rates—that, and the restoration of confidence by whatever means possible.

The following passage, which emphasizes the reactions of the business community to uncertainty, serves as a good review of the foregoing argument.

In the face of the social and political turmoil in Latin America, and particularly as a result of events in the Caribbean, private initiative maintained a wait-and-see attitude in 1961, and various disquieting and negative symptoms appeared: capital flight, freezing of investments, decline in certain productive activities, accumulation of stocks, etc. This behavior on the part of Mexican entrepreneurs constituted an obstacle for the country's development (and therefore aggravated even further the socio-political conditions that were originally respon-

---

[24] The stock of funds held abroad in 1962 has been estimated at $300,000,000.

sible for the business men's attitude) and spurred the government to more decisive action in the economic field. State intervention in the economy, therefore, should be interpreted simply as a policy that was inevitable in the face of the threat of crisis and in view of the vacuum left by private enterprise in the general economic activity, rather than qualifying as radical action aimed at modifying existing basic production relationships in the country.[25]

While the López Mateos administration was unfortunate in coming to power at the same time as Castro, its behavior at home should not have been responsible for a severe loss of confidence. It sought cooperation with business, particularly with the "New Group," in order to promote economic development. The instances of nationalization for which it was responsible were not very numerous, and they have been accompanied by adequate compensation. Further, they served necessary politicoeconomic ends. Nationalization has been a vehicle for demonstrating to the underprivileged that the government is vitally concerned with their interests. The low income groups then looked upon the properties as "theirs," and they also responded favorably to the subsequent price policy—a uniform subsidy in the film industry and price discrimination in electricity. In the latter industry nationalization performed the economic function of extending services beyond the traditional centers of demand, as well as the political one of furthering national pride and unity.[26] Despite some minor causes of concern, the issue of nationalization appears to have been introduced like a reflex action in times of distress. The lack of confidence, which certainly existed, was more probably a response to the realities of retarded growth. Lower profitability and enhanced risk led to capital flights and hence to inward shifts of the supply schedules of investment funds. This, combined with a fairly tight monetary policy, raised the cost of credit. Contributing to the decline in activity was a tendency on the part of entrepreneurs to expect rates of return close to 25 per cent per annum on their investments.

[25] Banco Nacional de Comercio Exterior, "The Mexican Economy in 1961," p. 22.

[26] Miguel S. Wionczek, "Electric Power: The Uneasy Partnership," in Raymond Vernon, ed., *Public Policy and Private Enterprise in Mexico*, pp. 109 and 99.

The other major view of Mexico's quinquennium of economic retardation focused on inadequate aggregate demand, with particular stress on the limited purchasing power of the low income consumers. This view was the more widely held of the two. It certainly had the blessing of many Mexican economists whose research efforts we have already reviewed. Corroboration came also, despite some hedging, from the research organ of the second of the two largest banks in Mexico. Once again because of the nature of the source, the relevant passage is presented at some length:

. . . Mexico's unprecedented industrial growth has been accomplished in a rather disjointed manner. Among the factors which have contributed definitely towards a lack of coordination, two are outstanding: a) a haphazard accumulation of capital through inflationary means; b) Mexico's marked dependence upon her exportation of raw materials.

These two factors have contributed towards a growing concentration of the national income for the benefit of only a few individuals, and they have also made our country highly dependent upon foreign markets, which are unstable and unreliable. The population sector with the higher incomes now constitutes the most lucrative domestic market. That is why the capital goods industries have grown disproportionately in comparison with consumer goods industries. But more recently, a tendency has set in towards a redistribution of wealth. Lately, wages and salaries of the lower income groups have tended to increase.

Nevertheless, production of consumer goods is at present more than the local market can absorb; the local market is small because it is limited to the higher income groups. But it is encouraging to note that business men have now realized that the market should not consist solely of the higher income groups, and that the purchasing power of the middle class has been increasing.

Mexico's economic growth is not benefiting the great majority of its population, so the improvement in the living standard of this majority is very slight. The purchasing power of the lower class has not expanded. Moreover, too much emphasis is laid upon improving our commercial balance with foreign countries, so as to earn foreign exchange, but the fact is overlooked that the internal market must be expanded in order to achieve a high degree of economic development . . .

It is necessary, therefore, to strengthen our internal markets, through the incorporation into the national activity of the majority of our population, composed mainly of the rural sector, which is our best potential market. The present Administration of Government fully realizes this, and has already adopted definite measures towards increasing the purchasing power of the rural population . . .[27]

To enhance rural purchasing power the authors recommend the promotion of diversified agricultural production. However, this calls for a strengthening of the demand for agriculture's products. A United Nations source was most accurate in 1955 in predicting that ". . . it is more than likely that agriculture will be unable to continue developing during the next few years without a steady expansion in domestic demand."[28] Despite the shifts in the relative prices of agricultural commodities in favor of domestic goods and at the expense of exported items, producers have not responded accordingly. All this suggests the complementarity of demands between agricultural and industrial commodities, with the inequalities of income distribution in each sector helping to account for the weak demand in the other.

Support of this second view also emanated from no less a source than the National Chamber of Manufacturers,[29] though associations of particular industries might adhere more closely to the first position. The Chamber has viewed income not only as unjustly distributed but as hampering the internal market. Industries serving the domestic market, it pointed out, were plagued with excess capacity. It held that reforms and enhanced productivity were necessary in agriculture because of the effects on rural purchasing power; similarly, smaller- and medium-sized firms should be encouraged because they cater to the internal market. Since economic development requires a center, the government's role is strategic, though of course the public sector is not to encroach upon the private one. The problem of governmental interference need not be a serious one, however, because of continuing shortages in public capital, as in transportation, electricity, gas, and petro-

[27] Banco Nacional de México, "Some Observations Upon Mexico's Economic Development," *Review of the Economic Situation of Mexico*, 35 (August, 1959), 3–4.

[28] UNESCO, *External Disequilibrium*, p. 46.

[29] Cámara Nacional de la Industria de Transformación, *Veinte años de lucha, 1941–1961*, esp. pp. 73–81.

chemicals. The Chamber hoped for investment coefficients (gross investment/GNP) of 25 per cent, with the government generating 40 per cent of total investment as well as 10 per cent of the national output. To finance these public expenditures the Chamber called for higher taxes upon the recipients of interest, rent, and the profits accruing from trade. Fiscal policy must generally serve as an arm of development.

It is a moot question whether the partial endorsement of this second position by the National Chamber of Commerce is even more astonishing than the virtually full support given it by the manufacturers. Commerce approved of the government's public works and of the various official programs for stimulating private industry. It further recognized the necessity of additional tax revenues, although it objected to the imposition of new types of taxes. It placed great value upon education and training as forces for raising both productivity and consumption. In a fashion more familiar to a North American, the Chamber also had faith in advertising, propaganda, and publicity as vehicles for stimulating consumption.

The evidence, and the positions of the majority of those who examined the evidence, reveal a fairly clear consensus. One is made aware first, and perhaps foremost, of the importance of demand in Mexico's economic growth. If Mexico's history at all exemplifies the process of development, the subject of demand has yet to receive the attention it merits in the theory of development. Regarding the components of demand, one can assert further that mass consumption did not contribute significantly to Mexico's early advance and that it in fact failed to do so in more recent years. Unfortunately the sources of demand which stimulated the expansion from the early forties to the mid-fifties did not always exhibit the same strength thereafter. Many Mexicans have interpreted this as the occasion for stimulating mass consumption in order to provide the basis for continued economic growth. This has directed them in turn to the nation's income distribution and to recommendations of lessened inequality. In the words of one informant, "It is necessary to reenforce the basic ideas of the Revolution." This has implied programs of education, social benefits, and agricultural development, especially irrigation works and altered land tenures. It has further implied a dynamic government. The latter has found it necessary to step up its public investment programs, not only to enhance the productivity of the low income group but to take up the slack in aggregate demand as well.

The propensity to save. Finally, have savings patterns reflected the nature of Mexico's income distribution? As the latter has altered, has there been any effect on the nation's propensity to save?

The evidence points to a savings shortage during the decade of the forties, particularly during the war years. According to the United Nations, ". . . the volume of domestic savings continued, in the first part of the period under review, to be insufficient to finance investment."[30] Private gross investment approximated only 6 per cent of the gross national product in 1939 and 1940. By the end of the decade and the beginning of the 1950's, the private investment coefficients had climbed toward 8 and 9 per cent. Given the typical values of capital-output ratios, the higher coefficients were associated with an additional 1 per cent of income growth per year.

Not surprisingly, the well-to-do have managed most of the saving in Mexico. For one thing corporate saving has greatly outweighted personal saving. In a recent year the latter accounted for less than 7 per cent of all private gross domestic saving, with undistributed profits giving rise to almost 50 per cent of the total and depreciation reserves to the remainder. The savings patterns of households further bear this out. In 1956 about 16 per cent of the population was responsible for almost 89 per cent of all personal saving.[31]

The effect of a family's income position upon its ability to save appears in greater detail in Table 39. The contributor to column four of this table has calculated the effects on saving of redistributing income more equally, first by 10, then by 50, and finally by 100 per cent. He finds that average family savings would be lowered from 101 pesos to 98.46, 90.63, and 60.27 pesos per month, respectively. As he points out, this assumes that families with changed incomes would possess the same propensities as those cur-

[30] UNESCO, Economic Commission for Latin America, *Recent Events and Trends in Mexico*, p. 10.

[31] Arturo González Cosío, "Clases y estratos sociales," in *México: Cincuenta años de revolución, II, La vida social*, p. 68, t. 9.

Growth, Equality, and the Mexican Experience

TABLE 39. Personal Savings and Monthly Incomes*

Range of Monthly Income (pesos)	Average Monthly Income (pesos)	Average Monthly Savings (pesos)	$\frac{S}{Y}$
<100	72.20	−22.49	−31.1
101–200	157.79	−27.09	−17.2
201–300	263.35	−23.76	−9.0
301–400	361.78	−7.55	−2.1
401–500	459.57	14.49	3.2
501–750	629.47	55.03	8.7
751–1,000	871.16	101.53	11.7
1,001–2,000	1,426.80	244.08	17.1
2,001–3,000	2,512.49	708.40	28.2
More than 3,000	4,918.28	1,874.15	38.1
Total	692.80	101.12	14.6

* The first three columns are from Ifigenia M. de Navarrete, "*La distribución del ingreso y el desarrollo económico de México*," appendix to table 10. Column 4 represents the calculation by Leopoldo Solís in his coreview of Mrs. Navarrete's book, *Comercio Exterior de México*, 11 (February, 1961), 89.

rently occupying a given income position. Technically the procedure assumes static consumption functions. Yet one might reasonably expect the analytical consumption functions to shift upward as a consequence of redistribution. If national income remained constant under these circumstances, saving would of course decline. However, there is no reason to assume constancy of income. If inadequate consumption is a bottleneck, income can rise together with the consumption function and thereby generate more savings ex post. When savings comprise the major shortage, the upward shift in consumption causes income to fall, or at least to rise at a slower rate. The optimum propensity to save or consume obviously varies with the underlying circumstances.

One could thus persuasively argue that as long as the private investment coefficient continued to expand, some increase in inequality of income distribution could benefit the economy. There is a question of degree, however. As Aubrey summarizes it, ". . . while investment increased sizably it did not grow nearly to an extent which would appear to justify the increasing inequity of social distribution from a development angle."[32] The combination of inflation, exceedingly favorable profits, and the rising inequality of income distribution that occurred from 1939 to the mid-fifties proved to be a wasteful way of inducing savings (see Table 40). Profit recipients apparently allocated one-fifth of their incomes to investment and the remainder to consumption. The economy tolerated a situation in which over 30 per cent of the national income was directed to satisfying the consumption needs of profit earners in order to encourage them to invest at a rate not exceeding 10 per cent of the GNP. These circumstances did not alter in later years. In 1955 and 1956 the business community reinvested 22 and 23 per cent, respectively, of its income, while it spent the balance upon consumer goods and services. Even these percentages overstate the amounts devoted to capital formation because they neglect foreign sources of funds; once these are included the percentages drop to 19 and 21 for the years in question.[33] During these years, also, the business community as a whole enjoyed more than 50 per cent of the total private consumption of the economy and in the process consumed over 40 per cent of the nation's GNP.[34] In the early sixties retained earnings as a proportion of profit continued to fluctuate between one-quarter and one-fifth. Investment was generally not forthcoming unless it could be recovered in three or four years. During the whole period the trade-off between growing inequality and more savings thus imposed a severe penalty upon the majority of Mexican people. Given this comparatively small contribution to capital formation, one can perhaps be excused for wondering if additional taxes for increasing public saving might not have expanded the economy's capital more rapidly.

By the late forties the private investment coefficient, $\frac{I}{Y}$, leveled off and the rate of increase in private investment, $\frac{\Delta I}{I}$, declined.[35] This of course rendered the case for a sharp and rising income inequality even less acceptable. Once investment begins to falter, much of the defense for a marked inequality disappears. Further,

[32] Aubrey, "Structure and Balance in Rapid Economic Growth," p. 523.

[33] Banco Nacional de Mexico, *Review of the Economic Situation*, 34 (January, 1958), 12.

[34] *Ibid.*, p. 9, t. 2.

[35] See chapter 2, Table 4, and chapter 7, Table 41.

TABLE 40. Profit Income and Private Investment, 1939–1954*

Year	Percentage of Total Profits Invested	Percentage of Total Profits Consumed	Profits Consumed ÷ National Income
1939	22.1	77.9	20.4
1940	22.0	78.0	22.3
1941	22.5	77.5	23.8
1942	14.8	85.2	28.1
1943	13.6	86.4	30.5
1944	15.2	84.8	31.9
1945	16.0	84.0	34.7
1946	18.4	81.6	36.8
1947	21.2	78.8	34.9
1948	21.4	78.6	33.7
1949	21.2	78.8	32.7
1950	19.1	80.9	33.5
1951	17.9	82.1	34.5
1952	18.4	81.6	35.9
1953	21.6	78.4	29.8
1954	21.0	79.0	30.8

* Adolfo López Romero "Desarrollo económico de México (1934–1959)," *El Trimestre Económico*, 29 (January–March, 1962), 51, tables 14 and 15.

if it is assumed that the investment coefficient reflects the propensity to save—that is, $\frac{I}{Y} = \frac{S}{Y}$—and if this is incorporated in familiar growth formula, $\frac{\Delta Y}{Y} = \frac{S}{Y} / \frac{\Delta K}{\Delta Y}$, it is possible to combine the underconsumption argument of the previous section with the present one regarding a constant saving propensity. If, as happened over 1957–1962, the rate of increase in income declines while $\frac{S}{Y}$ remained stable, $\frac{\Delta K}{\Delta Y}$ must rise. This in turn is certainly consistent with a rise in excess capacity, which was seemingly concentrated in the consumer goods industries. The marginal gross capital-output ratios averaged just below 2 for the period 1954–1957 and then climbed to 3.7 for the years 1958–1961.[36] The capital-output ratio could not of course be expected to increase indefinitely. Either steps had to be taken to improve $\frac{\Delta Y}{Y}$ or $\frac{S}{Y}$ had to deteriorate

[36] See chapter 2, Table 5.

to some degree. In fact the latter as well as the former occurred. The private investment coefficient, $\frac{I}{Y}$, remained stable while the flow of private foreign funds showed a slight relative increase. During 1939–1950 private external investment accounted for one-tenth of fixed gross private investment, but it had climbed to one-sixth during 1950–1959.[37]

In sum, the propensities to save have served as a barometer of the degree of inequality of income distribution, but not as a very good one. During the forties both the propensities and the inequalities tended to increase, but one could not judge from savings patterns that inequality had intensified to such a degree. Inflation played an important role in these relationships in that it had pronounced effects upon income distribution without affecting savings very much one way or another.[38] During the fifties the propensities to save no longer rose and in fact exhibited a slight tendency to decline. One would hope that this would have signaled an improvement in income distribution, but the latter actually worsened somewhat. During the entire two decades the income distribution apparently had to deteriorate steadily to call forth rising and relatively high savings propensities; a continued high, and even moderately rising, level of inequality was insufficient for this purpose. Phrased differently, a coefficient of elasticity relating the percentage increase in savings to the percentage increase in the degree of inequality of distribution would fall considerably below 1. Such a situation is of course intolerable in the long run, and it certainly cannot serve as a model of sustained development. Over a brief period (Mexico's history suggests as much as a quarter of a century) this situation may yield tolerably good results, particularly if the heightening of inequality is not accompanied by absolute declines in the planes of living of the lower income groups. Again in terms of the basic growth formula, $\frac{\Delta Y}{Y}$ and $\frac{S}{Y}$ can each expand over the shorter period, while $\frac{\Delta K}{\Delta Y}$ remains relatively stable. But, over the long run, this certainly cannot serve as a model of sustained development.

The view here is that by the late fifties the time had come for

[37] Alfredo Navarrete Romero, "El financiamiento del desarrollo económico," in *México: Cincuenta años de revolución, I, La economia*, p. 516, t. 3.

[38] See chapter 7.

Mexico to modify both its income distribution and its structure of demand. The occasion now called for greater equality, rather than less, and for a more rapid expansion in wage goods relative to the other components of demand. The investment coefficients and the realized savings propensities would be sufficiently high to permit rapid growth in that the changed circumstances would affect the inducements to invest favorably. With the pursuit of these policies, the relatively low growth rates of the late fifties and early sixties would simply appear as a cyclical phenomenon; without these necessary changes the Mexican economy might suffer long term stagnation.

What did this imply for specific governmental policies? The following three chapters, Seven through Nine, deal with various aspects of this question.

CHAPTER SEVEN

Perspectives on Inflation

Inflation and economic growth. Several of the foregoing chapters have focused upon the role of government in influencing economic development, while, of the following two, Chapter Eight directs attention to taxes (*impuestos*) and Chapter Nine, to expenditures (*gastos*). Here we consider the proposition that national governments can finance their projects at whatever rate they please; finance as such is no bottleneck. The issue of course concerns the extent to which a government is willing to play havoc with its standard of value. This seems the occasion for placing inflation in its proper perspective and for considering it as a mechanism for inducing growth if the tax system cannot be altered sufficiently.

Viewed *ceteris paribus*—that is, outside the framework of conflicting national objectives—inflation is evidently inequitable, and it *may* hamper growth because of its effect on productive investment. Virtually all of the indictments against inflation enumerated by E. M. Bernstein and I. G. Patel[1] have been experienced in Mexico. The two authors argue that the investment accompanying inflation does not tend to be pronounced, especially once the rise in prices gathers force. Further, they point out, any added investment is achieved at a relatively high cost, since inflation alters both the composition of consumption goods and the structure of investment. Savings tend to shift from the strategic areas of agriculture, indus-

---

[1] E. M. Bernstein and I. G. Patel, "Inflation in Relation to Economic Development," *International Monetary Fund Staff Papers*, 2 (November, 1952), 363–398.

try, and export goods to inventories, real estate, and foreign assets. The writers conclude with a strong statement in favor of stabilizing prices and of utilizing "much more efficient means of building up productive capital than is provided by continuous inflation."[2]

However, a comprehensive evaluation of the inflationary process calls for a consideration of several major policy alternatives. Is the over-all economic performance associated with price stability superior to one that includes inflation?

For the moment let us ignore the very wide ranges that can be traversed by both prices and real income and simply consider each in discrete terms. That is, either growth occurs (at the rate of some 5 per cent per year) or it doesn't, and either prices advance (perhaps about 10 per cent a year) or they remain absolutely stable. Ignoring the minus signs, which are less probable and which cannot be tolerated as a steady diet, four combinations are then possible. Of the four everyone would agree that zero income growth together with rising price levels, brought about perhaps by a reckless mismanagement of the country's economic affairs, represents the least desirable alternative. The combination of income growth and price stability is surely the most attractive of the lot. Serious disagreement may arise, however, over the priorities to be attached to the two remaining combinations. If the prevailing tax structure must be taken as given or subject to very gradual change and if the central bank is hampered in the exercise of its monetary policy, as is true in so many of the underdeveloped countries, the authorities might well be advised to seek a combination of growth and inflation in preference to stagnation and price stability. This may tend to be true despite the several difficulties reviewed by Bernstein and Patel. As long as additional expenditures contribute to growth, the economy enjoys a dynamism which should eventually assist even those who are most injured by the rise in prices, in part because of the steps which they themselves eventually take to assure their participation.

The problem is of course much more complex in the everyday world. For one thing, it evidently cannot be posed in such discrete terms. Assume that in addition to price and income stability and a combination of a 5 per cent income growth and a 10 per cent price

2 *Ibid.*, p. 384.

rise, it is also possible to choose 4 per cent increases in both income and prices. For the latter two combinations the marginal rate of transformation between income growth and price increases is 6 to 1. The third combination seems tempting, though the growth rate does come perilously close to being inadequate, given the usual population increase. The choice between combinations like the latter two depends in considerable part upon an economy's previous performance. If it has not yet enjoyed much progress a high rate of inflation may, if necessary, be a small price to pay for change. On the other hand if an economy has already experienced some momentum it may find it wise to restrict inflation at the expense of growth.

Generalizations about advances in income and prices are further complicated by the multiple sources of inflation. Inflation-inducing activities can promote economic growth under some conditions and exert a neutral or a retardative effect under others. Moreover, some economies are much more inflation-prone than others because of differences in supply conditions. As a consequence, world experience reveals no unique correlation between growth of income and advance of prices. As one source has phrased it: "While . . . annual rates of growth of 5 per cent or more have been attained in a few countries where the degree of inflation has been considerable, for the underdeveloped countries as a group there has been no consistent relationship between inflation and growth."[3]

Although this properly cautions against undue generalizations, it does also take note of a class of exceptions—of "a few countries" in which growth and inflation accompanied each other. There are some signs that Mexico belongs to this smaller group. For Mexico or other highly growth-oriented countries let us therefore hypothesize the growth-inflation curve that may be predicted on a priori grounds. Then the data can be brought in to ascertain whether the Mexican economy has behaved as anticipated.

In Figure 3 two growth-inflation curves are confined to the range in which price stability and income growth pose conflicting objectives; on every point of each curve a movement toward one goal gives rise to some surrender of the other. The percentage in-

[3] United Nations, Economic and Social Council, *World Economic Survey*, *1960*, p. 59.

crease in income, $\frac{\Delta Y}{Y}$, appears on the horizontal axis, and the relative change in the price level, $\frac{\Delta P}{P}$, on the vertical one. Since some economic growth occurs at stable prices, the curve begins to the right of the origin. It should then exhibit a positive first derivative. The initial behavior of the second derivative is far from clear, however. Conceivably $\frac{\Delta Y}{Y}$ may rise more rapidly than $\frac{\Delta P}{P}$ over a small range, so that the second derivative is initially negative (not shown). In relatively short order, however, the price level should rise more rapidly than real income, whereupon the second derivative becomes positive. In all probability it has been so all along.

Curve BB' represents the alternatives available to a relatively backward, low per capita income nation. In turn, AA' represents the alternatives available to the same country at a higher income level. The second curve should neither be identical with nor lie

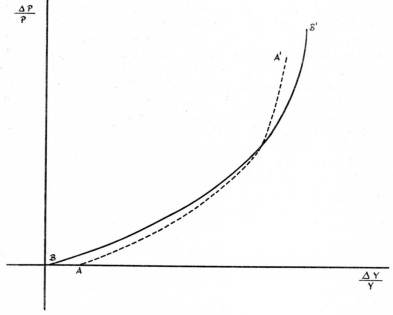

Figure 3. Hypothetical Relationship between Price Increases and Income Growth (in Percentage Terms)

parallel to the first. Given any validity to the structuralist view of inflation, the elasticities of cost and supply should have increased in the interim and the economy ought now to experience less inflation when aggregate demand expands. This causes the AA' curve to lie below and to the right of BB' at the outset. On the other hand a more advanced economy may find it more difficult to attain exceedingly high growth rates because of the size of its current base. Exceptional circumstances such a postwar recovery can intervene, but the maximum potential relative increase in income is probably lower for a richer economy. It is highly likely that AA' eventually intersects BB' and then rises to the left of BB'. Failing that, AA' should at least approach BB' in the upper ranges.

Figure 3 concerns the most interesting combinations of income growth and price increases in that it portrays conflicting objectives and implies significant policy decisions. Curves AA' and BB' are in effect transformation curves showing the trade-off between income growth and price stability. However, these dual goals are in conflict only over a particular range. In the areas denoting recession or depression, below the horizontal axis, both AA' and BB' should have positive first and second derivatives, though the curves should be quite flat because of price rigidities downward. Over this range the price stability and income growth objectives do not clash. The same measures that help stimulate a rise in incomes may also discourage price declines. Further, in the very high ranges the AA' and BB' curves should eventually bend backward. The behavior of the curves in this area is less predictable, since so much depends upon people's past experiences with, and the response to, inflation. A great deal also depends upon the factors contributing to the rise in prices. If a nation is compelled to live through the severe disruption in economic activity occasioned by the ravages of a war and the confusions of a post-war period, the curves will probably bend back. Once again the conflict between two broad objectives disappears, since a reduction in disorder and uncertainty leads to more favorable price and income results. The function would be negatively sloped in this range, although the degree of the slope is not easily foreseen.

Has the Mexican economy behaved in accordance with these a priori expectations? Since the foregoing functions have been designed as analytical schedules, one must assume that the experiences of two decades emanated from approximately the same universe and then proceed as if the ex post data represented alternative combinations in the same period.

The relevant price and income series appear in the first and second columns of Table 41, and they have been plotted in Figure 4. Neither economic theory nor the nature of the scatter suggests a simple linear relationship. A linear function might be drawn on the assumption that three abnormal war years, 1943, 1944, and 1951, belong in the range of a positive correlation between price increases and income growth—that is, within the portion represented in Figure 3. Another approach is to regard these three years as part of the backward-bending range, which depicts a negative relationship between income and prices, and to exclude them from any linear correlations. The exclusion yields somewhat better results, but in neither case does the coefficient of correlation exceed four-tenths. Moreover, the horizontal intercept lies beyond 5. If, instead, a nonlinear curve were drawn freehand (not shown) it would still cut the horizontal axis in the range of a positive $\frac{\Delta Y}{Y}$ but closer to the origin, and it would sweep upward in the fashion of Figure 3 toward the points represented by the years 1945 and 1955. This introduction of curvilinearity makes the case for inflation as an accompaniment of economic growth considerably more persuasive. The growth performance in the range of price stability now becomes quite unsatisfactory, while income continues to expand, albeit at a decreasing rate, until $\frac{\Delta P}{P}$ climbs as high as 15 per cent.

Why should this moderate correlation between income and prices have occurred? The answer that comes to mind most readily is couched in terms of a forced saving thesis. According to this view inflation should benefit profit recipients and hamper wage earners as well as recipients of fixed property returns, as it evidently did in Mexico. On balance the whole process is supposed to favor those who are the most likely to engage in capital formation. This is a time-honored view, perhaps applicable to the development experiences of many countries. The Mexican authorities were hardly culpable if they adopted it as a means of stimulating growth, and some in fact believe they may have done so. Tannen-

TABLE 41. Increases in the Price Level and Related Series, 1939 and Following*

Year	$\dfrac{\Delta P}{P}$ (%)	$\dfrac{\Delta \text{GNP}}{\text{GNP}}$ (%)	$\dfrac{\text{Profits}}{\text{Income}}$ (%)	$\dfrac{I_{private}}{\text{GNP}}$ (%)	$\dfrac{\Delta I_{private}}{I_{private}}$ (%)
1939	...	...	26.2	6.0	...
1940	4.0	1.1	28.6	6.4	11.1
1941	5.1	12.4	30.7	7.2	24.8
1942	10.3	13.3	33.0	5.0	−21.9
1943	20.8	3.7	35.3	5.0	4.2
1944	22.5	8.5	37.6	5.9	25.8
1945	11.3	7.6	41.3	6.6	19.1
1946	12.1	6.6	45.1	7.9	39.0
1947	8.8	1.4	44.3	9.2	19.4
1948	7.3	4.5	42.9	9.0	−0.3
1949	9.5	4.3	41.5	8.7	−3.5
1950	9.3	7.8	41.4	8.1	−2.4
1951	24.0	7.5	42.0	8.9	14.0
1952	3.7	4.0	44.0	8.0	−2.4
1953	−1.9	0.6	38.0	7.9	−0.9
1954	9.4	10.5	39.0	7.5	7.3
1955	13.6	8.7	42.5	8.7	23.9
1956	4.6	6.3	39.0	9.0	13.9
1957	4.3	7.7	38.0	8.9	7.1
1958	4.4	5.5	37.5	8.4	1.9
1959	1.2	2.9	36.5	8.0	0.9
1960	4.9	7.9	...	8.1	7.8
1961	1.0	3.5	...	7.5	−1.8
1962	1.8	4.8	...	...	...
1963	0.6	6.3	...	...	...
1964	4.2	10.4	...	...	...

* Columns 1, 2, and 4 are from chapter 1, tables 2, 3, and 4, respectively, while column 3 is from chapter 5, Table 27. The data in column 5 for 1939–1950 are taken from The Combined Mexican Working Party, *The Economic Development of Mexico*, p. 203, t. 25. The 1951–1961 rates of change in column 5 are based upon the private investment figures in Secretaría de Industria y Comercio, *Anuario estadístico de los Estados Unidos Mexicanos, 1960–1961*, p. 628, t. 16.4, deflated by the wholesale price indices for the years in question.

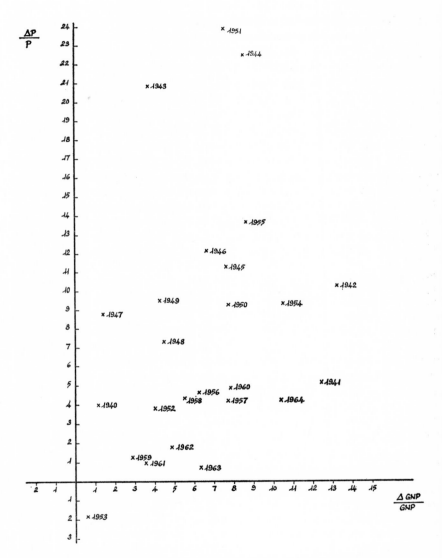

Figure 4. Price Increases and Income Growth (in Percentages) in Mexico, 1940 through 1964.

baum refers to "a seemingly deliberate policy of monetary inflation for the very purpose of stimulating industrial activity."[4]

One aspect of this argument possesses a degree of validity when applied to Mexico. Inflation did contribute moderately to profits (see Table 41, columns 1 and 3). About the most that can be said for the years 1940 through 1946 is that changes in prices and in the ratio of profits to income were each positive. Beginning in 1947, on the other hand, the strength of the relationship between prices and profits varies with one's interpretation. The trends for the profit share and the rate of increase in prices were each downward. On an annual basis, moreover, the profit share rose when the increase in prices was especially vigorous (at least 9 per cent) and fell when prices climbed only moderately. Yet for the whole period 1940 through 1959 a simple correlation between the annual rate of increase in prices and the annual change in the profit share yielded a coefficient of 0.2. On a yearly basis inflation thus correlated better with income growth than with modifications in profits.

If the price, output, and profits series are divided into periods of about half a dozen years and annual changes are ignored, the relationships are relatively close. Growth rates, price increases, and profit shares all attained their highest values during World War II. Thereupon the real GNP and the general price level rose at lesser rates, while the profits share fell off fairly uniformly. On the other hand there is again a noteworthy lack of any correlation between annual changes in the profit share and the real national product. In sum, changes in the profit share were only moderately related to inflation, and they could be correlated with rates of increase in income only on a long term basis. This in turn implies that both the first premise of the forced saving thesis, the stimulating effect of price movements on profits, and the second, the favorable impact of profits on growth, were at best partially fulfilled in Mexico's development. If income growth and price advances somehow stimulated each other, variations in the profits share did not serve as the prime mover.

The proposition that the correlation between changes in income and prices was not due to the behavior of the profit recipients re-

---

[4] Frank Tannenbaum, *Mexico: The Struggle for Peace and Bread*, p. 219.

ceives further corroboration from the series on private investment coefficients. Under the conditions of World War II the price level rose rapidly whereas the investment coefficient lingered in the vicinity of 5 or 6 per cent. Thereupon the price level declined while the private investment coefficient advanced, and it then fluctuated considerably as the investment coefficient exhibited a rather remarkable constancy beginning in the late forties. Some studies have dwelled on the negative correlation that actually occurred during the entire decade of the forties between savings propensities on the one hand and price increases and profit shares on the other. Thus until 1946 the marginal propensity to save lagged behind the average, but thereafter the marginal exceeded the average.[5] Or, in the same vein, ". . . the coefficient of saving of the group obtaining the greatest advantage from the shift in income distribution did not improve. Instead the savings coefficient tended to decrease over most of the period under review."[6] However, the period under discussion was not only brief but it reflected war and postwar influences as well. Perhaps one should not make too much of apparent negative correlations during the forties and simply record that no noteworthy positive relation existed between changes in the price level and changes in the investment coefficient.

The series on the rates of changes in real private investment (Table 41, column 5) should deliver the *coup de grace* to the forced saving thesis, insofar as Mexico is concerned. A diagram of the relationship between the rates of change in prices and private investment (with the latter on the vertical axis) would reveal a tremendous scatter and would suggest an almost vertical function. The linear correlation coefficient in this case is all of 0.3. If the idea of forced saving cannot bear the burden of explaining the moderate relationships between growth and inflation in Mexico, in what respects has it proved invalid?

The thesis is limited in that it tends to view the interrelationships among the several valuables in terms of a unidirectional flow. It

[5] The Combined Mexican Working Party, *The Economic Development of Mexico*, p. 183, t. 12; and Adolf Sturmthal, "Economic Development, Income Distribution, and Capital Formation in Mexico," *Journal of Political Economy*, 63 (June, 1955), 194–195.

[6] United Nations, Economic Commission for Latin America, *Economic Survey of Latin America, 1951–1952*, p. 88.

dwells upon inflation as an independent variable and neglects the factors which first cause price rises. In reality a burst of growth-inducing investment activity may place pressure upon productive services and lead to a shortage of final goods, whereupon prices proceed to perform their celebrated equilibrating function. Growth would thus give rise to inflation, not vice versa. Unquestionably experience in the everyday world is one of considerable mutual interaction. In general terms, however, the forced saving argument has undoubtedly concentrated too heavily on the hoped-for growth consequences of inflation and too little on the expenditures which may have generated the rise in prices.

This neglect of initiating forces pertains to private as well as to public activities. In 1955, for example, when private investment expanded by nearly one-quarter while prices advanced almost 14 per cent, the former was associated with the very high level of aggregate demand of that year and, in the course of things, affected prices. However, the forced saving argument tends particularly to ignore the role of governmental expenditures. These are of course not likely to be influenced very much by price changes, and hence they cannot occupy an important position in the thesis. If real public investment is sufficiently flexible, it should decline somewhat as prices advance, for budgetary reasons as well as for purposes of stability. On the other hand government purchases should also become more extensive, so that public investment in terms of current prices may hold steady. Yet the government's deficit spending has contributed in some measure to the rise in the general price level. From 1940 on, government expenditures rather consistently exceeded its revenues. This is not to say that the differences were astronomical or that they got out of hand. The deficits seldom exceeded 2 per cent of the GNP; more often than not they comprised a fraction of 2 per cent of the GNP, and in several years the government experienced surpluses. In all, the deficits averaged 0.7 per cent of the GNP from 1939 through 1963.[7] According to another estimate Mexico obtained 1.1 per cent of her GNP, and 22 per cent of her governmental resources from inflation.[8] Further, after World War II the Mexican government turned

[7] Ssee chapter 8, Table 45.
[8] Rodrigo Núñez, "Comment" [on Nicholas Kaldor, "The Role of Taxation

increasingly to the Export-Import Bank, the World Bank, and other foreign sources for its funds; this also should have exercised some restraint upon inflation. But whether or not it was characterized by caution and restraint, the deficit spending evidently did constitute an inflationary force.

The question of appropriate policy alternatives again arises. Assuming the prevailing tax structure as given, should Mexico, with its underdeveloped status and its need for economic advancement, have sacrificed growth-inducing expenditures to reduce deficit spending and counter inflation? Possibly, and to some degree, but the leadership and the community opted primarily for economic growth. Despite the growth-oriented program that was adopted, Mexico's railway system has remained inadequate, publicly financed irrigation has played a key but insufficient role in the development of agriculture, education is in great need of additional resources, and so on. If Mexico were to experience one of the highest growth rates recorded in the underdeveloped world, public expenditures, particularly public investment expenditures, could not be curtailed any more. This is the position adopted by Hansen, who sees a close parallel between the growths of Mexico and Japan. As he phrases it, each country ". . . undertook a program of economic development. In the process something happened to prices."[9] If inflation and the accompanying income inequality were inevitable consequences of public expenditures, these had to be borne to some extent if the economy were to continue growing. Strangely enough, a combination of faster growth and moderately high inflation probably had more favorable consequences for political stability than barely adequate growth and near price stability. Observers of Mexico's development have sometimes wondered at the willingness of workers to accept rising costs of living. Perhaps this reflects a traditional fatalism as well as the power of the dominant party. It may also be the result of a widespread belief that the government has been economically progressive and committed to the economic advancement of the Mexican people.

The proposition that growth first occurred and then something

in Economic Development"], in Joint Tax Council, *Fiscal Policy for Economic Growth in Latin America*, p. 97.

[9] Alvin H. Hansen, *Economic Issues of the 1960's*, p. 176.

happened to prices has a yet stronger basis. An examination of the bursts of inflation during the forties and fifties leaves no doubt that the major sources of the advance in prices lay not so much in the deficit financing of investment, whether private or public, as in the behavior of export demand. Rapid inflation attended World War II; the devaluations of the late forties was followed closely by the Korean war; and the devaluation of 1954 combined with the export boom of 1955. Gross additions to foreign reserves totaled 1,518,000,000 pesos from 1942 through 1945, 1,900,000,000 in 1949 and 1950, and 3,045,000,000 in 1954 and 1955.[10] The 1955 accumulation, about 2,578,000,000 pesos, was the largest on record. This was a reflection of the unduly sharp devaluation of the preceding year, made in response to an overestimation of the duration and amplitude of the 1953–1954 United States recession.

Ex post the resulting increases in prices may on occasion have been rationalized as applications of the forced saving view. Ex ante the officials recognized the cost of sharp inflation and the necessity of limiting its advance. However, they lacked the necessary tools. The fiscal apparatus could be described, with only slight exaggeration, as primitive. Confronted with this obstacle, the authorities endeavored to counteract inflation by restraining the expansion of credit, but monetary policy frequently bordered on the helpless. During World War II the authorities sought control of inflation through a policy of increasing reserve ratios. Early in 1941 they raised the ratio to 20 per cent, then without precedent in Latin America, and by the end of the year they had gradually elevated it to 50 per cent. In October 1942 excess deposits as of a given date were sterilized, while in May 1944 steps were taken to facilitate the investment of such deposits.[11] A decade later the monetary authorities still worked primarily with legal reserve requirements. They employed them not only quantitatively but qualitatively as well in order to promote stability, guard the liquidity of banks, and channel credit into the favored fields of industry and agriculture. In 1955 they resorted to marginal reserve requirements. Commercial banks then had to maintain 50 per cent of their total demand

[10] Víctor L. Urquidi, "La inflación en México," p. 43, t. 15.

[11] Víctor L. Urquidi, "Tres lustros de experiencia monetaria en México: Algunas enseñanzas," *Memoria del segundo congreso mexicano de ciencias sociales*, Vol. 2, p. 450.

deposits in various types of securities and 30 per cent of the total in approved government securities. These requirements in turn hampered the use of open market operations. Further, the authorities did not alter the rediscount rate frequently. The rate averaged 3 per cent in 1938 and 1939; it was then raised to 4.5 per cent by mid-1942 and remained at that level throughout the remaining 1940's and the 1950's.[12] The central bank used rediscounting as a weapon against inflation in a different fashion by granting the privilege only to those banks whose deposits were growing at less than a normal rate, defined as 6 per cent. Finally, the authorities reduced inflationary pressures by absorbing revaluation profits through the stratagem of exchanging foreign assets at the old rate of exchange.[13]

Had Mexico possessed adequate mechanisms for countering inflation at home (had Mexico not been underdeveloped) the export booms might primarily have advanced the Mexican economy. As it was, the favorable trade developments stimulated both growth and inflation.

The evidence thus indicates that the forced saving hypothesis has not been completely without merit, but that its relevance for economic growth may easily be exaggerated. On the other hand the correlation between economic growth and inflation has apparently been quite high. This suggests that growth probably played the more independent role—that inflation has been more of a function of growth than vice versa. Private and public capital formation, often financed through deficits, and a booming export business have all contributed to inflation, while price increases in turn served the cause of growth by inducing some added private investment. Presumably inflation would have an adverse effect on economic development in the range of exceedingly high rates of price increase combined with a falling rate of increase in income, but this phase has been encountered infrequently, if at all, in post-1939 Mexican history. Hence income growth rather than inflation appears on the horizontal axes in Figure 3 and Figure 4 in order

[12] International Monetary Fund, *International Financial Statistics, 1960,* p. 483, t. 174.

[13] Robert F. Emery, "Mexican Monetary Policy Since the 1954 Devaluation," *Inter-American Economic Affairs,* 12 (Spring, 1959), 75–77.

to call attention to this relative dependency of price increases upon income growth.

Monetary aspects of Mexico's inflation. Thus far the analysis of Mexico's inflation has been couched in terms of the Keynesian variables. A glance at the rise in prices from the vantage point of more orthodox monetary theory may also prove valuable. How did the stock, the turnover, and the price of money behave in the midst of rising commodity prices and incomes?

The money supply and national income in current prices each rose monotonically during 1941–1958, except for a slight dip in the total money supply in 1946 and a fall in the national output in 1953 (see Table 42). Over the period the total money supply climbed from 1,313,000,000 to 12,354,000,000 pesos—a 9.4-fold increase. Demand deposits especially contributed to this advance, since they moved from less than 40 per cent to more than 50 per cent of the total stock of money during the interval. Over the same time span the GNP rose from 8,800,000,000 to over 127,000,000,000 pesos—a 14.4-fold increase. The expansion of the money supply thus provided for almost two-thirds of the increase in money income, while the rise in income velocity accounted for the remainder.

Income velocity climbed from an initially high level of over 5 in the early forties to more than 10 by 1958. These are remarkable turnovers indeed. Clearly any money that the public authorities and private bankers were willing to create was sure to become money very much on the wing. Through most of the years in question the public apparently wanted a more rapid expansion of the monetary stock than occurred, and it compensated for the alleged shortcoming by utilizing the available supply at a considerably more rapid rate. Only in its short run annual changes did income velocity have few surprises to reveal. As expected, it declined during World War II and the Korean war. Even during these periods, however, the magnitudes remained relatively high.

Monetary theory suggests an evident relationship between income velocity and interest rates. As the demand for funds exceeded the supply and velocity rose, interest rates should have behaved in similar fashion. Since commodity prices rose during every year but one after 1939, one would further expect the prices of stocks to follow suit and those of bonds to decline, perhaps with some lag.

TABLE 42. Money Supply and Income Velocity, 1941–1958*

	(millions of pesos)			
	(1)	(2)	(3)	(4)
				Income Velocity
Year	Total Money Supply	Demand Deposits	GNP	(Col. [3] ÷ Col. [1])
1941	1,313	511	8,800	6.70
1942	1,789	764	10,700	5.98
1943	2,615	1,133	13,700	5.24
1944	3,314	1,542	17,700	5.34
1945	3,543	1,882	20,500	5.79
1946	3,461	1,732	26,100	7.54
1947	3,548	1,779	29,000	8.17
1948	3,762	1,814	31,700	8.43
1949	4,193	1,946	35,200	8.39
1950	5,108	2,491	40,577	7.94
1951	6,466	3,278	52,311	8.09
1952	6,827	3,325	58,643	8.59
1953	7,241	3,548	58,437	8.07
1954	7,791	3,809	71,540	9.18
1955	9,441	4,878	87,349	9.25
1956	10,602	5,563	99,323	9.37
1957	11,579	6,149	114,225	9.86
1958	12,354	6,531	127,152	10.29

* Columns (1) and (2) are from Banco Nacional de México, *Review of the Econom* *Situation of Mexico*, 36 (October, 1960), 16; each figure is for the end of a given yea Column (3) is from chapter 1, Table 1 of the present work.

Table 43 indicates Mexico's experiences in these financial areas during the decade of the fifties. The prices of the securities with variable yields acted as anticipated. The prices of fixed yield securities, however, did not. Nor, by and large, did the discount rates on short term paper. The rigidity of the rediscount rate may in part have influenced the behavior of the interest rates, particularly the short term variety; yet the long term rates have exhibited greater stability. In the case of a relatively advanced economy, the

Gurley-Shaw model of money substitutes[14] might account for relatively steady interest rates in the face of economic expansion and rising prices, but this approach does not appear appropriate for the Mexican economy. The major explanation of the inelasticity of demand for bonds seemingly lies in Mexico's continuing underdeveloped status: "Mexicans seek a sure profit, small risk of loss, and easily saleable securities."[15] Bonds can be cashed easily, and they have carried annual yields approximating 8 per cent. As a consequence, fixed yield securities have accounted for 97 per cent of all transactions on the Mexico City Stock Exchange, and a like percentage is undoubtedly approached over the counter. To be sure, firms have endeavored to push stock sales in response to the higher prices. They issued stocks valued at 3,473,000,000 pesos in 1959, compared to 2,423,000,000 pesos in 1951.[16] By comparison new bond issues merely advanced from a total value of 1,575,000,000 pesos in 1951 to 1,723,000,000 pesos in 1960. Yet the public continued to exercise a preference for bonds.[17]

The effects of inflation on the balance of payments. Discussions of the effects of inflation customarily consider growth, income distribution, and the balance of payments. The last of these still has to receive some attention.

In the conventional textbook case, changes in the balance of payments may provide the initial impetus to inflation or they may contribute to an inflation that has its origin in other circumstances. The problem in the first instance is one of squandering foreign exchange through high import propensities; severe inflation or balance of payments difficulties are not likely. The more frequent analytical procedure is to assume equilibrium and then to permit some other force, typically deficit financing, to be directly respon-

---

[14] John G. Gurley and Edward S. Shaw, "Financial Aspects of Economic Development," *American Economic Review*, 45 (September, 1955), 513–538.

[15] Banco Nacional de México, *Review of the Economic Situation of Mexico*, 37 (April, 1961), 15.

[16] *Ibid.*, 37 (August, 1961), 5.

[17] By 1964, however, prosperity and rising incomes encouraged purchasers of securities to turn increasingly to equity shares yielding 5 per cent and more. See "Mexico: Booming Urban Economy," *Hispanic American Report*, 17 (July, 1964), 596.

TABLE 43. Selected Financial Series, 1950–1959*

Year	Stocks—General Price Index	Bonds—General Price Index	Market Discount Rate
1950	131.6	102.7	. . .
1951	184.7	103.4	. . .
1952	187.0	102.1	10.30
1953	182.6	102.8	10.41
1954	197.6	102.9	10.41
1955	216.6	102.6	10.21
1956	252.4	102.5	10.21
1957	271.4	102.4	10.32
1958	248.4	102.4	10.62
1959	242.0	102.4	11.35

* Columns 1 and 2 are from Banco Nacional de México, *Review of the Economic Situation of Mexico*, 36 (August, 1960), 6. Column 3 is from International Monetary Fund, *International Financial Statistics, 1962*, 188 ff. The first two columns pertain to quotations on the Mexico City Stock Exchange.

sible for a rise in prices. This of course discourages exports and encourages imports, with balance of payments difficulties as the evident consequence. While the import surplus serves as a partial antidote to inflation, the authorities cannot afford so placid an interpretation of their trade difficulties. They must resort to some device, such as devaluation, to activate exports and/or reduce imports. Yet this once again is an inflation-inducing force which tends to create additional balance of payments difficulties, which may call for more correction, which tends futher to promote inflation, and so on. The model is thus apparently an explosive one, yielding an ever-rising price level and periodic balance of payments difficulties. The situation is further aggravated by the high ratios of exports and imports to national product for the poor, relatively small countries. Small wonder that those who value price stability highly also devote much attention to international trade and balance of payments positions.

In Mexico, as was noted in the first section of the present chapter, export booms have often been the major contributory factor to the rise in prices. Insofar as inflationary pressures have resulted from other forces and have thereby threatened her balance of payments position, Mexico has responded primarily in terms of periodic devaluation of her currency. The country entered World War II with an exchange rate of 4.86 pesos per U.S. dollar. In 1948–1949 ensued a series of devaluations which reduced the value of the Mexican currency to average *de facto* rates of 6.91 during August 1948–April 1949 and 8.13 during May 1949–June 1949. A rate of 8.65 began in July 1949. Finally, in April 1954 the value of the peso was reduced to 12.50 pesos per dollar, and it has so remained through the time of writing. Through much of this entire period Mexico in fact resorted to devaluation with something of a vengeance. From 1937 on, except for the years 1944 through 1947, Mexico undervalued the peso relative to the Mexican and United States wholesale price indices. Insofar as wholesale prices are adequate criteria, devaluations actually tended to prolong trends rather than offset overvaluations.[18]

Unlike other Latin-American countries, Mexico has not utilized multiple exchange rates to cope with her balance of payments problems. Nor has she resorted to exchange controls, but rather has at all times maintained the free convertibility of the peso. Foreign investors especially appreciate such abstentions, as well as the frequent employment of broad and diffuse policy measures. This awareness of foreigners' preferences may very well have influenced the government to adopt such policies. On the other hand the Mexican government has certainly not operated on a completely nonselective basis. It has particularly wished to control the composition of imports so as to add to the country's rate of capital formation. Further, depreciation has some implications for the terms of trade, of which the Mexicans have been highly conscious. If one ignores the many complications attending the gains from international trade and focuses on the single feature of the unit terms of trade, it is possible to maintain that depreciation leads to a transfer of benefits to other nations because of the relatively lower export prices.[19] Possibly to offset these effects and most assuredly to supplement the hoped-for benefits of devaluation,

[18] UNESCO, *External Disequilibrium in the Economic Development of Latin America: The Case of Mexico*, pp. 58–62.

[19] This of course is the view of Raúl Prebisch. See his "Commercial Policy in the Underdeveloped Countries," *American Economic Review: Papers and Proceedings*, 49 (May, 1959), 251–273.

the Mexican government has turned to discriminatory techniques. These have taken the form of differential import duties and, occasionally, direct import controls.[20]

There is no evidence that on balance the devaluations and the accompanying selective instruments hampered growth, and they may have been salutary. The price increases from 1948 to 1950 were no higher than the average of the whole 1939–1957 period. In 1955 the general wholesale index rose almost 14 per cent, but, as noted previously, the year was one of unexpected high aggregate demand. As had been intended, exports expanded considerably after the devaluations. Whereas Mexico's deficit on her current account averaged 650,000,000 pesos during 1946–1948, she enjoyed export surpluses of 229,000,000 and 189,000,000 pesos, respectively, in 1949 and 1950. In 1954 her deficit was 1,318,000,000 pesos; in 1955 this had fallen to 336,000,000, despite the advances in domestic prices. (In the following three years, however, the deficit soared to annual averages of 2,277,000,000.)[21] From 1950–1951 to 1956–1957 the annual rate of increase in the exports of merchandise averaged 13 per cent.[22] There is evidence, also, that the 1954 depreciation stimulated Mexican exports for at least four years. As a result of the change of that year the value of the peso fell nearly 45 per cent. Then, in the ensuing four years, Mexican prices increased an estimated 45 per cent. This development would evidently have eliminated the advantage introduced in 1954 had it not been for the behavior of United States prices, which rose about 8 per cent in the interim. The net Mexican price increase over the four years thus approximated 37 per cent, still almost 8 per cent short of the previous reduction of the value of the peso.[23]

Since the prices of most of Mexico's exports were set in external markets that are insensitive to changes in the peso's value, Mexico was in a good position to profit from her own altered rates of foreign exchange. The increase in export income then improved Mexico's budgetary position because of her resort to export

[20] Antonio Carillo Flores, "Mexico Forges Ahead," *Foreign Affairs*, 36 (April, 1958), 499.

[21] Urquidi, "La inflación en México," p. 41, t. 14.

[22] United Nations, Economic and Social Council, *World Economic Survey, 1959*, p. 75, t. 2–10.

[23] Emery, "Mexican Monetary Policy," p. 83.

duties. Export tax receipts rose from 98,000,000 pesos in 1948 to 540,000,000 in 1950, and from 646,000,000 pesos in 1953 to 1,551,000,000 in 1955.[24] The accompanying reduction in budgetary deficits in turn encouraged a continuation of the government's expansionist policy, part of which aided exports. This was especially valuable for agriculture, since cotton, coffee, and other farm commodities have comprised a significant fraction of Mexico's export trade.

The devaluations of course tended to reduce imports in the aggregate, thereby reinforcing the protectionism provided by import duties and stimulating the production of import substitutes.[25] The ratio of domestic capital goods production to equipment imports increased from 0.59 to 1.09 during 1947–1949 and from 0.84 to 1.07 during 1953–1955.[26] The Mexican authorities have been well aware of the necessity of controlling the composition of imports—immediately after depreciation because of the declines in aggregate imports and in due time because of approaching balance of payments difficulties. As a consequence they have aimed for policies that would prevent Mexico's precious export proceeds from being allocated indiscriminately. They have generally, though not consistently, endeavored to use foreign exchange as an instrument of development and a fashion designed to strengthen Mexico's long run trading position.

Table 44 summarizes the patterns of imports that accompanied her two most recent devaluations. At these times capital goods accounted for nearly one-half of the aggregate value of imports, while materials comprised over one-quarter of the total. Finished consumer goods averaged only 18 per cent of the import value. These percentages had not altered much by 1960; capital goods then accounted for 48 per cent, materials for 34 per cent, and consumer goods for 18 per cent.[27] Further indication of the structure

[24] Combined Mexican Working Party, *Economic Development of Mexico*, p. 340, t. 118; and United Nations Statistical Office, *Statistical Yearbook, 1955*, p. 500, t. 178.

[25] The discussion of the favorable effects of devaluation is based on United Nations, Economic Commission for Latin America, *Economic Survey of Latin America, 1956*, pp. 143–145.

[26] UNESCO, *External Disequilibrium*, p. 49.

[27] Nacional Financiera, "Economic Indicators, 1961," p. 2.

of imports is to be found in the rates of increases experienced by different types of imported commodities. The average annual rates of increase from 1940 to 1958 registered as follows for the various classes of goods:[28]

	%
Total	7.5
Consumer durables	3.4
Consumer nondurables	4.2
Fuels	12.7
Metals	9.9
Other raw materials	−5.1
Building materials	6.6
Equipment for industry, agriculture, and transportation	9.7

On the basis of the foregoing, one would conclude that the Mexican economy has increasingly taken to the domestic production of consumer goods and that the country's imports have concentrated on capital items. One would further conclude that an international demonstration effect has not interfered seriously with Mexico's economic development. Since only 18 per cent of all imports assumed the form of finished consumer goods, this implies some 3 per cent of the GNP, a modest figure indeed. By the same token the purchase of luxurious consumption goods from overseas would not constitute a serious problem. Necessitous goods made up some proportion of the total, and it can be argued that the remainder was necessary for incentive purposes.

However, these remarks concerning the composition of imports need to be qualified in at least one respect. In many instances Mexican firms imported parts and materials into the country and transformed them into finished consumption items. Should these be included under consumption, as has in fact been done in the Economic Commission for Latin America study cited in Table 44? Then imports would be divided almost equally between capital and consumption goods. Since Mexico is virtually self-supporting in food and has placed high duties on textiles, a considerable percentage of total imports would be of the luxurious type. Seen in this light, local processing may have added to domestic employ-

28 Urquidi, "La inflación en México," t. 6.

TABLE 44. Types of Imports as Percentages of Total Imports,
for Selected Years*

Item	1948–1950		1954–1955	
Consumer Goods	47		46	
Durables		8		6
Nondurables (finished)		11		11
Nondurables (unfinished)		28		29
Fuels	4		8	
Capital Goods	49		46	
Agricultural equipment		4		4
Industrial equipment		24		23
Transport equipment		10		11
Metals		5		4
Building materials		6		4

* Based on United Nations, Economic Commission for Latin America, *Economic Survey of Latin America, 1956*, p. 145, t. 102.

ment and output, but in a fashion consistent with the consumption patterns discussed in Chapter Six. Income inequality has now apparently led to a considerable malallocation of foreign exchange.

One mode of classification yields a ratio of consumer goods imports to total imports of almost one-fifth, while a second results in a ratio of one-half. It is no easy task to choose between them. Goods near completion might be regarded largely as consumption items while those closer to the raw materials stage would be placed in the investment category. Given the nature of much of the processing, this procedure would probably yield a result closer to the one-half than to the one-fifth mark. Apparently Mexico has possessed the tools for deploying her foreign exchange in the service of economic development, but the structure of her income distribution combined with the fairly high consumption propensities of her well-to-do have rendered the effort only moderately successful.

Despite the considerable success attending the use of currency devaluation to correct balance of payment difficulties, the method does have a serious limitation. Depreciation may perform well when administered in occasional and unpredictable doses, but an economy will not tolerate continual treatment of this sort. In the latter circumstance capital flight becomes a virtual certainty. This factor undoubtedly influenced the authorities' decision not to devaluate after 1954. In one writer's words, "The trauma produced by the [1954] devaluation has made the Mexican government highly sensitive to even a hint of further depreciation."[29] In the absence of depreciation, Mexico has lived with some severe balance of payments problems; in fact the average annual trade deficit over the period 1957–1962 approximated $300,000,000 U.S. To make up this deficit and to promote growth with less inflation, the López Mateos administration found it advisable to concentrate on foreign borrowing. When devaluation was still feasible, however, it performed an extremely important task. Owing to a number of institutional and technical constraints, Mexico in the forties and fifties could grow only with inflation. The latter in turn could well have played havoc with the balance of payments, the ability to import capital goods, and therefore with growth itself if there had been no offsetting mechanism. The several acts of depreciation provided such a mechanism. By holding the balance of payments deficits precariously in check, they permitted Mexico to buy time for economic development. The country thereby moved closer to economic maturity, to a time when it would be less troubled by problems of inflation and balance of payments. Viewed in this fashion, depreciation may have promoted increases in the price level in the short run, but in the last analysis it served as a valuable disinflationary force.

This chapter has dealt with the case in which a country has no option but to accept inflation as a cost of development. It is evidently more desirable that growth occur in the context of relatively stable commodity prices and exchange rates. In the future, developing nations may in fact find it highly advisable to pursue the objective of growth with a minimum of inflation as vigorously as possible. If, as a second alternative, a sufficient number of countries adopts the Mexican model of occasional currency depreciation, the device of devaluation itself (though not necessarily its precise timing) becomes readily predictable. By the same token it becomes less workable in that it gives rise to pronounced capital

[29] David H. Shelton, "The Banking System: Money and the Goal of Growth," in Raymond Vernon, ed., *Public Policy and Private Enterprise in Mexico*, p. 169.

flights and the eventual adoption of various restrictive devices, such as exchange controls. Whether a nation would adopt the first or second path depends not only upon the relative values assigned to growth and price stability but also upon the currently accepted explanations of inflation. That is, a nation's economic leaders might opt for the second alternative because they favor growth over price stability and/or they attribute inflation to the structural maladjustments associated with the nation's economic backwardness. They would turn more to the first alternative if they favored price stability and also if they explained inflation in terms of additions to aggregate demand and the monetary supply.[30] Yet a third alternative would contain elements of the first and second but would rely strongly upon a political solution. That is, a nation could give top priority to rapid economic growth and seek to manage its affairs so as to experience a very moderate increase in prices. Failing the latter, it would mitigate its balance of payments difficulties through devaluation, hoping at least to make its timing an element of surprise. Failing a policy of depreciation, it would then not resort to controls on international transactions but rather point with pride to its rate of growth and its ability to develop, probably fabricate a strategic position in the cold war if it did not already possess one, hope for political moderate majorities in the legislatures of the economically advanced countries, and appeal for aid. If, in spite of all this, aid were not forthcoming it would be forced to concentrate on either the first or second set of alternative policies.

[30] For an analysis of structural inflation in Mexico see Marnie W. Mueller, "Structural Inflation and the Mexican Experience," *Yale Economic Essays*, 5 (Spring, 1965), 145–194. The author finds that with economic development in Mexico, the structural maladjustments in agriculture and the public sector decreased, but foreign trade behaved in opposite fashion.

CHAPTER EIGHT

Taxation, Saving, and Consumption

Mexico may have experienced economic growth at the expense of price stability after the late thirties, but this does not appear to have been an optimum course. Inflation is clearly a cost. Would not the authorities have been well advised to have heightened their tax revenue in order to cover the cost of government expenditures and reduce the pace of inflation? More particularly, should they not have tapped the incomes of the beneficiaries of inflation by introducing a higher degree of progressiveness into their tax structure?

At this point some general bench marks regarding the role of government in economic development would be useful, and Walter Heller's work on the fiscal needs of the underdeveloped countries seems tailor-made for this purpose.[1] Heller observes that the ratio of government expenditures to the gross national product in the poor countries has typically approximated 12 per cent. In Mexico, from 1939 through 1963, $\frac{G}{GNP}$ never rose above 11.7, dropped as low as 6.6, and averaged 9.7 (see Table 45, column 1). True, a very low percentage of the federal budget, only 10 per cent in more recent years, was directed to military affairs, but this might have served as an opportunity to devote more public resources to economic ends. Moreover, 12 per cent is merely a statistical norm;

---

[1] Walter W. Heller, "Fiscal Policies for Under-Developed Countries," in United Nations Technical Assistance Administration, *Taxes and Fiscal Policy in Under-developed Countries*, pp. 1–22; reprinted in Richard Bird and Oliver Oldman, *Readings on Taxation in Developing Countries*, pp. 3–30.

TABLE 45. Government Expenditures and Revenue as
Percentages of GNP, 1939–1963*

Year	Expenditures	Revenue	Surplus(+) or Deficit(−)
1939	11.3	11.4	0.1
1940	11.7	10.3	−1.4
1941	11.1	10.0	−1.1
1942	10.6	9.1	−1.5
1943	10.5	9.9	−0.6
1944	9.2	9.1	−0.1
1945	10.0	8.3	−1.7
1946	8.6	8.4	−0.2
1947	9.7	8.4	−1.3
1948	9.9	8.7	−1.2
1949	10.7	10.6	0.1
1950	11.1	10.3	−0.8
1951	10.3	9.4	−0.9
1952	11.0	10.4	−0.6
1953	9.4	8.6	−0.8
1954	11.1	9.0	−2.1
1955	10.2	9.1	−1.1
1956	8.7	9.3	0.6
1957	8.5	8.5	0.0
1958	9.1	9.3	0.2
1959	8.4	7.6	−0.8
1960	9.8	8.4	−1.4
1961	8.5	7.6	−0.9
1962	6.6	6.6	0.0
1963	6.9	6.9	0.0

* The 1939–1951 data are taken directly from The Combined Mexican Working Party, *The Economic Development of Mexico*, p. 338, t. 117. The percentages for 1952–1963 have been computed from the statistics on revenue and expenditures that appear in the 1957, 1962, and 1963 editions of the United Nations *Statistical Yearbook*. The figures for 1962 and 1963 are based upon revised estimates.

The allegedly balanced budgets for 1957, 1962, and 1963 result from rounding. Somewhat more accurately, the data in the surplus or deficit column should read −0.03, −0.01, and −0.06, respectively, for the three years in question.

other poor countries may have been allocating insufficient amounts to governmental activities.

In this vein Heller suggests that taxes are generally not too high if they reach 15 per cent of national output and that up to that level they tend to be superior to inflation. Most poor countries are in a position to tolerate additions to their tax revenues, with the precise increases depending on such technical and institutional factors as the savings and consumption habits of the higher income groups. Mexico could thus have increased its tax revenue as a percentage of its GNP, for taxes probably would not have eaten seriously into saving. Yet the tax revenue was never as high as 11 per cent of GNP after 1939, it may have dropped below 7 in 1962–1963, and it averaged all of 9 per cent during the whole 1939–1963 period (see Table 45, column 2). By Heller's criteria Mexico's tax receipts have clearly been too low. This situation has in turn led to several unfavorable consequences for Mexico's economic development. An obvious case in point is given by the inadequacy of public investment in vital areas such as irrigation projects. A somewhat less evident instance is to be found in the weakening of monetary policy. The continual budgetary deficits have created inflationary pressures and promoted monetary tightness and inflexibility. *Ceteris paribus,* monetary policy has contributed to relatively high interest rates and, presumably, to reductions in private investment.

Professor Heller then turns to fiscal structure and to a discussion of the redistributive aspects of fiscal policy. Here he leans toward some form of progressive taxation on the grounds of both incentives and equity. He sees progressive taxes as having less disincentive effects in the poor countries than in the richer ones because of the share of land rent in national income, the tendency of large estates to keep land idle or undercultivated, and the use of higher incomes for luxuries, speculation, and hoarding. In addition he favors a simple and direct tax system that leaves few loopholes for tax avoidance. In these matters Mexico's tax system once again fails to meet his standards. In this instance, however, one might wish to dispute the validity of the standard itself. Mexico's experience suggests that progressiveness is not necessarily a virtue throughout the course of a country's economic development but rather that the degree of progressiveness ought to alter as per capita income expands. The country's tax system may be criticized, however, in that it has not responded quickly or sharply enough to the need for greater progressiveness when it arose. No one, on the other hand, could argue with the statement that Mexico's taxes have failed to meet the criterion of simplicity. In a fashion typical of Spanish American countries, Mexico's tax structure has concentrated on numerous indirect taxes. Its direct taxes, when employed, have been schedular in nature; that is, tax liabilities have depended on the type of economic activity, an attribute which results in undue complexity and discrimination and which raises opportunities for tax avoidance beyond those usually made available to ingenious citizens. This complexity undoubtedly reduced the degree of progressiveness.

It should be worth while to examine Mexico's fiscal arrangements in some depth in order to gain an impression of just how involved, discriminatory, and low yielding the tax structure of a poor country can be. At the outset let us ignore the changes that have occurred in Mexico's fiscal apparatus and simply outline the general pattern that prevailed during the fifties.[2] While this aspect of the discussion concentrates on a tax system that has since undergone considerable revision, it should serve to illustrate how an archaic tax system—or, more generally, how lagging institutional reform—may retard economic growth. Thereupon we can turn to the modifications experienced over time. Throughout, attention will be directed to the distinction between direct and indirect taxes, or between levies on income and those on expenditures.

The central government, the Federal District, the states and territories, and the municipalities have collected taxes in Mexico. Of these the first named has accounted for about three-quarters of the total revenue. While the several governments have not emphasized "direct" taxes, they have tapped business and personal incomes, distributed and excess profits, capital, social security participation, the production of minerals, commercial receipts, and export proceeds. On the occasions when firms and households found it necessary to pay business and personal income taxes to the central

[2] This description owes much to the Combined Party, *The Economic Development of Mexico*, p. 105 and pp. 340–341, t. 118; and Harvard University, International Program in Taxation, *Taxation in Mexico*, especially pp. 47–49 and chapter 12.

government, seven different schedules confronted them. Any tax-payer was subject to several schedules if he earned his income from more than one source. The schedules in question related to the following income resources:

I. Commerce
II. Industry
III. Agriculture, stock breeding, and fishing
IV. Labor
V. Independent professional and similar activities
VI. Personal income from capital
VII. Income from licenses or government concessions, including those permitting the use of the subsoil (Royalties were taxed under this schedule.)

Individuals were further responsible for a flat 15 per cent distributed profits tax, while firms incurred a relatively minor liability on their excess profits.

Of the remaining allegedly direct taxes noted in the preceding paragraph, the one levied on capital primarily concerned gifts and inheritance, but it also covered winnings from lotteries and games. Social security contributions came from both employers and employees, with the "patrones" legally responsible for twice as much as their hired hands and the state matching the payments of the workers. The last three categories of direct taxes, those pertaining to mineral production, commerce, and exports, were essentially taxes on gross income, and as such were less easy to avoid or evade than net income taxes. Students of the subject have tended to regard them as essentially taxes on profits and, consequently, as complements to the income tax. They thereby have dubbed them "direct."[3] In the case of the tax on mineral production, the classification seems fairly valid. This tax was computed as a percentage of the official price of a product; hence a firm could not shift its burden readily, for it was in no position to adjust its price. The argument seems justified also in the case of the tax on export proceeds, since the relevant prices were determined largely in world markets and could not be altered in response to the imposed tax. These duties on export proceeds have included both general

[3] This is the view of The Combined Mexican Working Party toward the taxes on mineral production and exports, in *The Economic Development of Mexico*, p. 105.

and surtax features. Introduced in 1938, abolished in 1947, and adopted once more in 1948 after the devaluation of that year, they have tended to serve as contracyclical shock absorbers. The commercial receipts tax, known also as the tax on mercantile income, was a sales tax and as such did not meet the requirements of a direct tax. It normally embraced a levy of 1.8 per cent of gross sales revenue by the federal government and one of 1.2 per cent on the part of states, although firms dealing in certain necessities, new and essential goods, and products otherwise covered by federal excises were either partially or completely exempted from the tax.[4]

The indirect category included excises imposed at the various levels of production, levies on natural resource exploitation other than the production of minerals, transportation taxes, stamp taxes, and import duties. Among the items subject to excises were tobacco, matches, cotton, cement, beer, alcohol, petroleum products, electric energy, and communications. The natural resource levies were computed as percentages of the prices of the taxable products. The stamp taxes were particularly directed at transactions involving tangible property; house rents, for example, were taxed in this fashion. The duties on imports were similar to the export taxes in that they possessed general and surtax components, but they were directly related to the prices of the affected commodities. A final category of nontax receipts included fees (*dereches*) for particular services, such as the granting of permits, as well as returns on government enterprises and properties.

To trace the changes in the tax structure over time, we can first compare the situations in 1939 and 1951. Most of the taxes and schedules discussed in the foregoing paragraphs were also in existence by the beginning of the fifties. Those which were "direct" embraced taxes on income, excess profits, capital, mineral production, and exports; while "indirect" taxes included duties on imports, natural resources other than mining, transportation, and sales and consumption, industrial excises, and miscellaneous taxes such as those on insurance premiums and "nonmercantile documents." If this classification is acceptable, the direct taxes as a

[4] Harvard University, International Program in Taxation, *Taxation in Mexico*, pp. 344–349.

percentage of over-all receipts of the federal government increased from 27.5 in 1939 and 1940 to 47.5 in 1950 and 1951. In the meantime indirect taxes fell from 53.5 per cent to 38.3 per cent. This shift can be attributed to a number of factors: the built-in progressiveness of the direct taxes as well as an increase in the number of persons subject to them; the 1948–1949 introduction of export duties, the excess profits tax, and tax on mercantile income; the rise in the profits share; and certain reforms in tax administration, especially the introduction of advance payments in 1943. The last factor seems to have been especially important, since direct taxes climbed from 29.8 per cent in 1942 to 38.4 per cent in 1943 while indirect taxes were falling from 49 per cent to 37.5 per cent of total receipts.[5] On the other hand several circumstances permitted potentially taxable income to remain in private hands. For example, individuals receiving different functional returns could utilize several schedules and subdivide their incomes so as to reduce their tax liabilities. The maximum marginal rate on business profits was only 33 per cent, and the effect of the excess profits tax minor. Apparently the stamp tax on rents was evaded through failures to report rental increases, while the sales tax frequently was not paid.

More recent studies have been concerned with the modification in direct and indirect taxes since the late forties. According to one pair of investigators,[6] the following percentages prevailed during the 1948–1952 period:

Year	Direct Taxes Total Tax Revenue	Indirect Taxes Total Tax Revenue
1948	46.1	53.9
1949	54.8	45.2
1950	53.1	46.9
1951	54.2	45.8
1952	55.2	44.8

[5] However, direct taxes again yielded less revenue than indirect taxes from 1944 through 1948. See The Combined Mexican Working Party, *The Economic Development of Mexico*, p. 133, t. 118.

[6] A. Calderón M. and A. Suárez C., "Impuesto sobre la renta," *Revista de Economía*, 16 (December, 1953), esp. 372, t. 2.

A United Nations publication reports that for 1953–1957 indirect taxes made up 42 per cent of total revenue,[7] which is somewhat higher than the 1950–1951 Combined Party statistic cited in the preceding paragraph. For the years 1955–1957, according to another United Nations source,[8] direct taxes, including export duties, accounted for 43 per cent of the total revenue of the federal government, while three categories of indirect taxes (turnover, imports, and others) made up only 38.5 per cent. Assuming the data to be comparable, little change thus occurred from 1950 to 1957. The percentage of total revenue accounted for by indirect taxes remained stable, while the proportion taking the form of direct taxes may have fallen by some 3½ percentage points. This decline accentuated considerably after 1957. Given the same classification as in the later United Nations study, direct taxes averaged 52.7 per cent of total tax revenue in 1956–1957 and then decreased, with little variation within the four-year period, to 46.6 per cent during 1958–1961.[9] Not since 1948 had direct taxes accounted for less than half of the tax revenue.

The evidence thus indicates a gain in direct tax revenue at the expense of indirect taxes during the forties (especially in 1943 and 1949), a general stabilizing of the ratio of direct to indirect taxes until 1957, and a decline in the relative significance of direct taxes over 1958–1961. The Mexican government apparently pursued fairly reasonable tax policies during the forties. As has been suggested in previous chapters, savings constituted an important bottleneck during that decade, and it can be argued that adoption of direct taxes at a much faster rate might have reduced the rate of capital formation. By a perversity not uncommon in economic development, however, a greater concentration on direct taxes would have been desirable during the fifties because of the growing limitations in consumption demand. Although the relative importance of direct taxes tended to be lower in Mexico than in other nations

[7] UNESCO, Economic Commission for Latin America, *Inflation and Growth: A Summary of Experience in Latin America*, p. 68, t. 7.

[8] United Nations, Statistical Office, *Statistical Yearbook, 1957*, p. 500, t. 178.

[9] José María Naharro, "Production and Consumption Taxes and Economic Development," in Joint Tax Program, *Fiscal Policy in Latin America*, p. 282, t. 9-2.

with similar per capita incomes,[10] the necessary changes were then not forthcoming. In sum, insofar as direct and indirect taxes provide a measure of progressiveness or a lack of it, Mexico's tax structure generally satisfied Heller's progressiveness test during the earlier decade but not during the later one.

Possibly, however, the direct-indirect tax dichotomy is only remotely related to the issue of progressiveness. Some note has already been taken of the difficulties of classification. More generally, the theory concerning tax shifting and the incidence of tax burdens is too weak to support a clear cut distinction between direct and indirect taxes. For example, the ability to shift income taxes depends among other things upon whether a firm or industry is operating in the long or the short run (that is, whether it can close its plant) and upon whether it is in equilibrium at the time a given tax is imposed. In the case of Mexico, small entrepreneurs have probably been able to shift the taxes on their business incomes to their customers, and exporters have apparently passed some of their tax burdens back to agriculture. The new income taxes on house rents, which have generally replaced the old stamp taxes, will undoubtedly be shifted in considerable part to the tenants.[11]

Since the groupings are so fluid, let us simply separate taxes on income from those levied on expenditures, as in Table 46. This new classification of course does not match the previous one; for example, taxes placed upon mineral production and commerce no longer appear with the income taxes. The data cover the years 1941–1958 and are divided on the basis of three successive national administrations. For the 1941–1952 interval the findings based upon the income-expenditures classification parallel the conclusions previously cited. During 1941–1951 income taxes assumed greater significance and expenditures taxes fell off relatively, though the changes were not as marked as in the case of direct and indirect taxes. After 1952, however, expenditures taxes continued their relative decline, although indirect taxes remained relatively constant; and income tax revenues rose slightly in percentage

[10] Douglas Dosser, "Indirect Taxation and Economic Development," in Organization for Economic Cooperation and Development, *Government Finance and Economic Development*, p. 17.

[11] These several observations regarding the shifting of particular taxes in Mexico follow from interviews with several Mexican economists.

TABLE 46. Taxes on Income and Expenditures, 1941–1958*

	1941–1946 Totals (millions of pesos)	% of Total	1947–1952 Totals (millions of pesos)	%	1953–1958 Totals (millions of pesos)	%
Total Revenue	7,211.12	100	21,549.9	100	50,567.0	100
Tax Revenues	6,068.4	84.1	17,566.5	81.5	39,795.1	78.6
(1) From Incomes	2,561.7	35.1	8,214.2	38.1	19,855.4	39.3
Domestic incomes	1,319.8		4,919.9		12,528.8	
Exports	1,105.7		2,957.7		6,877.1	
10% additional	132.8		189.8		53.1	
Others	3.4		146.8		396.4	
(2) From Expenditures	3,506.7	48.6	9,352.3	43.4	19,939.7	39.5
Industry	1,363.7		3,041.1		6,874.4	
Imports	878.3		2,803.2		6,319.0	
Commerce	91.0		1,324.0		43.0	
Timber	598.5		419.6		500.5	
Natural resources	388.6		1,138.2		2,008.2	
Mercantile receipts	. . .		420.1		3,929.9	
Others	186.6		207.1		264.7	
Nontax Revenues	1,142.8	15.9	3,983.4	18.5	10,712.7	21.2

* Juan Delgado Navarro, *Desarrollo económico y justica social en México*, pp. 134, 204, and 248.

terms, while direct taxes fell off somewhat. The income-expenditures classification thus yields a more definite trend than does the one couched in terms of direct and indirect taxes. The relative decline in mineral production, the taxation of which is regarded as direct in the one instance and as involving an expenditure in the other, may in part explain the discrepancies. In any event, the two sets of findings agree on the broad outlines: the changes in the tax structure were fairly significant in the 1940's, but at best moderate during the course of the 1950's.

If these developments did transpire, they have important implications for economic advancement and income distribution. On the face of it, there may be no necessary correlation between the progressiveness of a tax system and its degree of reliance upon direct and/or income taxes. Indirect or expenditures taxes can be aimed at high income goods, and direct or income taxes, particularly of the schedular type, can be manipulated to strike at the lower income wage earning groups. However, these particular, unusual properties have not characterized the Mexican tax system.

Indirect or expenditures taxes have been at least moderately regressive. One need only glance at the list of items that have borne domestic excises to ascertain that the authorities have taxed wage goods. Tobacco has stood out in this context, as has the sales tax. However, the effects of the latter have been rendered less certain by the introduction of several types of exemption.[12] Included among the products that have been wholly exempt from excise taxation have been activities otherwise subject to special federal taxes, new and essential industries such as motion pictures and transportation, goods produced by small craftsmen, and, particularly, various necessitous goods and services such as basic food items (tortillas, milk, meat, vegetables) and energy sources (coal, gas, electricity). The exemptions have only been partial in other instances. Sometimes, as in the instances of gasoline and telephone and telegraph services under federal concession, only the federal rate of 1.8 per cent has applied. In other cases the federal and state taxes have each been reduced by one-half. Illustrative of this group are food items not entirely exempt, medicine, soap and detergents, the sales revenues of small stores with assets of less than 5,000 pesos, and the receipts of hospitals, restaurants, barbershops and beauty parlors, printers, and millers. Many of the exemptions have aided the lower income groups, but it is equally evident that they have not all been designed for such a purpose and that they frequently assisted the upper income groups as well.

Import duties have functioned primarily to protect domestic industries and to conserve foreign exchange by reducing the imports of items that contribute relatively little to economic development. To the extent that the high income groups have continued to purchase luxurious consumers' goods like whiskey, porcelain, lace, and certain kinds of toys from abroad and have paid the accompanying high rates of more than 100 per cent, the duties have tended to be progressive. On the other hand import levies

---

[12] Harvard University, International Program in Taxation, *Taxation in Mexico*, pp. 345–349.

have also directed against fairly basic goods, such as clothing and canned foods. The lower and middle income groups typically reacted to these by turning to less satisfactory, often high priced, domestic substitutes. Whenever the duties successfully provided protection to particular commodities, consumers frequently had to pay higher prices for the restricted goods, with the degree of the price increase depending upon such variables as productivity, the elasticity of supply, and the degree of price competition in the domestic market. All things considered, the total effects of import duties on income distribution appear too diffused to pursue.

Domestic indirect or expenditures taxes seemingly imparted a degree of regressiveness to the tax system, while import duties exerted no perceptible influence along these lines. Fortunately, the effect of the former taxes on income distribution is roughly measurable. In 1950 the indirect taxes of the federal government comprised 6.5 per cent of aggregate private consumption expenditure,[13] but at the same time took 18 per cent of total wage income.[14] Since wage earners consume most of their disposable income, they assuredly contributed a higher percentage of their income than the average. Indirect taxes thereby tended to be regressive.

Income taxes dominate the discussion below. In the present context let us note that they possessed the usual nonregressive property; that is, they were not designed to strike deliberately at the lower income groups. In fact, taxes on wage income had some progressiveness built into them in several ways. The rates at the low income levels were so insignificant that in some labor-management work contracts the employer agreed to pay the workers' income taxes as a type of fringe benefit. Persons in the middle income wage and salary range were probably least able to avoid and evade tax payments. Those in the very high salary brackets were subject to progressive rates in order to prevent them from raising their salaries and bonuses to avoid taxes on profits. These sources of progressiveness did not greatly affect the entire tax structure, since the total tax revenue derived from salaries was relatively low. The

[13] The Combined Mexican Working Party, *Economic Development of Mexico*, p. 343, t. 119.

[14] Horacio Flores de la Peña, *Los obstáculos al desarrollo económico: El desequilibrio fundamental*, p. 95.

taxes on property incomes were similarly of relatively low yield and moderate progressiveness. For example, earners of profits were subject to the following schedule:

Per Cent of Profits	Marginal Tax Rate (%)
Up to 15	0
Between 15.01 and 20	5
Between 20.01 and 30	10
Between 30.01 and 40	15
Between 40.01 and 50	20
In excess of 50	25

In sum, the effects of Mexico's taxes upon income distribution were not atypical: the indirect or expenditures taxes tended to be fairly regressive while the direct or income taxes tended to be moderately progressive. These conclusions combined with the previous ones—namely, that the proportion of direct or income taxes to total tax revenue tended to increase during the 1940's, remained approximately at the same level until 1957, and decreased during 1958–1961—suggest that in the earlier period the tax system changed so as to contribute less to income inequality, while during the fifties the degree of progressiveness first remained largely unaltered and then declined. For both decades the tax system was undoubtedly regressive. One Mexican researcher has estimated that in 1959 only nine of fifty-seven federal taxes possessed some progressive features and that they accounted for only 45 per cent of the government's tax revenue.[15]

The tax system was not sufficiently progressive, particularly during the fifties, and it did not yield adequate revenue.[16] These blemishes led to considerable discussions of tax reforms, which in turn centered around the necessity of assigning a greater role to income taxes. These taxes shall not occupy our attention. We shall look first into the income tax structure of the late fifties and then into the reforms that were decreed in December 1961 and put into effect in January 1962. Among the items to be considered are the

[15] Lorenzo Dávila Reig, *La estructura federal impuestos en México.*
[16] Ramón Fernández and Ricardo Acosta, *Política agrícola*, p. 182.

schedular aspects of income taxation and the great need for a simplified tax.

Table 47 reveals the remarkably low rate at which income has been taxed in Mexico. Column one serves as a useful reminder of the generally low percentage of total tax revenue to national income, while the remaining columns indicate how sparingly taxes have affected the incomes of persons and firms. Column four is a demonstration of the earlier point regarding the low income tax rates placed upon wages and salaries. Columns two and three show the relative contributions of firms earning profits and persons receiving property incomes; apparently the latter particularly contributed very little to the national treasury. In column five all three types of income taxes appear as ratios of national income. The results generally support the previously noted trends in direct or income taxes, including the discontinuities which occurred in 1943 and 1949. Given these data it is possible to assert, with only slight exaggeration, that Mexicans as a group simply did not pay income taxes. This broad proposition of course conceals specific differences. Interest on government securities was exempt from income taxation, for example, but royalties were subject to rather high rates.

By the same token the income taxes paid by some given income category were low relative to the income earned. In the late forties and early fifties profits taxes approximated 1.7 per cent of the nation's income. During these years recipients of profits and mixed incomes together received between 65 and 70 per cent of the national income. Hence, *firms* were allocating no more than 2.5 per cent of their profits to income taxes. If it be suggested that mixed incomes should not be included with profits—not only on conceptual grounds but also because of the poor payments record of small firms—the percentage rises somewhat. In 1954, for example, firms devoted over 3.5 per cent of their profits to income taxes. *Personal* taxes on property income, in turn, totaled about 0.45 per cent of the national income in the early fifties. At the time non-profit property returns comprised about 6.5 per cent of the national income; let us assume these were received by individuals rather than firms. Also, about 80 per cent of total profits, which implies about 33 per cent of national income, was declared as dividends.

TABLE 47. Selected Taxes as Percentages of National Income, 1939–1960*

Year	Total Tax Revenue National Income	Profits Taxes National Income	Capital Taxes National Income	Taxes on Workers' Income National Income	Total Income Taxes National Income
1939	6.6	0.5	0.1	0.1	0.7
1940	6.1	0.6	0.1	0.2	0.9
1941	5.5	0.5	0.1	0.1	0.7
1942	5.1	0.6	0.1	0.1	0.8
1943	5.9	1.2	0.4	0.1	1.7
1944	5.6	1.4	0.4	0.2	2.0
1945	5.2	1.1	0.3	0.1	1.5
1946	5.1	1.1	0.3	0.2	1.6
1947	5.4	1.3	0.4	0.2	1.9
1948	5.2	1.1	0.3	0.2	1.6
1949	6.5	1.3	0.5	0.2	2.0
1950	6.7	1.4	0.5	0.3	2.2
1951	8.1	1.8	0.5	0.3	2.6
1952	8.1	2.0	0.4	0.3	2.7
1953	7.5	1.5	0.4	0.5	2.4
1954	7.9	1.4	0.4	0.4	2.2
1955	8.5	1.7	0.5	0.4	2.6
1956	8.6	2.1	0.5	0.5	3.1
1957	7.9	1.9	0.5	0.6	3.0
1958	7.5	1.8	0.4	0.6	2.8
1959	7.7	1.8	0.4	0.6	2.8
1960	7.7	2.0	0.4	0.7	3.1

* The first four columns are from Ifigenia Martínis de Navarrete, "Naturaleza de la reforma fiscal," *Comercio Exterior*, 12 (March, 1962), 140. The 1960 figures are provisional.

Hence property returns to individuals approached 40 per cent of the national income. Collectively these data indicate that persons receiving property incomes devoted all of 1.1 per cent of their earnings to the payment of income taxes.

These results point not only to the need for increasing the yield from income taxes, but they possess some rather disturbing implications for functional income distribution as well. Most economists would undoubtedly favor a higher tax burden for rentiers than for profit recipients, on the grounds that at least some decision makers may turn out to be innovators and assumers of risk. Yet the data on functional income distribution and the above calculations reveal that while profit recipients (including earners of mixed income) received about ten times as much income as the rentiers, they paid, partly as a result of the double taxation to which they were exposed, about twenty times as much in income taxes. Further, a comparison of labor income and income tax revenue from wages and salaries shows this group contributing about 2 per cent of its income—that is, less than the profit recipients but more than the rentiers.

The schedules that prevailed before the 1961–1962 modifications provide more detailed indications of the effect of income taxes on income distribution. The first schedule reproduced is number IV (in Table 48), which pertains to labor income. It includes a marginal tax rate that begins at 1.5 per cent for 300 pesos per month and rises to 46 per cent for monthly incomes of 50,000 pesos, at which point the progressive feature is terminated. Table 49 introduces four separate schedules with identical brackets. The schedules in question are I, II, III, and VI, which are applied, respectively, to business earnings in commerce, industry, and agriculture and to the various personal incomes from property.

The remaining schedules are sufficiently like these to render their reproduction in full unnecessary. In Schedule V, designed for professionals, technicians, artisans, and artists, the marginal rates were, respectively, 1.4, 1.5, and 1.6 per cent on annual net income brackets beginning at 2,000, 2,400, and 3,600 pesos, and 30.0, 31.5, and 33.0 per cent, respectively, for incomes beginning with 312,000, 750,000, and 1,000,000 pesos.[17] Schedule VII pertains to incomes from licenses and transfers of government concessions. It features a proportionate tax of 10.2 per cent that applied at all levels as well as a progressive one that began with 8.5 per cent on incomes up to $2,400 and then rose to 31 per cent for a total of 41.2 per cent on incomes in the range beginning with 500,000 pesos.[18] Only schedules VI and VII contain no exemptions.

[17] Secretaría de Hacienda y Crédito Público, Dirección General del Impuesto sobre la Renta, *Ley del impuesto sobre la renta*, pp. 56–57.
[18] *Ibid.*, p. 82.

TABLE 48. Rates of Taxation of Wage and Salary Income
(Schedule IV), 1960*

Monthly Income (thousands of pesos)		Percentage Applied to Income Exceeding Lower Limit
Lower Limit	Upper Limit	
0.0	0.3	exempt
0.3	0.4	1.5 (+$1.40)
0.4	0.5	1.6
0.5	0.6	1.7
0.6	0.7	1.8
0.7	0.8	1.9
0.8	0.9	2.0
0.9	1.0	2.1
1.0	1.5	2.6
1.5	2.0	3.1
2.0	2.5	3.6
2.5	3.0	4.1
3.0	4.0	5.1
4.0	5.0	6.1
5.0	6.0	7.1
6.0	7.0	8.1
7.0	8.0	9.1
8.0	9.0	10.1
9.0	10.0	12.0
10.0	12.0	16.0
12.0	14.0	18.0
14.0	18.0	22.0
18.0	22.0	26.0
22.0	28.0	30.0
28.0	34.0	34.0
34.0	40.0	38.0
40.0	50.0	42.0
50.0	and up	46.0

* Secretaría de Hacienda y Crédito Público, Dirección General del Impuesto sobre la Renta, *Ley del impuesto sobre la renta*, p. 47.

TABLE 49. Rates of Taxation of Miscellaneous Incomes
(Schedules I, II, III, and VI), 1960*

Annual Income (thousands of pesos)		Percentage Applied to Income Exceeding Lower Limit		
Lower Limit	Upper Limit	Commerce or Industry (Schedules I and II)	Agriculture (Schedule III)	Property Income (Schedule VI)
0.0	2.0	exempt	exempt	} 10
2.0	2.4	3.8	1.90	
2.4	3.6	3.9	1.95	10.4
3.6	4.8	4.1	2.05	11.6
4.8	6.0	4.3	2.15	11.9
6.0	7.2	4.5	2.25	12.1
7.2	8.4	4.8	2.40	12.3
8.4	9.6	4.9	2.45	12.5
9.6	10.8	5.1	2.55	12.8
10.8	12.0	5.3	2.65	13.1
12.0	18.0	6.4	3.20	14.0
18.0	24.0	7.5	3.75	15.0
24.0	30.0	8.6	4.30	16.1
30.0	36.0	9.8	4.90	17.1
36.0	48.0	11.1	5.55	18.2
48.0	60.0	12.3	6.15	19.2
60.0	72.0	13.5	6.75	20.3
72.0	84.0	14.7	7.35	21.4
84.0	96.0	15.9	7.95	22.3
96.0	108.0	17.2	8.60	23.5
108.0	150.0	19.4	9.70	24.6
150.0	200.0	20.3	10.15	25.6
200.0	250.0	21.7	10.85	26.0
250.0	300.0	23.0	11.50	27.9
300.0	350.0	24.8	12.40	29.0
350.0	400.0	25.7	12.85	30.0
400.0	450.0	27.1	13.50	31.1
450.0	500.0	28.6	14.30	32.2
500.0	750.0	30.0	15.00	33.1
750.0	1,000.0	31.5	15.75	34.6
1,000.0	and up	33.0	16.50	36.1

* Secretaría de Hacienda y Crédito Público, Dirección General del Impuesto sobre la Renta, *Ley del impuesto sobre la renta*, p. 26 for column 3, p. 39 for column 4, and p. 71 for column 5.

At this point it would be helpful to present summary data of the comparative tax liabilities of the very low and the very high income taxpayers. The task is complicated by the schedular nature of the system, however, since the differences in liabilities can be determined only with sufficient knowledge of the sources of income. Further, no standard procedure exists for computing the degree of progressiveness of a tax. The method here adopted involves a comparison, within any given schedule, of the tax burdens of persons in low brackets with those for whom the marginal rates have become constant (see Table 50). While the liabilities of the affluent taxpayers are modest, the schedules appear to be fairly progressive because of the low rates for those in the low brackets. If one moved on to still higher incomes the degree of progressiveness would continue to rise, though at a declining rate. This follows from the fact that the margin exceeds the average rate at high income levels, so that the average would increase at a decreasing rate as it approached a stable margin asymptotically. However, the upper points chosen are relatively high, and they represent points of discontinuous change. All in all, they do not seem unreasonable for comparative purposes.

TABLE 50. Tax Burdens of Low and High Income Receivers, pre-1961–1962 Reforms

	(1) At the Upper Limits of the Low Brackets			(2) At the Lower Limits of the High Brackets			(3) (2)(c) ÷ (1)(c)
Schedule	(a) Tax Lia-bilities (pesos)	(b) Incomes (pesos)	(c) Taxes/Incomes (%)	(a) Tax Lia-bilities (pesos)	(b) Incomes (pesos)	(c) Taxes/Incomes (%)	
I, II	15.20	2,400	0.6	260,058	1,000,000	26	43.3
III	7.60	2,400	0.3	130,029	1,000,000	13	43.3
IV	1.40	300	0.5	13,577	50,000	27	54.0
V	5.60	2,400	0.2	260,058	1,000,000	26	130.0
VI	(variable)	up to 2,400	10.0	300,602	1,000,000	30	3.0
VII	(variable)	up to 2,400	18.7	206,000	500,000	41.2	2.2

In the first five schedules the lower points are governed by the level of exemptions. The resulting range of zero tax liabilities can lead to curious results. If the exemptions were removed, one would normally be prepared to say that the income tax structure would become less progressive. Because of the device employed, however, the imposition of a tax rate of 1 per cent on heretofore untaxed incomes of 2,000 pesos per month would allegedly render the system more progressive, since the lowest incomes subject to the tax would now be assessed at a lower rate. A heightening of the level of exemptions, with no other modifications in the income tax rates, would serve the dual purpose of rendering the tax system less regressive, while permitting the proponents of greater progressiveness to "demonstrate" that the income tax was only mildly progressive! Another disturbing feature appears in the exemption of certain forms of income generally enjoyed by the higher income groups. This was especially true of interest income. Purchasers of interest bearing securities issued by any government, the Nacional Financiera, public enterprises, and industrial corporations approved by the government, together with the holders of savings deposits in banks, were all exempt from the payment of personal income taxes under Schedule VI.

On the basis of the foregoing figures, a minor—a very minor—case can be made for the proposition that Mexico in the late fifties required additional public revenue more than she needed a greater progressiveness in her tax system. The elements of yield and progressiveness were only moderately separable, for any important increase in tax revenues simply had to come from the middle and upper income groups. Moreover, too much must not be made of the degree of progressiveness of the income tax as such, since it bore the brunt of the struggle against the regressiveness of the whole tax system. Finally, as already noted, the official income tax rates do not indicate the possible degree of avoidance and evasion. Along with the requirements of greater yield and progressiveness, the income tax was very much in need of simplification.

The several schedules and the different types and levels of exemptions merely touch upon the complexity of Mexico's income tax before the 1961–1962 reforms. Firms in industry and commerce, otherwise subject to schedules I and II, could pay taxes upon their gross incomes if their sales fell below 100,000 pesos a year.[19] They were exempt from payment altogether if their annual sales fell below 10,000 pesos. (The numbers of firms managing to report gross incomes that were either just under 100,000 or 10,000 pesos must have been impressive indeed.) From 10,000 to 100,000 pesos, the tax liability of a given firm depended both upon its sales revenue and its place within a sevenfold classification (not to be confused with the seven schedules) of different branches of economic activity. Every activity within industry or commerce was thus assigned a number from 1 to 7. Jewelry and cabarets were in category 7, photography in 6, paper and tobacco in 5, radios in 3, lottery tickets in 2, table sets in 1, and so on—with the income tax law containing pages upon pages devoted to this classification. To determine his tax liability, the manager of a firm first checked the sales proceeds he was reporting and then located the number to which his business had been assigned. The situation for agricultural enterprises, under Schedule III, was similar, except that the option applied to firms with sales proceeds under $200,000, the rates were lower, and the classification merely distinguished between firms which were involved in exchange and those which were not.[20]

What, however, of the firms in commerce and industry whose proceeds exceeded 100,000 pesos and those in agriculture who enjoyed more than 200,000 pesos of sales per year? No reader could be so naïve as to believe that these firms had no option but to meet their tax liabilities directly under schedules I, II, or III, respectively. Once again classifications based upon types of economic activity played their peculiar role.[21] To these larger firms, however, the income tax tables revealed not specific tax liabilities but rather the percentages to be applied to gross sales revenue to determine taxable net income. Among others, the percentages were 22 for cement, 20 for telephones, 16 for wooden furniture, 15 for cotton and bananas, 13 for civil aviation, and 10 for vanilla and for fish products otherwise not specified. In computing its liability a firm could follow the above formula or delve into its own accounts in order to derive the tax base, whichever obligation was the lower. One can undoubtedly be too disparaging in reporting facts such as

19 *Ibid.*, pp. 94–119.
20 *Ibid.*, pp. 119–122.
21 *Ibid.*, pp. 123–132.

these. In particular, the option of employing gross sales revenues in computing income tax liabilities may be advisable in countries where citizens are not accustomed to tax payments and take evasion as a matter of course. However, the various schedules, options, and classifications were unquestionably in need of simplification, and Mexico would have profited greatly from the adoption of a global, as opposed to a schedular, tax system.

The reforms of 1961–1962 stopped far short of meeting the requirements of higher tax rates and reduced complexity. While the economic technicians pressed for these modifications and the government was highly aware of the needed reforms, the opposition to radical change was sufficiently powerful to cause the authorities to proceed cautiously. Resistance to broad reform came not only from relatively big business, which certainly would have paid a considerable share, but also from small business, the self-employed, and the professionals. All this should occasion little surprise, for other countries have experienced similar opposition; recall, for example, the Poujadists in France. Even organized labor adopted a wait-and-see policy. The government was thus confronted with a situation in which major tax changes were desirable economically but well-nigh impossible politically. In the face of this difficulty the authorities chose Marshall's "Natura non facit saltum" or Robertson's "Blondinianism"—that is, gradualism. One might hazard a guess that other countries requiring tax reform for development, such as those embraced by the Alliance for Progress, will have to choose similar paths. To quote one source on this subject: "The fiscal and administrative framework cannot be suddenly and completely modified; it would be senseless to disregard the traditions and the mentality of the population concerning the determination and payment of taxes."[22]

While the authorities ultimately intended to adopt a global income tax, and in fact espoused such a tax on television, for the time being they decided to continue with the schedules.[23] In so

[22] Banco Nacional de Comercio Exterior, *Comercio Exterior de México*, 9 (April, 1963), 9.

[23] The new schedules appear in Secretaría de Hacienda y Crédito Público, "Ley federal del impuesto sobre la renta," *Boletín Oficial*, 8 (February, 1962), 197–270. Also, for the 1962 average income tax rates as percentages of taxable income see Ifigenia M. de Navarrete, "Comment" [on Richard Goode, "Per-

doing they left *business* income taxes relatively unchanged. For schedules I and II, the marginal rates at the low income levels were now about one or two percentage points higher, while the highest marginal rate, now set for annual incomes over 2,000,000 rather than 1,000,000 pesos, was 39 per cent compared to the previous 33 per cent (see Table 51, column three). The alterations in these schedules seem to have been designed more to increase tax revenue than to affect the degree of progressiveness. This was less true of Schedule III, presumably as a consequence of the vast disparities in income in the agricultural sector (see Table 51, column four). Again the marginal tax rate was raised by a few points at the lower income levels, but the marginal rate in the highest income range expanded from 16.5 per cent to 25 per cent. Schedule V was subject to virtually no changes, the marginal rate in the lowest income bracket being raised slightly from 1.4 per cent to 3 per cent and the rate for incomes exceeding 1,000,000 pesos per year remaining precisely at 33 per cent. Excess profits taxes remained unaltered. Taxes on normal business profits could not average more than 30 per cent, while those on all profits might rise to more than 40 per cent with the inclusion of dividends and excess profits.

Accelerated depreciation, heretofore a special privilege made available in certain activities at the discretion of the authorities, now became a general feature. Further, firms might accelerate at more rapid rates, although in this respect, as in so many others, the reforms did not advance as far as the economic technicians had recommended. Administration improved to some degree. Eliminated was the system of *calificación*, whereby a tax official was charged with the responsibility of estimating the tax liabilities of the small- and medium-sized concerns who kept no records of their activities. Henceforth the burden of proof was to fall upon these firms, with the officials reserving the right to check tax declarations. Continued, but with modification, was the practice of classifying economic activities when using gross incomes to determine the tax base. This privilege of utilizing gross income was extended to firms whose sales totaled less than 300,000 pesos per year, rather

sonal Income Tax in Latin America"], in Joint Tax Program, *Fiscal Policy for Economic Growth*, p. 178, t. 6-3.

TABLE 51. Rates of Taxation of Miscellaneous Business Incomes
(Schedules I, II, and III), 1962*

Annual Income (thousands of pesos)		Percentage Applied to Income Exceeding Lower Limit	
Lower Limit	Upper Limit	Commerce or Industry (Schedules I and II)	Agriculture (Schedule III)
0	2	exempt	3.2
2	3.5	5.0	3.6
3.5	5	6.0	4.0
5	8	7.0	4.6
8	11	8.0	5.2
11	14	9.0	5.8
14	20	10.0	6.5
20	26	11.0	7.2
26	32	12.0	7.9
32	38	13.0	8.6
38	50	14.0	9.4
50	62	15.1	10.2
62	74	16.2	11.0
74	86	17.3	11.8
86	100	18.4	12.6
100	125	19.5	13.5
125	150	20.6	14.4
150	175	21.7	15.3
175	200	22.9	16.2
200	250	24.1	17.1
250	300	25.3	18.0
300	350	26.5	19.0
350	400	27.8	20.0
400	500	29.1	21.0
500	750	30.4	22.0
750	1,000	31.7	23.0
1,000	1,250	33.1	24.0
1,250	1,500	34.5	25.0
1,500	1,750	36.0	25.0
1,750	2,000	37.5	25.0
2,000	and up	39.0	25.0

* Secretaría de Hacienda y Crédito Público, "Ley federal del impuesto sobre la renta," *Boletín Oficial*, 8 (February, 1962), 210–211 for column 3 and p. 217 for column 4.

than 100,000, as previously. A greater progressiveness was built into the tax, and firms grossing more than 300,000 pesos were denied the privilege completely.

In accordance with Mexico's needs, somewhat more extensive revisions occurred within the *personal* income tax categories. Schedule IV rates were altered to yield more revenue and, in some

TABLE 52. Rates of Taxation of Wage and Salary Incomes
(Schedule IV), 1962*

Monthly Income (thousands of pesos)		Percentage Applied to Income Exceeding Lower Limit
Lower Limit	Upper Limit	
0.5	0.6	2.10 (+$4.50)
0.6	0.7	2.15
0.7	0.8	2.21
0.8	0.9	2.27
0.9	1.0	2.57
1.0	1.5	3.54
1.5	2.0	4.50
2.0	2.5	5.45
2.5	3.0	6.55
3.0	4.0	8.30
4.0	5.0	9.85
5.0	6.0	11.20
6.0	7.0	12.40
7.0	8.0	13.50
8.0	9.0	14.60
9.0	10.0	15.65
10.0	12.0	17.75
12.0	14.0	19.75
14.0	18.0	23.07
18.0	22.0	26.41
22.0	28.0	30.65
28.0	34.0	34.12
34.0	40.0	40.10
40.0	70.0	48.03
70.0	and up	50.00

* Secretaría de Hacienda y Crédito Público, "Ley federal del impuesto sobre la renta," *Boletín Oficial*, 8 (February, 1962), 219–220.

respects, to correct deficiencies in progressiveness (see Table 52). Relatively high labor incomes were now subject to marginal tax rates of 50 per cent, as opposed to 46 per cent in prereform days, but the level of exemptions was very considerably lowered from 3,000 to 500 pesos per month. The major changes in Schedule IV actually appeared at the intermediate levels; the $9,000–$10,000 bracket, for example, had its marginal rate raised from 12 per cent to 15.65 per cent. Additional progress was made in tapping personal property incomes. In the case of schedules VI and VII the marginal tax rate rose to 50 per cent for incomes from 840,000 pesos and up, compared to the previous 36.1 per cent for incomes over 1,000,000 pesos (see Table 53). But undoubtedly more important than the changes in the rates were the inclusions of new types of taxable income. Recipients of interest income in excess of 7.2 per cent now became liable under Schedule VI, though at relatively low average rates (between 2 and 5 per cent) because of the exemption permitted. Further, a capital gains tax on incomes from the transfer of real estate and bearer securities appeared for the first time. Though it may be found in the law in connection with Schedule VI, this tax presented a different rate structure. The rates rose gradually from 5 per cent for gains of less than 100,000 pesos and for assets held more than four years to 20 per cent for gains of more than 400,000 pesos and assets held less than one year. The pattern was particularly designed to penalize short periods of holdings rather than large gains, a feature which was in keeping with the major objective of reducing speculative activities in real estate and securities. The tax was made nonretroactive beginning January 1, 1962.

Personal income from property was further to be taxed under two schedules, VII and VIII. The new Schedule VII, which replaced the former one on income from licenses and concessions, pertained to dividend income. The rates in this instance reflected the underlying administrative problems. Mexican securities have always been predominantly of the bearer type, in which case the owner's name appears neither on a certificate nor in the books of a company, and the bearer of a certificate need merely clip a coupon and present it for payment of dividends. Needless to say, this practice has made the evasion of one's tax obligations a relatively easy matter. As part of the reform, the authorities encour-

TABLE 53. Rates of Taxation of Personal Property Income
(Schedules VI and VIII), 1962*

Annual Income (thousands of pesos) Lower Limit	Upper Limit	Percentage Applied to Income Exceeding Lower Limit
0	2	10.0
2	5	11.3
5	8	12.6
8	14	13.9
14	20	15.2
20	26	16.5
26	38	17.9
38	50	19.3
50	62	20.7
62	75	22.1
75	100	23.5
100	125	24.9
125	150	26.4
150	200	27.9
200	250	29.4
250	350	30.9
350	408	32.4
408	480	36.0
480	720	40.0
720	840	45.0
840	and up	50.0

* Secretaría de Hacienda y Crédito Público, "Ley federal del impuesto sobre la renta," *Boletín Oficial*, 8 (February, 1962), 228 and 234.

aged the bearers of securities to place them with financial institutions in order to facilitate identification of ownership. Their inducement was a flat tax of 15 per cent which represented no change from the previous assessment; otherwise the recipients of dividends were legally liable at a rate of 20 per cent. The new Schedule VIII embraced not only covered rents and royalties but embraced one of the most publicized and significant of the recent reforms, namely, the inclusion of incomes from house rentals in the income tax law. While the recipients of rental incomes of 1,000 pesos or less per month continued under the stamp tax, those receiving more than this minimum now paid income taxes at flat 3.5 per cent rates. Unfortunately, the new taxes on rents may have been as easily shiftable as the older stamp taxes. The last schedule, IX, is the former VII, concerning royalties from governmental concessions and licenses. In this instance also some greater progressiveness was in evidence. Whereas the marginal rates had previously moved from an initial 18.7 per cent to 41.2 per cent for annual incomes over 500,000 pesos, the new marginal rates began at 20 per cent and advanced to 55 per cent for incomes over 2,000,000 pesos.

Finally, the reforms introduced a complementary rate on the cumulative incomes of individuals which moved the income tax in the direction of a single schedule. Persons who earned incomes in excess of 180,000 pesos per year ($14,400) and who received two or more different types of income were now required to total their incomes from the several sources and to apply to that sum a surtax that began at a rate of 3 per cent and continued to 15 per cent for annual incomes beyond 1,450,000 pesos ($116,000). However, some of the schedules did rise to relatively high rates. Hence it was deemed equitable to exempt a taxpayer from the complementary tax whenever his total tax payment exceeded (only) 30 per cent of his personal income. To render the several reforms even more palatable politically, the Federal District also abolished its taxes on legacies and inheritances, on the grounds that collection was slow, costly, and rather easily evaded and that the first business at hand was the improvement of the income tax. The Bankers' Association of Mexico *et al.* promptly gathered their forces to urge the state governments to follow suit and surrender the taxes in question. They did not urge in vain.

How valuable were these several reforms in improving upon the yield, progressiveness, and simplicity of the income tax?

To obtain some ideas of the changes which took place in yield and progressiveness we can again compare the tax burdens of the low and high income recipients subject to any particular schedule (see Table 54). The measures utilized suggest a modest increase in the progressive taxation of personal property incomes but a rather considerable reduction in the progressiveness attending the taxation of all other incomes. On the other hand the reforms performed admirably in raising the yield. By 1964 income tax returns were 35 per cent higher than they had been in 1963, while the rate of increase in 1965 was expected to be 26 per cent. The total tax revenue of the federal government increased 14 per cent in 1963 and 17 per cent in 1964.

It is in the areas of improved administration and, it is hoped, changed attitudes toward the payment of taxes that the reforms may yield the highest returns. To assist each taxpayer in "the fulfillment of his fiscal obligations," the authorities established a Federal Taxpayers Register. Because of limitations in computers and other resources the government initially exempted from registration all taxpayers under Schedule IV whose monthly income fell below 10,000 pesos and those under Schedule V whose annual earnings were less than 125,000 pesos; the ultimate plan, of course, was to register everyone engaged in economic activity. Otherwise the registration of taxpayers began on June 1, 1962, with the President of the Republic and his Secretary of the Treasury being the first to submit their names. By April 1963 about 2,500,000 persons had completed their registration, and by 1964 the number of taxpayers had climbed to 4,500,000. There had been only 700,000 in 1958.[24]

Despite the considerable improvements, few observers were prepared to argue in 1963 and 1964 that Mexico's public revenue was adequate for its needs or that either the income tax or the entire tax system was sufficiently progressive. While economic technicians spoke of the need for more government expenditures for both investment and social welfare, government revenue still remained at an incredibly low ratio of about 8 per cent of national output. The 1963 and 1964 federal budgets each embraced deficits of approximately 1,000,000,000 pesos. The whole tax structure with its various schedules, classifications, omissions, and discriminations remained exceedingly complex and inequitable. Deductions were in need of revision; a wage earner with a monthly income of 4,000 pesos, for example, paid his income tax at a rate of 5 per cent irrespective of the number of his dependents.[25] The payment of taxes on interest income under Schedule VI involved

24 "Mexico: Booming Urban Economy," *Hispanic American Report*, 17 (July, 1964), 595.
25 Navarrete, "Naturaleza de la reforma fiscal," p. 142.

TABLE 54. Tax Burdens of Low and High Income Receivers post-1961–1962 Reforms

	(1) At the Upper Limits of the Low Brackets			(2) At the Lower Limits of the High Brackets (thousands of pesos)			(3)	(4)
Schedule	(a) Tax Liability (pesos)	(b) Income (pesos)	(c) Taxes/Income (%)	(a) Tax Liability	(b) Income	(c) Taxes/Income (%)	(2)(c) ÷ (1)(c)	Former Index of Progressiveness
I, II	75	3,500	2.1	623.9	2,000	31.2	14.9	43.3
III	102	3,500	2.9	365.1	1,500	24.3	8.4	43.3
IV	4.5	500	0.9	24.4	70	34.9	38.9	54.0
V	60	up to 2,000	3.0	257.9	1,000	25.8	8.6	130.0
VI, VIII	(variable)	up to 2,000	10.0	286.4	840	34.1	3.4	3.0
IX	(variable)	up to 2,000	20.0	915.1	2,000	45.8	2.3	2.2

not only the partial exemption already noted but complete exemptions as well. Some cases in point concerned special securities of the government, paper issued by international credit institutions in which the Mexican government was a partner, and income from reinsurance with foreign insurance companies. Because of the existence of several schedules, firms and individuals realized that the same income could incur vastly different tax liabilities. Thus if a firm or person earned 50,000 pesos ($4,000) per month the tax liability would depend upon the source of income as follows:

	(%)
Wages and salaries (Schedule IV)	30
Commercial or industrial enterprise (Schedules I and II)	24
Agricultural enterprise (Schedule III)	16
Dividends (Schedule VII)	15
Interest in excess of 7.2% (Schedule VI)	2 to 5
Rent (Schedule VIII)	2 to 3.5

Evidently Mexico required another dose of tax reform once it again became politic to do so.

The occasion arose again rather quickly in 1965, in part because of the economy's performance in 1964. Further, business interests participated in the planning of the new law, so that the newest reform, like the preceding one, encourages private investment. Little purpose would be served in discussing the reforms in detail;[26] suffice to say that they moved Mexico significantly toward a modern income tax. The new provisions rid the system of the nine schedules and simply classified tax payers into three large groups: firms, persons obtaining income from work, and persons receiving income from property or capital. Enterprises paid only one tax on their total incomes, and, among other things, now enjoyed carry-back privileges. Individuals similarly were subject to merely one tax liability, without any distinction between income from labor and income from investments, when their earnings exceeded 150,000 pesos a year. Recipients of wages and salaries were to be

---

[26] For a summary of the major revisions see "The Fiscal Reform," *Comercio Exterior*, 11 (January, 1965), 3–4. For the law itself see "La Nueva ley del impuesto sobre la renta," *El Mercado de Valores*, 25 (January, 1965), 13–36 and 49.

taxed on only 80 per cent of their incomes. The authorities have claimed that the latest reforms will reduce the relative tax burden of the low income groups.

The country had indeed come a long way in less than a decade. Confronted with an institutional obstacle of extremely serious proportions, Mexico possessed enough flexibility to modify her behavior and resume her vigorous economic development. The whole episode was characteristic of her post-Revolutionary experience and further helps explain why she has grown rapidly relative to other nations. Hence it is not a major criticism to assert that there were some neglected opportunities in the comparatively brief interim between the need for tax reform and its actual implementation.

CHAPTER NINE

Government Expenditures for Education and Welfare

A reprise and an overture. The last several chapters have witnessed the argument that Mexico in the late fifties and early sixties could have benefited from a combination of added tax revenue, less deficit financing, less inflation, and greater income equality. Although these goals were pursued in considerable measure, government receipts and expenditures were not permitted to contribute sufficiently to economic growth at that time.

A survey of the government's budgets during the early 1960's indicates that the authorities allocated approximately 40 per cent of the expenditures to investment for development, 10 per cent to investment for welfare purposes, and 25 per cent for welfare services, or 75 per cent for the three purposes combined. Had government revenues totaled 16 per cent of the GNP while the budget was virtually balanced and the above proportions were maintained, the expenditures within each of the above categories could have expanded without seriously threatening price stability. Public investment for development and for welfare could then have approached 7 per cent and 1.5 per cent, respectively, of the national product, so that the two combined could have yielded an additional 2 per cent or more. Further, total expenditures on education and welfare services might have approached 4 per cent of the national output, or about 1.5 per cent beyond that actually experienced during the period. Undoubtedly reductions in voluntary saving would have partially offset these gains, but enough has been said of savings propensities in Mexico to suggest the probability of an over-all net gain. Further, it is erroneous to think in static terms. An expanded program on the part of the government would be expected, on balance, to introduce favorable multiplier effects into the private sector and to stimulate activity there.

The events of 1963–1964 suggest the benefits to be gained from such programs.[1] It would evidently be foolhardy to argue that the limited tax reforms of 1961–1962 were responsible for the resurgence of the economy. Much of the spurt might easily have been associated with the expanding phase of the business cycle. Then, too, the balance of payments became favorable during 1962–1964 despite the declines in Mexico's three chief export commodities, and these developments were only remotely related to the previous reforms. Yet the data are certainly consistent with the hypotheses voiced so frequently in these pages—that the late fifties and early sixties required tax reforms which would direct resources to the government and permit it to take steps to improve upon the productivities and incomes of the low income groups and stimulate mass consumption in the process. In 1963 Mexico's GNP grew at a rate of about 6 per cent in real terms. "Consumption climbed owing to increased income from wage hikes, higher employment levels, and the increase in current expenditures by the government."[2] During the year the government sector as a component of aggregate demand expanded 6 per cent in real terms, and the production of consumers goods advanced 7.6 per cent, with significant increases in nondurables as well as durables. During the following year the GNP and the government's contribution to it again kept pace, each expanding by a whopping 10 per cent in real terms. In manufacturing the volume of consumer goods rose 13 per cent, and production goods, 14 per cent. Price increases in both years were moderate, in 1964 because of the bumper harvest of that year and in both years because of the idle capacity still to be found in Mexico's consumer goods industries. Nevertheless, by 1964 the investment component was exhibiting a great deal of strength (see Table 55).

Beyond these macroeconomic considerations arise the specific

[1] The data in this paragraph are from current issues of Banco Nacional de Comercio Exterior, *Comercio Exterior*, and Nacional Financiera, *El Mercado de Valores*.

[2] "The Mexican Economy in 1963," *Comercio Exterior de México*, 10 (March, 1964), 5.

TABLE 55. Selected Investment Series, 1960–1964*

Item (%)	1960	1961	1962	1963	1964
Private Investment / Total Investment	63.2	56.9	56.3	50.7	53.6
Public Investment / Total Investment	36.8	43.1	43.7	49.3	46.4
Private Investment / GNP	9.6	8.5	8.0	7.6	8.6
Public Investment / GNP	5.6	6.4	6.2	7.4	7.5
Total Investment / GNP	15.2	14.9	14.2	15.0	16.1
ΔCapital Stock / ΔGNP	...	4.4	3.1	2.5	1.8
$\Delta I_{private} / I_{private}$	...	−9.3	−0.9	1.2	24.8
$\Delta I_{public} / I_{public}$	...	17.9	1.4	27.2	11.0
$\Delta I / I$	...	0.7	0.1	12.6	18.0

*United Nations, Economic Commission for Latin America, *Economic Survey of Latin America, 1964*, p. 103, t. II-58. The last three rows have been taken directly from this source, and the first six have been computed from the data presented on gross fixed investment in 1950 prices. The 1964 figures are provisional estimates.

problems of the allocation of the government's resources. Insofar as this involves capital outlays for economic growth, the criterion to be pursued is the familiar one of the rates of return over cost, assuming these can be determined. Such a criterion could also effectively promote greater income equality. In particular, irrigation works, extension services, and similar forms of assistance to agriculture should bear rates of return that exceed the rate on the economy's marginal project.

In addition, expenditures on education are generally believed to yield a high social dividend. Ignorance evidently constitutes a significant cause of poverty, while education contributes to progress because of its correlations with science and rational decision making. However, these heart-warming generalizations still do not serve as guides for specific investment policies in the realm of education. Many troublesome issues arise because of intangibles and the difficulties of measurement. Moreover, education is quite expensive during the present, and it may not produce noticeable results until some vaguely defined future. At what rate, then, should the authorities seek to improve the educational system, given the many other development needs confronting their nation? Further, what types of education are to be promoted? Should the focus be on primary or on advanced education, and in the latter case on technical training or a broad liberal education? What shall be the regional distribution of the outlays? Do urban or rural areas particularly require help?

Of the outlays designed to relieve income inequality the government consumption expenditures are undoubtedly the most controversial. These are evidently intended to relieve familiar forms of socioeconomic distress such as those accompanying dependency or illness. Critics of such programs point to the relatively high costs involved and charge that poor countries cannot afford to divert precious resources from growth promoting ends. "Welfare statism," they are likely to remind us, did not arrive in the more advanced economies until they had attained considerable progress. Simply because the line between investment and consumption is so thin, however, productivity considerations may lurk in these outlays. A diseased or debilitated worker obviously cannot perform an adequate day's work. Moreover, granted that programs with the highest returns should be encouraged, perhaps other criteria are important as well. Should there then be a blanket indictment of "welfare statism"? May this not require disaggregation as does education or virtually every other aspect of the problem of equality? Conceivably some social services can be offered relatively early in the development process while others come with a lag.

A brief review and evaluation of Mexico's experiences with

education and social service might throw some light on these issues of composition, timing, and sequences. Guide lines are especially needed in the case of social services, where little work has been done.

Government expenditures for education and welfare during the forties and fifties. The point of departure is given by total welfare developments during a period when the data are more readily available, during the 1940's and 1950's. As might be expected, public welfare expenditures became more prominent in the later decade. Less predictably, these expenditures had already attained considerable magnitude during the forties.

A survey, first, of public *investment* expenditures for welfare in the forties shows these to have been modest compared to total government investment for economic development. Investment under the category of both social and municipal construction averaged about 12 per cent of public investment and therefore less than 5 per cent of total investment during the 1939–1951 period. The vast percentage of expenditures in this category, 79 per cent from 1939 through 1946 and 67 per cent from 1947 through 1950, was concentrated on the municipal works—on water supply, sewage, slaughterhouses and markets, the pavement of streets, and so on. After 1947 low-cost housing increased to some extent. Hospitals and educational institutions comprised the remaining categories, with the expenditures on each of these typically ranging from 1 to 2 per cent of total public investment.[3]

The data on educational, health, and welfare *services* reveal a somewhat different development. From 1939 to 1950 the average annual rates of increase in volume and per capita volume were 6.9 per cent and 4.2 per cent for educational services and 10.8 per cent and 8.1 per cent, respectively, for public health and welfare services. That is, during these years educational services expanded at nearly the same rate as did the total national product, while the growth rates for health and welfare exceeded the total growth rates by substantial margins. (Undoubtedly, the low base partially accounted for these performances.) Education, health, and welfare services further paralleled the total product in exhibiting,

[3] The Combined Mexican Working Party, *The Economic Development of Mexico*, p. 99 and p. 195, t. 20.

even to a greater degree, a lower rate of growth in 1946–1950 than in 1940–1945.

Expenditures on education services averaged 9.5 per cent and public health and welfare services, 6.4 per cent of total public outlays during the decade.[4] Since investment in education, health, and welfare came to some 12 per cent of public investment and public investment averaged about one-third of total government expenditures,[5] this implies another 4 per cent of total public outlays to health, education, and welfare. Approximately 20 per cent of all government expenditures was thus allocated to health, education, and welfare.

By 1956–1957 *investment* in education and public health and welfare had moved up from its previous 12 per cent to about 22 per cent of total public investment. Municipal works had declined to approximately 13 per cent of public investment, while education, public health, and low-cost housing each now accounted for about 2.5 per cent.[6] From 1952 through 1958 *public consumption* expenditures moved up at annual rates of increase averaging 6.9 per cent; by 1956–1958 the average came to 13.6 per cent.[7] By the same token total expenditures on education, health, and welfare as a percentage of the outlays of the federal government were rising. In 1960 they had reached 30 per cent and by 1962 they surpassed one-third of the total. Social security and welfare outlays alone rose from 4.5 per cent in 1955 to 8.7 per cent in 1962.[8] In brief, outlays on education and welfare were expanding more rapidly than either the economy as a whole or all remaining government expenditures.

Developments and issues in education. Attempts at improving and expanding the educational system began in the early 1920's, when the federal government established its Department of Education. The emphasis at the outset was at the bottom. Education was to become free, secular, and allegedly compulsory up to the age of

[4] *Ibid.*, p. 100 and pp. 326–327, t. 112.

[5] Based on *ibid.*, p. 336, t. 116.

[6] International Bank for Reconstruction and Development, "Mexico's Public Investment Program, 1957–1958," Report No. WH-59 (July, 1957), t. 58.

[7] Víctor L. Urquidi, "La inflación en México," p. 39, t. 2.

[8] Nacional Financiera, *El Mercado de Valores,* 22 (October 15, 1962), 613, t. 2.

fourteen. Much was accomplished in those early days by truly dedicated, all-purpose, frequently migratory teachers, who each received all of 1 peso a day from the federal department.[9]

Needless to say, resources have been meager and the actual program has fallen short of stated ideals. Yet the country has experienced steady progress in its endeavor to promote literacy. In 1910 and in 1930 the illiteracy rate for the population aged ten and over approximated 70 per cent. By 1950 it had been reduced to 50 per cent and in 1960, to 38 per cent. By the sixties the country was in the midst of an Eleven Year Plan, designed to provide at least an elementary school education for every Mexican child by 1970. This was indeed to be an expensive crash program.

[It] requires the construction, over a period of 11 years, of 39,265 classrooms, of which 11,825 are being built in urban zones and 27,440 in rural regions. It also implies the establishment of 51,090 new positions for teachers, of which 23,650 will be for urban schools and 27,440 for rural classes. Urban schools will have two shifts of students and one in rural schools.[10]

It is hoped that starting salaries of 100 pesos a month with fringe benefits and promises of ultimate raises would be sufficient to attract the required teachers' services.

Confronted with these data, one struggles for standards. Is a reduction in illiteracy of somewhat over 30 per cent in three decades significant? In several respects the answer is in the negative. The changes do not necessarily reflect developments in formal education as such; for example, of the estimated 6,900,000 literate persons in 1940, only 2,800,000 had attended school.[11] In 1960 many children were still without formal instruction of any kind, and the majority did not attend school beyond the first year. Most of the schools have been without sufficient operating funds.

[9] See Frank Tannenbaum, *Mexico: The Struggle for Peace and Bread*, chapter 6. For a detailed historical study, as well as a selected bibliography, see Rámon Eduardo Ruiz, *Mexico: The Challenge of Poverty and Illiteracy, passim*.

[10] Octaviano Campos Salas, "Economic Panorama of Modern Mexico," *Comercio Exterior de México*, 9 (February, 1963), Supplement, 5. For illiteracy data, see *ibid*; G. Benham and H. A. Holley, *A Short Introduction to the Economy of Latin America*, p. 14; and Nathan L. Whetten, *Rural Mexico*, p. 420, t. 86.

[11] Tannenbaum, *The Struggle for Peace and Bread*, p. 170.

Yet, by various criteria, Mexico has expanded its primary education at a relatively satisfactory rate. Various United Nations publications reveal that Mexico's literacy compares favorably with other countries at approximately the same per capita incomes. Or, if the rate of increase in the total national product be adopted as the criterion, expenditures on education have at least kept up with rates of economic growth and have in more recent years exceeded them. Yet another criterion makes use of the degree of industrialization, as measured by the proportion of gainfully occupied males outside agriculture.[12] By this standard Mexico's struggle for literacy has been reasonably successful. Since the percentage of the total work force occupied in agriculture declined moderately from 65 per cent in 1940 to 54 per cent in 1957,[13] the decline in illiteracy over the same period seems impressive by comparison.

In short, given the difficulties of determining the returns to education, particularly in poor and poorly statisticized countries, and given also the many tasks to be performed in such communities, some rule of thumb must place constraints upon those who view education as the perennial infant industry. A reasonable solution is to relate the expansion of primary education to the economy's over-all growth rate in the earlier period of development and then to expand literacy at a faster rate during a later phase. Then more resources are available, and it may become particularly necessary to improve the productivity of the low income groups. For the most part, Mexico has pursued this rule.

These remarks regarding aggregates still leave unanswered innumerable questions about the allocation of funds for primary education. The only one to be noted at this point concerns urban-rural differences. Without any doubt Mexico's primary educational system has favored urban pupils.[14] In 1940 four-fifths of all persons aged ten or over and residing in localities of over 10,000 inhabitants were able to read and write, while only two-fifths of

[12] See Hilda H. Golden, "Literacy and Social Change in Underdeveloped Countries," *Rural Sociology*, 20 (March, 1955), 1–6.

[13] See chapter 5, Table 29, of the present work.

[14] Ramón Eduardo Ruiz, *Mexico: The Challenge of Poverty and Illiteracy*, esp. chapter 11. Ruiz indicates that much of the discrimination against the rural sector is to be attributed to its political weakness (p. 207).

those living in smaller communities were literate.[15] A decade later barely 50 per cent of the rural inhabitants and over 80 per cent of those in the urban areas were reported literate.[16] A decade after that less than 10 per cent of all rural pupils were in the two final primary grades (fifth and sixth), but the urban schools typically offered the full primary cycle through the sixth grade.[17]

In some respects these differentials were deplorable. Given the usual isolation and fatalism of the countryside, primary education can act as a powerful force for change, and conceivably it can yield among the highest marginal returns in the economy. To have concentrated on the urban schools appears to have been yielding to expediency. Yet much can again be said for the Mexican approach. Education per pupil tends to be considerably more costly when the unit is small, so that the rate of return over cost tends to be greater in the urban school. This is especially likely when subsistence farmers resist the establishment of educational institutions; in their way of life, literacy tends to be of little import and it can easily languish once it is attained. Under these circumstances, attacks upon rural isolation through the construction of roads and the establishment of agricultural extension services can initially be much more effective than formal education. Urban residents, on the other hand, immediately require at least a primary education in order to cope with an industrializing economy.

The federal and state governments appear to have been less dedicated to the advancement of postprimary education in the aggregate, despite occasional claims to the contrary. In 1958, after the country had experienced its marked economic development, only 332,400 students were enrolled at the advanced levels. Somewhat more than half of them were in preprofessional or prevocational schools—that is, at the secondary, preparatory, and prevocational levels. Prevocational and vocational students made up only 5.7 per cent of the total. The postprimary group as a whole represented about 6 per cent of those, aged fourteen to twenty-nine, who were

[15] Whetten, *Rural Mexico*, p. 420, t. 85.

[16] John H. Adler, "Public Expenditures and Economic Development," Joint Tax Program, *Fiscal Policy for Economic Growth in Latin America*, p. 145, t. 5-4.

[17] Howard F. Cline, *Mexico, Revolution to Evolution: 1940–1960*, pp. 199–200.

eligible for advanced work.[18] Five years later an official study uncovered the disturbing fact that of each one thousand children who entered primary school any given year, only seventeen completed the sixth grade; and, of course, there were further casualties in the transference from the primary to postprimary levels. The dropouts occurred essentially for economic reasons.

The frustrating problem of standards once more arises. Was Mexico delinquent in not stimulating postprimary education more actively? In confronting this issue one would again seek some correlation between economic and educational development. More specifically, did a lack of well-educated and/or well-trained individuals hamper Mexico's growth?

The answer to this would seem to be a negative one insofar as professional and white-collar skills are concerned. Mexico has been rather well endowed with national and state universities. The most celebrated of these, the U.N.A.M. (Universidad Nacional Autónoma de México), is the continent's oldest university and now thrives on a mammoth and colorful campus just outside Mexico City. Nearly one-third of its student body, which numbered seventy thousand at the time of writing, works for graduate degrees in medicine, engineering, and law. Other institutions, such as the Polytechnic Institute (1936) and the Institute of Technology (1942), similarly are of fairly high quality. At many of the more advanced institutions, degrees in commerce (accounting, secretarial work, and so on) have proved highly popular. Moreover, the scions of the wealthy have simply furthered their studies in other countries when they have found Mexico's system inadequate; for example, the number of Ph.D.'s in economics from United States and other foreign universities is not inconsiderable.

There is evidence, however, of insufficiencies at the middle levels. We have already noted the small proportions of students enrolled in technical courses as well as the tendency for intermediate students to concentrate on preprofessional studies. If one had the wherewithal to enter a secondary school one generally could proceed further with his training. Mexico's educational system thus reflects not only the level and rate of increase of its national income, but its income distribution as well; it seems to have performed

[18] *Ibid.*, p. 203.

tolerably well at the extremes but not in the center. In more recent years the Mexican government has awakened to these shortcomings. In 1963, for example, it planned to open thirty vocational training schools in nineteen different states. The schools were to be primarily at the grade school levels. Ten were to feature industrial training and to be located in urban areas, while the remaining twenty were to be agricultural-rural. The industrial schools were to train for a variety of occupations, such as general mechanics, electrical mechanics, masonry, and carpentry, while the agricultural schools trained for full time jobs on modern farms.[19]

This was precisely the type of program Mexico required in order to advance the productivity of its lower income groups and to promote economic growth and equality of income distribution simultaneously. Because of both the leadership and the literacy required during the initial periods of economic development and because of the possibilities of on-the-job training, formal vocational training did not at first seem to deserve high priorities in the outlays for education. But Mexico was subsequently ready for, and could afford, relatively more formal instruction at the middle levels.

Trends in social security and social welfare. Mexican specialists in social security tend to distinguish between *la seguridad social* and *el seguro social*. The first pertains to the concept or idea of sustaining those prevented from participating in an economically productive life because of sickness, disability, unemployment, and the like, while the second refers to the system of institutions for implementing the concept.[20] As in the case of the labor movement, both the idea and the institutions made some progress in Mexico in the nineteenth century, but the institutional development was relatively retarded. In 1813 Morelos, one of Mexico's greatest heroes, already spoke of the obligation of Congress to moderate both opulence and indigence and to augment the incomes of the poor. Later, pensions were provided for various classes of civil servants. Mail

[19] Paul P. Kennedy, "Mexico Launches Education Drive," *New York Times,* May 5, 1963, section 1, p. 4.

[20] Miguel García Cruz, "La Seguridad social," *México: Cincuenta años de revolución, II, La vida social,* pp. 501–502. The historical review of Mexico's social security system that now ensues is based primarily on this source, pp. 503–519.

employees, for example, were granted higher pensions in 1856 because their lives were threatened by roaming bandits. No further developments occurred during the Díaz regime.

As the 1910 Revolution progressed it generated a great deal of propaganda for the economic protection of the worker. Much of it saw realization in Chapter Four of the Constitution of 1917. Among other things, the employer was to help implement the idea of *la seguridad social.* According to Section Fourteen of Chapter Four he was responsible for accidents and illnesses incurred on the job, and he was to pay an indemnity in the case of death or a permanent disability. Section Twenty-nine encouraged the federal and state governments to establish institutions that would provide insurance for old age, sickness, accidents, death, and unemployment. Accordingly, in the 1920's, civil servants were again provided with pensions upon retirement. However, in a sense these two sections hindered the development of a social security system at the national level. Since employers and government-sponsored labor unions were already providing union members with fringe benefits, this provided an argument for those opposed to a comprehensive social security system; and because Section Twenty-nine had ambiguously called for action by both the national and state governments, this became the occasion for a struggle between "states righters" and proponents of action by the federal government. For approximately a quarter of a century those in favor of state programs tended to have their way. In 1921 the National Congress defeated a proposed social security bill; in 1928 Obregón, who favored a social security system financed by employers, employees, and the state, was assassinated (on the issue of re-election) before he could assume office; in 1929 President Portes Gil instituted a constitutional reform which made *el seguro social* a public right and explicitly called for enabling legislation, but the state governors fought the reform and kept the issue alive; and in 1932 President Ortiz Rubio announced that a social security law would be ready in several months, but for political reasons he was soon ousted from office. It is difficult to determine whether the opponents of a national system were genuinely interested in states rights, whether they were motivated primarily by selfish concerns, or whether they had carefully considered the ability of the economy to support a comprehensive social security system.

In the interim a haphazard and chaotic social aid "program" came into existence. Pensions, banks of popular credit, postal savings, *pequeños cajas de socorros* (institutions of charity), and cooperative societies for aid in receiving medical services, pharmaceuticals, and legal advice dotted the scene. Most of these developments occurred in the Federal District, which in 1924 established an institute of social services known as La Beneficience Pública.[21] In other parts of the country only one or two of these social services were to be found, while in the most remote and rural parts of the nation no such benefits were in evidence.

Then in 1934 Cárdenas, as the National Revolutionary Party (PNR) candidate, ran on a platform that supported legislative enactment of a social security system. While in office he proposed legislation on three different occasions. Through his efforts a compromise was reached, and in 1941, under Avila Camacho, the enabling legislation passed. Led by Miguel García Cruz, a commission worked for two years in studying various systems in Europe and the United States. Finally, on January 19, 1943, President Avila Camacho proclaimed the Social Security System law, virtually twenty-six years after the Constitution was adopted. Affiliation was to begin July 1943, and benefits and services would start in January 1944. The Instituto Mexicano del Seguro Social (IMSS), the Mexican Social Security Institute, was established as a separate and independent agency and presented with a loan of more than 500,000,000 pesos from the Hacienda Pública (Ministry of the Interior) to build and equip four hospitals in the Federal District.

As the IMSS is currently managed, the President of Mexico appoints its director general for a six-year term concurrent with his own. The head of the IMSS is aided by a Governing Board, or General Assembly, of thirty members, ten from the government who are presidential appointees, ten from the employers, elected by the various industrial chambers, and ten from the workers, elected by the unions. The director general is responsible to the Governing Board, which is the ultimate authority. In addition the members of the Technical Commission, made up of four persons

[21] Xavier de la Riva Rodríguez, "Salubridad y asistencia médico-social," *México: Cincuenta años, II*, p. 391.

from each of the three sections and elected by the Governing Board, serve as the administrators and legal representatives of the Institute; their terms also run for six years and they may be re-elected. A six-member Commission of Vigilance, designated by the Governing Board and made up of two representatives from each of the three sectors, is responsible for the auditing and general supervision of the management.[22]

The first three years of the IMSS were difficult ones, as much energy and time were spent in the courts fighting cases of anti-constitutionalism. The courts handled each case separately according to the Mexican law of *amparo*, since modified, which then required that the interpretation of a law be limited to the particular case being heard. Despite these difficulties, the system began to thrive. Centers were soon established in the Federal District, and in Monterrey, Guadalajara, and Puebla. Additions to staff included lawyers, engineers, architects, economists, accountants, social workers, and administrators, but the initial activities of the IMSS were concentrated in medical care. During the period 1944–1952, 42 clinics and 19 hospitals with nearly 1,700 beds opened their doors for service.

The evident philosophy of the IMSS has been to reduce to a minimum the various risks faced by man. According to one informant associated with the system, risks are viewed as threefold: natural (fires, droughts, earthquakes), biological (illnesses, injuries, maternities), and social (primarily ignorance). The system focuses on the relief of the second of these, but it mitigates the third as well—as in the community development projects to be described below. Table 56 summarizes the types of assistance given by the IMSS during 1959–1960. Included are the usual afflictions associated with social security coverage, except that unemployment is excluded. Old age retirement pensions led in funds allocated, but orphans and widows were the most numerous recipients of benefits.

By the end of 1952 those eligible for IMSS benefits numbered over 1,100,000 persons. Of these, some 435,000 were members and the remaining 706,000 represented their dependents. A decade

---

[22] The details of the Institute's organization are given in Instituto Mexicano del Seguro Social, *Ley del seguro social.*

TABLE 56. Benefits Received from IMSS, 1959–1960, by Types of Assistance*

Class	Recipients Number	%	Value Amounts (pesos)	%
Orphans	14,944	35.90	6,385,340.61	12.72
Widows	10,067	24.18	9,850,870.47	19.63
Retired	6,527	15.68	17,513,166.37	34.89
Disabled	4,803	11.54	10,859,083.51	21.63
Parents	225	0.54	86,519.16	0.17
Dangerous professions				
Permanently disabled	2,328	5.59	3,059,281.65	6.10
Orphans	1,667	4.01	1,249,879.10	2.49
Widows	759	1.82	971,911.12	1.94
Parents	307	0.74	216,762.92	0.43
Totals	41,627	100.00	50,192,814.91	100.00

* García Cruz, "La seguridad social," p. 566, t. 6.

later the social security system had expanded to include over five million potential beneficiaries. In addition, many more persons received medical care, old age insurance, and pensions from other public agencies. A member's family is eligible for all the benefits which he may receive. Further, the term "family" is broadly defined indeed. It includes the spouse, either one who is legally married or one who has cohabited for at least five consecutive years, children under sixteen years of age, and the parents of the member and his spouse, provided they are old and require financial help from the member.

By 1956 the IMSS had extended its program beyond the construction of hospitals and had established the first of the Centros de Seguridad Social Para El Beinestar Familiar, or neighborhood centers located in worker residential areas. These were designed to educate the members of the IMSS and their families in the history of art and folklore of Mexico, in the more modern methods of food preparation, and generally in methods of hygiene and health care. Nurseries in these institutions can relieve mothers for a few hours a day and thereby permit them to attend classes in reading, writing, sewing, handicrafts, homemaking, and hygiene. At these centers mass wedding ceremonies have frequently taken place, to legalize many of the cohabitation families. Since so many of the workers employed in urban industries have recently arrived from the rural areas, the centers further help orient them to city living and, incidentally, acquaint them with the benefits they can derive from the social security system. The neighborhood centers encourage youths to remain in school and help keep them off the streets. Some offer employment services on the side, though this is not organized but is rather a matter of personal contact between the director of the center and local employers. In 1962 nearly forty such centers thrived in Mexico, with half of them located in Mexico City. Additional ones were under construction.

A yet more ambitious and comprehensive IMSS undertaking consists of the large housing developments in various cities of Mexico. All residents of these housing units have someone in the family who belongs to the IMSS and who has thus established the initial eligibility. Most families work outside the *unidad* (development), but some are employed to provide the services required to keep the community functioning. Frequently these developments are nearly cities within themselves. They possess their own schools, medical centers, and shopping facilities. Some sell inexpensive furniture and appliances, typically on a credit, noninterest basis. The recreational facilities may include a theater, a swimming pool, and equipment for pursuing various artistic interests. Much of what transpires at a *unidad* is part of an educating and adjusting process—whether it assumes such simple forms as acclimating the residents to locked doors, electric lighting, and toilet facilities, or it makes the services of the development psychologist or psychiatrist available to them. One *unidad* in Mexico City includes professional persons such as doctors, newspapermen, and officials of the IMSS itself. The rents these people pay and the quality of housing they receive are above standard, in keeping with the higher income which they earn. Their presence there is the result of their ability to educate the other members by example. The same *unidad* also illustrates the cooperative spirit which can arise in such a development. When some of the residents struck their jobs, others set up a relief fund to help support them during their period of economic stress.

Since these social security arrangements and the increased outlays on education have still failed to touch significant portions of the population, the federal government has turned to yet another device for redistributing national income. It has established a trading corporation to subsidize the purchases of the low income groups, especially in the Federal District. From 1937 to 1961 the Corporation was officially known as CEIMSA (Compañiá de Exportadores y Importadores, Sociedad Anónima), but in the latter year it assumed the more appropriate title of CONASUPO (Compañiá Nacional de Subsistencies Populares, S.A.). One branch of the company has dealt in basic cereals and beans throughout Mexico, a second has specialized in milk in the Federal District, and a third has dealt with fifteen basic food products, clothing, and shoes in the Federal District. In 1962 a branch was created to deal with feed, eggs, and fish, and plans were afoot to sell family baskets. In its various operations the corporation has often purchased items, especially food, at guaranteed prices, it has incurred storage and marketing costs, and it has then sold its goods at prices that failed to cover total unit costs. Only on occasion has the price exceeded the cost. Recently private banks have participated in the program by providing warehousing services and much of the immediate financing. This arrangement has, of course, not altered the service offered by the public sector, that of absorbing the differential between cost and price.

The government has generally covered its operations through the issuance of securities. Unfortunately this has provided the basis for a further expansion of credit, and it has in turn led to some combination of over-all monetary restraint and inflation. Both outcomes of course tend to restrict the demand for additional goods and services; such a result must follow if, given constant resources, subsidies induce purchases of necessities. In the short run monetary restraint is less likely than inflation to injure the very low income groups that the subsidy program is designed to assist, while in the longer run monetary restraint could conceivably be more damaging to their interests if it interfered with economic growth unduly. In brief, there are some indirect and diffused offsets to the activities of CONASUPO. In all probability the corporation has assisted the low income groups by directly raising their real purchasing power.

Conclusions concerning social security and public welfare. The theoretical literature typically contains a warning against undue

welfare legislation at the onset of development programs. Many
of the arguments against undue haste in this field are reasonable
and valid: the economy cannot afford it; government expenditures
that do not enhance output are inflation-inducing; the disincentive
effects can be extremely dangerous; and so on. Because of these
problems, social security measures and labor legislation are typically cited among the disadvantages of a late start. In effect, is this
introduction of humanism into the process of development necessarily disruptive and discouraging to economic growth?

The answer to this question probably revolves around the basic
differences between rural and urban living—and rural and urban
hopes and fears. The basic problems of the small farmer, once he
is freed of the worst abuses of the landlord and the middleman, are
those of ignorance in technical matters and a general lack of sophis-
tication in the ways of the world. He is typically illiterate, tradi-
tion-bound, and as uninformed about social phenomena as he is
about alternative ways of producing and marketing his product.
Above all else he needs technological assistance and the resulting
heightened productivity. This and an improved transportation system help him overcome his great insecurity, the danger of famine.
In the event of illness or accident he requires, at zero or exceedingly low cost to himself, the services of a medical practitioner. Beyond this, however, the extended family and/or the village help
provide for his basic needs. If he or his immediate family is involved in a personal tragedy, time-honored institutions facilitate
his adjustment, in economic as well as noneconomic terms. From
the point of view of the donors of welfare services, moreover, he is
relatively difficult and expensive to reach.

Urban dwellers possess different needs, particularly once they
have disassociated themselves from rural backgrounds. Much has
been made of their *anomie*, or in the disintegration of their values
and their inability to find meaning in life. Much can also be made
of the fears they now possess regarding unemployment, accidents,
illness, and so on. Further, though this has not been true of Mexico, many of the new countries do not possess the basis for political
stability, whereupon the frustrations of the urban work force may
lead to civil disorder.[23] As noted in Chapter Three, these needs

23 See Charles P. Kindleberger, *Economic Development*, chapter 13.

help explain the relatively early formation of labor unions. Historically, unionism's greatest contribution to worker welfare has probably been not some material benefit but a greater sense of security, dignity, and control. If this has been true of the relatively rich countries it must have applicability for the poorer ones, particularly for those experiencing more rapid rates of development.

It is further to be noted that in Mexico the allocation of resources within the social security field has been more discriminatory than in education. In the latter instance the urban areas received priority, but the authorities did focus on mass primary education. In the case of social security there has been a similar concentration on urban areas, but the program has further been selective in its choice of eligible persons and their families. For the most part, services have been offered as a package. One received many benefits if he were a member, very little if he were not.

That the system should have concentrated initially on urban residents, it has just been argued, is most understandable. The administrative costs were thereby reduced and the more economically vulnerable workers received protection. That the program should also have promoted a worker elite does at first seem less tenable. This was inequitable, and it tended to make administrative efficiency a major criterion in the extension of the social security system. Yet, how could the system have supported itself otherwise? And it had to support itself, for it could not afford widespread transfer payments any more than it could tolerate the likely byproduct of a serious inflation. Thus unorganized employees, such as the construction, casual, and domestic workers, long did not receive social security benefits, their urban residence notwithstanding. Since they frequently did not possess permanent employers, records regarding them were difficult to maintain. If they were eligible for membership in the IMSS, they might not be aware of their opportunities. If, finally, they possessed sufficient awareness they either tended to fear employer retaliation or they could not force employers to maintain adequate records. Unions, on the other hand, could check on the accuracy of records and thereby helped prevent evasion of the law.

It will be remembered that by the early sixties the IMSS had still refrained from assisting the unemployed; this form of social welfare has trailed in Mexico. The rationale for neglecting it is not evident. The taxes associated with a public unemployment insurance program can effectively reduce inflation, especially when the government takes advantage of the high ratio of young people in the work force and so arranges the rates that workers' contributions greatly exceed their benefits. Such a tax would be equitable, given the relation of industrial wage rates to those of the casual worker or the farm employee. Since managers of firms rather than illiterate peasants are called upon to keep records, the tax should also be feasible, although, as in other Mexican social security programs, the employers' cooperation may have to be verified and not taken for granted. The lack of governmental protection against unemployment is probably explicable in terms of the benefits offered organized labor. As noted in Chapter Three, the process of discharging an employee is encumbered by severance pay and similar devices. Legally the employer rather than the state must bear some of the burden of unemployment, although economically he may at least partially shift this burden backward to the work force or forward to the consumer of his product. This system leaves something to be desired, particularly during the times when unemployment is the consequence of aggregate weakness rather than any particularized inefficiency.

The foregoing review has also shown that Mexico's social welfare measures have not been confined to the IMSS. Prior to the Revolution the Mexican government provided its employees with retirement pensions, but this did not spread to the private sectors. During the Revolution employers were made financially responsible for the occupational disabilities of their employees, an instance in which employer responsibility is considerably more justified than in the case of unemployment. In accordance with the high priority assigned to medical services, a host of agencies, private as well as public, national as well as decentralized, has provided free or inexpensive medical facilities. This concern with medical care is appealing on humanitarian grounds, and it is also economically sound in that it represents a form of social welfare that may particularly affect the prime age groups. Like education, medical care improves the quality of the work force and influences growth as well as the distribution of income. Once again the effect on productivity serves as an important criterion. In fact, the more evidently a welfare measure contributes to improved productivity, as in health, education, and the furthering of social transformation, the less significant becomes the self-support rule mentioned earlier in this section.

Whether other nations can wait twenty-five years after becoming development-oriented to introduce comprehensive social welfare programs is highly doubtful, for few possess Mexico's political stability. Economically a government may not be able to embark upon a massive nonsupported welfare program, but politically it may have no other recourse. There is obviously no ready answer to this, and Mexico's history offers few clues because of the country's fortunate political position. Of some relevance is the marked rural-urban migration which occurred in Mexico as a result of the relative neglect of agriculture in the country's development programs. This would suggest the possibility of reducing the ranks of the urban proletariat through extensive improvements in the rural sector. Furthermore, the Mexican government has frequently utilized its welfare programs as a means of enhancing labor productivity, and it has engaged in various projects (neighborhood centers, housing developments) which have conveyed the impression of an officialdom interested in the lot of the common man. To the extent that the government has promoted security by backing, or at least not interfering with, the development of unions, it has further expressed its interest in labor's welfare, though it then wooed labor's elite rather than the *lumpenproletariat*. Also, for Mexico the establishment of the IMSS may have been belated, but the timing was not terribly unfortunate. When, in the forties, the nation experienced both her major growth spurt and a rising income inequality, she was also taking her first steps to render the growing inequality less severe. Later, when she presumably required less income inequality, her social security system already thrived. In 1953 the contributions to the IMSS totaled 325,000,000 pesos, the benefits paid, 253,000,000, and the additions to reserves, 72,000,000. By 1959 these had jumped to 1,290,000,000, 1,046,000,000, and 244,000,000, respectively.[24]

In sum, Mexico's experience with social welfare suggests improved labor productivity and institutional self-support as the major criteria for determining the desirability of particular pro-

[24] García Cruz, "La seguridad social," p. 537, t. 2, and p. 561.

grams. With the passage of time, the first of these tended to assume a growing relative importance. Unfortunately these propositions imply a rather high degree of discrimination and inequity in the early periods of economic advancement, as evidenced particularly in the diverse treatment accorded those in the urban and rural areas.

CHAPTER TEN

Political Democracy and Economic Development

This chapter deals briefly with the political features of Mexico's development.[1] Its purpose is to throw some light on the relationship between economic development and equality within the political realm. The issue at hand is whether a democratic framework is appropriate for a poor, largely illiterate country as it embarks upon and experiences economic development.

Of the properties associated with democracy, the following (not unrelated ones) seem to be the most significant: an adherence to certain basic civil liberties which, among other things, perform the function of protecting the minority points of view; a decision making based ultimately on the wishes of the majority; and the control of the power of the executive through the rule of law and the enhancement of the other major branches of government. To these, traditional political theory would add the existence of at least two parties and the toleration of a loyal opposition. Do these several attributes, then, tend to enhance the rate of economic growth? These questions are moot, and their presumed answers, highly complex.

It is tempting to assert that a developing country should possess the basic civil liberties which are made available to the minority as well as the majority groups. These rights are important ulti-

---

[1] For purposes of the present study there is no need to examine Mexico's political system in detail. Those interested in Mexico's government may appeal to several good works on the subject. See Howard F. Cline, *Mexico, Revolution to Evolution: 1940–1960*, chapters XIII through XIX and bibliography, pp. 365–366.

mately and for their own sake, but they can also be of value immediately because of their effect on economic development. Their existence tends to encourage constructive criticism, permit geographic and social mobility, promote political stability, and turn men's attentions away from political complaints and toward problems of economic advancement. Particularly if there is to be a resort to science and knowledge derived from experience, the rights to criticize and evaluate are required for advancement. Yet the example of the U.S.S.R. indicates that such rights may be minimal, and Ghana, which jailed its loyal opposition, frequently showed signs of rapid economic progress. Further, a totalitarian system may restrict mobility and yet direct it so that it serves economic ends.

Whether a second property of democracy, majority rule, is conducive to development is still more debatable. Does democracy itself really suffer if the illiterate, isolated peasant or tribesman, unaware of the issues, unaware perhaps even of the existence of the nation-state of which he is allegedly a member, fails to cast a ballot? Is not one's vote equally meaningless or worse if one simply behaves as his *hacendado*, or equivalent, dictates? Moreover, when politicians heed the popular will, they may very well fail to perform the exceedingly unpopular acts, such as altering centuries-old traditions or raising the tax rates, which are necessary for development. On the other hand the act of voting performs a social-psychological function that furthers development. It helps make the public politically aware, and it renders economic progress more of a grass roots phenomenon. It assists nationalism in its struggle with the parochialism and divisive ethnic attachments that interfere with economic change. Perhaps, also, it serves to relieve tensions and promote political stability. And may not a popular support be of value to public officials when they seek reforms that may harm the country's elite?

The above would seem to suggest that civil liberties and majority rule may be desirable for economic development but that they are not indispensable in the short run. The other attributes of democracy appear to be even more expendable as a nation initially interests itself in economic development. This tends to be true of the existence of more than one party. If a single party has already embraced the aspirations of the vast majority in matters of independence, prestige, and improved planes of living, the creation of synthetic issues and synthetic parties is pointless. Should a genuine opposition with different points of view arise openly, this could easily cause prolonged dissension and disrupt long term planning. If the principle of orderly succession has yet to be accepted, multi-parties may lead to serious instability and disorder. A conceivable argument in favor of a multiparty system is the proposition that the current administration is thereby diverted from extremely serious errors. Possibly, but this is true when party differences revolve around matters of over-all objectives and basic policies. When all parties are committed to economic growth, the differences are typically technical ones, and these are not solved best through the political process. By the same token a country should develop its economy more rapidly when decision making is concentrated and the chief executive is in a position to *act*. A strengthening of the powers of the legislature and the judiciary might well lead to stalemates and indecisiveness which interfere with the country's growth. The chief executive must, however, pursue reasonably predictable policies. If he is inclined to whim and caprice he obviously creates an uncertainty which disturbs the private sector of the economy.

These propositions have some disturbing implications for political democracy taken as an entity. If some elements must be sacrificed or postponed until the economy experiences sustained development, this affects whatever attributes may be compatible with economic growth. What, for example, is the fate of the freedom to criticize if the opposition parties are weak or cannot come into existence? Are the rule of law and the ability to predict officialdom's actions consistent with a powerful executive and a weak judiciary? In effect, can a nation at all further political democracy if it seeks to promote rapid economic progress?

Mexico has responded to these various questions by assigning priorities to economic development and encouraging democratic forms whenever they have not interfered with the economic objective. The answer, that is, has lain in a responsible leadership and in a Mexico strongly led. Most particularly, no chief executive has ever forgotten how Mexico was once rocked by violence, rebellion, and revolution. Each has sought to prevent open dissension before it could occur by negotiating and cooperating with the country's various nonextremist groups. This has on the one hand narrowed the range of action of the chief executive but it has also strengthened his hand in implementing policies. He has acted swiftly to maintain order on the occasions of small and sporadic outbursts of organized violence. To provide further for political stability and prevent the conflict that might arise if a president sought to perpetuate his power, the 1917 Constitution has asserted that no man shall succeed himself; and since 1928 no ex-president has openly sought noncontinuous terms of office.[2] In sum, Mexico's leadership has responded intelligently to the obvious lessons of Mexico's history. In few other developing nations has so high a value been placed on civil peace, not only as a good in itself but as a prerequisite for economic development.[3]

At the same time, Mexico has moved considerably toward political democracy. Let us listen to Oscar Lewis, writing on Mexico's political development after 1940:

One of the most impressive gains has been the growth of political democracy and a much greater sense of national unity. The role of the military in political life has been markedly reduced, and Mexico has enjoyed years of stability and peaceful elections. It has a free press, freedom of speech, and freedom of worship. There are no political prisoners, and Mexico is still a haven for political refugees from other countries in the Western hemisphere.[4]

The general impression conveyed by this summary is correct, but the passage does tend to be overly laudatory. For example, the government controls the distribution of newsprint, a situation to be envied by any would-be censor. It is understood that neither the press nor any other medium of communication is to criticize the president openly, for he represents law, order, and the gains of the Revolution. The government may from time to time issue instructions to the press as particular circumstances arise. Yet the govern-

---

[2] However, Calles is generally recognized as having been Mexico's most powerful political figure from 1928, the year he officially surrendered the presidency, to 1935, the first full year of Cárdenas' administration.

[3] Martin C. Needler, "The Political Development of Mexico," *American Political Science Review*, 55 (June, 1961), 311.

[4] Oscar Lewis, "Mexico Since Cárdenas," *Social Research*, 26 (Spring, 1959), 18–19.

ment has employed its powers sparingly. As a result ". . . publications are fairly free,"[5] and Mexican residents are permitted easy access to the newspapers and journals of other countries. The government can also regulate the freedom of assembly and in fact requires official permission in many instances. This is again a potentially dangerous power. Nevertheless, the government typically grants permission, and at times, as it did in the case of a particular student protest, it does not give permission and then winks at the transgression.

The right to worship is indeed free, and the separation of church and state has been preserved. On the other hand the government has placed constraints upon religious institutions. Church buildings belong to the nation, which shall determine "which of them may continue to be devoted to their present purposes" (Article 27 of the Constitution). Nor can the church acquire, own, or administer private real property or make loans upon it.[6] Before the presidency of Cárdenas, some of the states prescribed the ratios of priests to total population and required marriages for the priests. Explanations of these restrictions are of course again found in Mexican history. In the early 1820's the church possessed about one-half of the country's land, and after Independence and through the Revolution it continually identified itself with foreign and/or ultraconservative interests because of its fears of popular governments and political instability. The more recent years have witnessed some healing of the breach between the state and the church. By 1964 Díaz Ordaz, scheduled to become Mexico's chief executive, was being described as the "first Catholic President."

The Mexican government thus potentially possesses powers reminiscent of the police state, but it has tended to employ them in a fashion which, in exceedingly large measure, has yielded an open society.

Further, Mexicans have the suffrage; for Mexican women this has been true since the mid-fifties. Registration is compulsory. Yet approximately one-third of those eligible to vote have exercised

---

[5] S. Walter Washington, "Mexican Resistance to Communism," *Foreign Affairs*, 36 (April, 1958), 512.
[6] Frank Tannenbaum, *Mexico: The Struggle for Peace and Bread*, p. 110.

their franchise, despite the many efforts of the government (presumably for the previously noted social-psychological and educative reasons) to enhance popular interest in elections. It is essentially the presidency that matters, and in selecting the chief executive the Mexican people have less of an effective choice than do the voters in other nations where the candidates are more evenly matched and the results are less of a foregone conclusion. Mexico has in fact realized her economic progress under the leadership of a single dominant party. It was established in 1928 as the National Revolutionary Party and known since 1946 as the Party of the Institutional Revolution (PRI). This party has simply attracted a wide variety of elements to its fold, at first through constituent organizations of agrarian, labor, and military sectors, and after 1938 through membership on an individual basis. It has thereby succeeded in winning one presidential contest after another. In order to attract so many diverse interests to a single organization, the PRI has found it necessary to become middle of the road, nonideological, and pragmatic.[7] Given its success in reducing ideological disputes and preventing the splintering into many atomistic groupings, it has found it possible to concentrate on the specific tasks of economic development.

Mexico, it is to be noted, is a country of one successful majority party not a country of one party. The law permits the existence of the Communist Party, although the Communists cannot participate in elections because of a legal membership minimum. Of the several minority parties in existence the most continuous has been the National Action Party (PAN). It has been backed by the Roman Catholic clergy, many of the wealthy, and, on occasions, the Sinarquistas, or ultra-Rightists. Persistently, and presumably hopefully, the PAN exposes its candidates to the experience of defeat in presidential elections. However, it has won seats in the Chamber of Deputies and at times has shown considerable strength. In the congressional election of July 2, 1961, for example, the Party made the Cuban revolution a major issue and received 250,000 votes as against more than 500,000 votes for the government candidates in the Mexico City area. This was the largest vote

---

[7] Robert E. Scott, *Mexican Government in Transition*, p. 176.

ever registered by the PAN in the Federal District for a congressional election.[8] On the other hand PAN is not likely to provide an alternative government in the near future.

Since the business interests frequently prefer membership in the PAN and other minority parties to affiliation with the PRI, the government has devised other instruments for cooperating with them. According to the law, an industrial or commercial firm with the mere capitalization of over 500 pesos must belong to one of the chambers, which collectively make up the national federations. In 1957 industrial firms became members of one of fifty-one chambers, classified on the basis of function. These chambers in turn form CONCAMIN (Confederación de Cámaras Industriales de los Estados Unidos Mexicanos). In the same year commercial firms were organized functionally and geographically into 254 chambers, which in the aggregate comprise CONCANACO (Confederación de Cámaras Nacionales de Comercio). The Secretary of the Economy determines which particular chamber any firm is to join, and a representative from this department attends all national meetings of both federations. CONCAMIN and CONCANACO each present the business interests with the opportunity to participate in policy making, despite their lack of representation in the PRI. The government consults with these organizations continually, particularly when new legislation and administrative regulations affect business interests. Needless to say, these organizations seek to present their point of view to the government (more specifically, to the secretariats of the Presidency and the Economy).[9] While the federations possess only semiofficial status, they engage in the behind-the-scene compromises and negotiations which have so greatly reduced the incidence of open clashes within Mexico's society.

We have already had occasion to observe that labor leaders have frequently served the interests of their rank and file with something less than full force and that they have enjoyed superior posi-

---

[8] Marion Wilhelm, "Mexicans Hand Reds Stiff Rebuff at Polls," *Christian Science Monitor*, July 11, 1961, p. 12.

[9] For statements regarding these Chambers, see Frank R. Bradenburg, "Organized Business in Mexico," *Inter-American Economic Affairs*, 12 (Winter, 1958), 26–50, esp. 32; and Scott, *Mexican Government in Transition*, pp. 283–286.

tions within the establishment.[10] Moral righteousness is all too easy in such a case. One can well charge "betrayal" and "fraud." But Mexico has long been confronted with problems of inflation and a distorted, quite inequitable wage structure. An arrangement between the governmental and labor hierarchies may be unfair to organized labor, but it serves the unorganized and other elements of the economy. In any event it represents one additional means available to the authorities for reducing the sources of friction and delay that might otherwise interfere with the government's development programs.

A further means of expediting action has been the reliance placed upon a relatively strong president. His powers may have been attenuated to some degree because of the necessity of conciliating a wide range of interest groups, but they are substantial nevertheless; certainly the legislature and the judiciary appear extremely weak by comparison. The chief executive can initiate legislations, he has the right of veto, and he cannot easily be impeached.[11] So much has the bicameral legislature been a rubber stamp that his budget is passed without discussion and without questioning.[12] According to some rumors, undoubtedly exaggerated, Mexicans tend to retire from their lifetime occupations to seats in Congress. The judiciary similarly shows few signs of independence, especially when the president takes a firm position on a given issue. Once chosen, the candidate for president has sufficient power within the PRI to act as the prime agent in the selection of candidates for Congress, the Supreme Court, and state governorships.[13] As president his authority is of particular significance in a federal system in which the national government is so powerful; for example, most of the tax revenues of the states and municipalities accrue to the central government. Finally, as the incumbent president approaches retirement he presides over the selection of his successor in a procedure known as the *tapado*. The term signifies concealed or bottled up and has reference to the fact that the

---

[10] See chapter 3.
[11] Raymond Vernon, *"The Dilemma of Mexico's Development,* p. 63.
[12] Scott, *Mexican Government in Transition,* p. 264.
[13] Washington, "Mexican Resistance to Communism," p. 512.

new president's identity is not revealed until the outgoing president has canvassed the views of the party.[14]

In brief, Mexico's political system virtually defies classification as either democratic or authoritarian. Many of its elements can be designated democratic, and yet by the same token it is lacking in some of the properties associated with a democracy. Frequently the differences between Mexico's political institutions and those of countries generally regarded as democratic are highly subtle and merely matters of degree. Many nations have experienced a growing concentration of power in the chief executive, but the evidence suggests that this has been more extensive in Mexico. In addition, the authorities have possessed the power to eliminate opposition if they so willed, and on occasion they have exercised their power to restrict criticism. Their much more frequent response has of course been to embrace the opposition, unless it was of the very extreme Right or Left, and to work out the differences in behind-the-scenes fashion. However, negotiation within a single party cannot provide a complete substitute for a popular democracy in which more than one party has a reasonably good chance of winning an election. More so than in the cases of two or several parties, the single party presents the economically powerful and the politically aware with the opportunity of dominating decision making. With respect to each of the properties of a political democracy, Mexico thus approaches authoritarianism sufficiently to give solace to the nation's critics and it is sufficiently democratic to give support to her defenders. Under the circumstances it is best to eschew labels, focus on specifics, and adhere to the single conclusion that Mexico has tended to pursue the democratic ideal insofar as her poverty and developmental needs have permitted her to do so.

On the other hand, Mexico's political system has been adequate —highly adequate—for the tasks of economic development. Until the late fifties few would have quarreled with this appraisal. At that time, however, Mexico's economic growth appeared to have slowed down considerably. While many economic factors were responsible for this poorer performance, it is certainly legitimate to inquire whether the political system had become less appropriate

[14] Keith Botsford, "Mexico Follows a 'Solo Camino'," *New York Times Magazine*, April 26, 1964, pp. 64 and 67.

for economic development. And beyond that, what may the near future possibly hold in store for Mexico's political institutions?

In a celebrated work Raymond Vernon has proposed that Mexico's political system has begun to impede her economic growth.[15] In his view, the chief executive has been losing his ability to act decisively. The corroding force is the diffusion of power. The president has always engaged in a trying balancing act: on the one hand he has required a concentration of power and a minimum of negotiation and compromise in order to govern with vigor, but he has also had to counter mounting opposition and permit continual entry into the inner councils of government. Because this second force could not be denied, the strength of the Mexican president has increasingly become a "mirage." Vernon writes: ". . . in his [the President's] ceaseless effort to achieve unanimity, in his concern to extend the reach of the PRI the full distance to both the right and left, he is held to a course of action which is zigzagging and vacillating when it is not blandly neutral."[16] Since much of the stimulus to development must come from within, the president's attempt to placate diverse interests has contributed very significantly to Mexico's economic retardation. Finally, Vernon discusses the possibilities of a stable multiparty system; given the PRI's tradition of conciliation, he does not foresee this as a likely prospect in the near future.

Certainly any analysis of the forces affecting Mexico's economic development, whether past, present, or future, must emphasize the role of government. Assuredly the government has some critical functions to perform if Mexico's economy is to grow rapidly. However, can the degree of political weakness—which Vernon overstates, in my judgment—be attributed so extensively to a conciliatory single party? In opposition to Vernon's thesis, one could ask why, for example, so sharp a *discontinuity* in the diffusion process occurred in the late fifties. Hasn't it been true for some time that the PRI has been broadening its base of support? The counterargument might then be that the Mexican economy was long able to prosper because of external windfalls which stimulated foreign

---

[15] Vernon, *The Dilemma of Mexico's Development*, pp. 128–136 and chapter 7.

[16] *Ibid.*, p. 189.

demand; with a return to a more normal export situation, the growing diffusion of political power had a greater impact. This position, which is not without merit, does permit one to cope with the question of discontinuity, but on economic grounds, not political ones. Moreover, it immediately raises other issues. How would Vernon explain the rapid economic headway that resumed in 1963 and 1964? Hasn't he employed a long term political trend to account for a short term economic phenomenon? Further, his reasoning in effect implies that the central government has long been fairly ineffective in promoting economic development because it has always placated so many diverse interest groups. The historical record will simply not support such a view. Broadly based the party has indeed been, but this has not prevented the government from being a most active and dynamic entrepreneur. In fact, the central position in this chapter has been precisely that the cooperation between groups of varied interests has reduced open conflict and that it has permitted the government to stimulate the country's economy.[17]

The government indeed seemed less equal to the tasks confronting it during the late fifties and early sixties than it had heretofore. This relative weakness was the consequence of not only a greater challenge, attributable to a decreasing dynamism elsewhere in the economy, but also of some diminution in the power of the government to act. Many words have been devoted in this work to the first of these problems. One reason for the second difficulty, the government's inability to move more rapidly, is a disarmingly simple one. In order to expand its activities the central government found it necessary to reform its tax system and increase its revenue. The governmental authorities, economic technicians, and a handful of enlightened laymen aside, no one took kindly to the

---

[17] In his study, *The Dynamic of Mexican Nationalism*, Frederick C. Turner has called attention to the role of nationalism in mitigating dissension among special interests in Mexico. He sees nationalism as having been inspired by the Revolution and fostered by the post-Revolutionary governments to reduce conflict and stimulate economic growth. In his words: "Paradoxically, invocations of nationalism that cloak the demands of special interests embody divisive forces in society, while nationalism as a means of resolving the conflict of special interests is a unifying, cohesive social force. The myth of nationalism and national unity is . . . one means of resolving intergroup conflict" (page 6).

idea of paying more taxes, certainly not in a country where the tradition was one of non–tax payment. Because of the dangers of noncompliance, the government had to compromise and move more slowly in its reform efforts than it might have wished.

A second possible explanation of political weakness is in a sense in direct contrast to the one presented by Vernon: political power may be insufficiently diffused. If the president could act with less restraint, precisely toward which areas would he direct his attention? Surely a high proportion of the government's expenditures would be utilized to assist the least privileged members of the community, most importantly in agriculture but in the urbanized pursuits as well. Indeed the prime task might be that of improving the productivity of these groups. Yet these are the elements with a very minimum of political power. They are the ones who possess little or no political awareness and few voices in the inner councils of party and government. Undoubtedly they contribute very significantly to the two-thirds who do not vote in the national elections. On very rare occasions they may protest their lot by organizing armed bands, but for the most part history has trained them to be nonexplosive. As in the case of tax reform, the impeding factor was the *lack* of a broadly based support for the measures necessary for rapid growth. Again, those favoring a given set of actions were basically the officials and the technicians.

It is in these respects, I believe, that the politics of the late fifties and early sixties differed from the preceding years. The early measures necessary for economic growth tended to be of benefit to those associated with the PRI and/or the government. The later measures were not. Political power and economic needs were less closely associated. Viewed in this fashion, a further diffusion of power within the PRI could very well be beneficial, not harmful, to development. This would of course be the political counterpart of the eventual movements toward greater income equality and the more rapid growth of consumption demand discussed in several of the preceding chapters. Moreover, insofar as the past is a guide the process of diffusion should continue for a considerable time to come. With its openness and flexibility, the PRI will probably embrace new opposing forces as they arise. If it fails to do so, Mexico will lose its lauded political stability.

Mexico's history rather vaguely suggests that the type of democracy which North Americans are most inclined to emphasize —the political—appears the least necessary for economic growth. The executive may be benevolent and permit the existence of many democratic forms, but a true popular democracy, at least as it is conceived in orthodox political theory, may not arise until greater equality has been achieved in the socioeconomic realms. Mexico's moderately "authoritarian," or modestly "democratic," political system may at times have erred economically, but it may yet emerge as a model to be studied and pursued by other developing countries. The system has resulted in order and stability, and it has permitted the nation to devote its energies to economic and social development.

CHAPTER ELEVEN

Conclusions: Income Distribution and Demand in Economic Development

1. It is time to return to the issues posed in the first chapter. The question of "the" relationship between growth and equality, it was asserted, cannot be answered because of multitudinous equalities or inequalities. One must first pluralize or disaggregate equality, and then, and only then, can one address himself to the question of relationships. In some instances the relationship between growth and a type of equality is negative and then positive; in other cases, always positive; and so on.

The first task is therefore one of identifying the various types of equality or inequality.[1] Such classification is, however, a dangerous pastime. The classifier can easily be attacked on the grounds of arbitrariness, since the subject does not always embrace clear-cut distinctions. Moreover, he is readily subject to parody, for the possibilities are virtually endless. (Do all adult males possess an equal opportunity to admire well-groomed girls? No? But never mind, the problem exists only in the short run. Economic development should redress this inequity.) Here we shall briefly review Mexico's experiences with a half-dozen or so of the seriously important categories.

For the most part, Mexico illustrates the mutual interactions which tend to accompany successful economic development. A

---

[1] For one notable attempt at a classification of egalitarianism, see Robert J. Lampman, "Recent Thought on Egalitarianism," *Quarterly Journal of Economics*, 71 (May, 1957), 234–266.

revolution tears at the roots of feudalism, furthers national sovereignty, and establishes a dynamic and strong central government. This encourages activity on the part of domestic private entrepreneurs, which in turn heightens the existent inequality of income distribution. The latter affects saving, consumption, and incentives rather favorably, although it is perhaps invariably associated with activities that do little to encourage growth. The expansions in national income and capital formation provide opportunities for employment and training which make inroads upon the vast disparities in productivity. These advances provide a counterforce, probably an insufficient one, to the growing inequalities in income and consumption. Yet the rise in national income increasingly permits the provision of economic security to households, while the marked income inequality makes such provisions desirable on humanitarian grounds and perhaps imperative on political ones. During the period when income distribution continues its march toward greater inequality, the government already seeks to take steps to reverse the trend once this becomes necessary. These measures can further be sharpened when limited consumption and inadequate investment inducements, rather than limited savings, become the major obstacle to further growth. The government may now find itself in a difficult period, however, since those whom it must now assist may have little representation within it. The required discontinuous change and the attack upon current political-economic power may thus be extremely difficult to engineer. Forced to respond less readily than the economic occasion calls for, the government nevertheless does act, and the society slowly begins to take on greater equality in most of its aspects. Hopefully, as socioeconomic advancements affect most of the nation's citizens, the more stringent requirements of a popular democracy may in due time be fulfilled.

Per capita income and the various types of equality, or inequality, make up the major ingredients of this development. Let Y_p represent per capita income and, as in Chapter One, let D_1, D_2, D_3 . . . D_n symbolize the various components of inequality. More specifically, let D_1 through D_6, respectively, signify the following: social mobility or equality of opportunity, equality of income distribution, equality of consumption, equality in productivity, equality in the degree of economic security, and political democracy.

Then the experience of Mexico suggests the following sequences and relationships, the latter being couched in *ceteris paribus* terms.

Social mobility, D_1, and per capita income, Y_p, tend to reinforce each other, so that the relation between them is positive irrespective of which is regarded as the independent variable. The value of D_1 should rise considerably as economic development ensues.

As Y_p rises, D_2, the equality of income distribution, should fall over an extended period of time. However, its decline eventually tends to slow down and (on the basis of the evidence supplied by the economically advanced countries) to reverse itself.[2] Ignoring the indirect influences operating through Y_p and other variables, a decrease in D_2 may directly hamper D_1. On the other hand the effect of a rise in D_1 upon D_2 is indeterminate, depending upon just who may enjoy the superior economic opportunity.

The relationship between Y_p and D_3, the equality of consumption, generally parallels the relation between Y_p and D_2. A happier circumstance would be one in which D_3 was relatively high at all times.[3] Then a low D_2 might truly serve economic development because of the implications for the propensity to save.

The relation between the equality in productivity, D_4, and Y_p is very difficult to ascertain. The evidence here is scanty. Moreover, as some low income persons acquire more skills, productivity is rendered more equal with respect to the top and middle groups but less so compared to the remaining low income groups. If a nation manages its economic development relatively well, overall D_4 should not deteriorate in the short run, and it may even rise. In the long run the relation between Y_p and D_4 should certainly be positive. It is to be noted that D_4 need not all parallel D_2, the equality of income distribution, in its behavior. This is true for a variety of reasons, including the relatively low price and income elasticities in agriculture, the highly elastic supply curves of labor in urban pursuits, the prevalence of customary prices and wages, and the effects of inflation. Hence D_4 may rise much earlier than D_2, irrespective of whether it first falls when Y_p begins its advance.

Equality in economic security, D_5, may initially be negatively

---

[2] The behavior of D_2 is explored in later sections of this chapter.

[3] See Paul W. Strassman, "Economic Growth and Income Distribution," *Quarterly Journal of Economics*, 70 (August, 1956), 425–440.

related to Y_p, largely because of the disadvantaged and unprotected families in the urban areas. Insofar as it correlates positively with Y_p, it does so with a considerable lag. The effect of rising economic security upon per capita income is indeterminate, depending largely on the forms which security measures assume. When they affect D_4, so that the relation between D_5 and D_4 is positive, they stimulate growth.

Since political democracy is not likely to flourish when economic development ensues, D_6 certainly tends to respond positively to Y_p. However, D_6 may exhibit yet a greater lag than D_5, depending on how one envisages a democratic form of government. Early exogenous changes in D_6 (whether positive or somewhat negative, as under communism) sometimes affect Y_p immediately, but such was not the case in Mexico. Finally, D_6 should bear a positive relation to each of the remaining D's.

Mexico's history thus indicates the intricacy and the complexity in the relationships between economic advancement and the various forms of equality. D_1 and D_6 both tend to rise with Y_p, and even the latter is true only when one discounts communism. Moreover, D_1 should expand together with Y_p, while D_6 may react with a considerable lag. With the growth of Y_p, both D_4 and D_5 may initially decline, but D_4 should rise earlier and advance more rapidly once it does reverse itself, whereas D_5 should move upward somewhat belatedly and very slowly. Finally, D_2 and D_3 may long move downward, with D_3 reversing itself somewhat earlier. Very considerable differences thus appear among the D's in the direction of change, the period of time involved in the movement in either direction, and the rate of change in either direction.

To call attention to the complexity of the relationships is also to counter the fairly popular notion that economic development requires inequality. Depending upon the phase or stage of development, a heightened equality is positively related to economic growth in many respects. This truth is obscured by the conspicuous, and initially converse, role played by income distribution. In due time, as the equality of distribution of income itself exhibits a tendency to rise, all of the designated components of equality tend to be on the upswing. Each of these trends is evidently subject to some upper limit, but these are issues for rich economies. Mexico in the 1960's, with her $300+ per capita income, could still benefit from the promotion of greater equality in its various dimensions.

More generally, the various components of equality interact so that they tend to be propelled in the same direction over long spans of time. If the culture respects and promotes education, the students may play a major role in toppling a political dictatorship; that is apparently what happened to Syngman Rhee in South Korea. If formal training and/or on-the-job experience permit members of the lowest class or caste to become more productive, their social status is likely to rise and they are less likely to find themselves objects of discrimination; Mexico's Indians represent a case in point. If the socioeconomically underprivileged in somewhat richer countries possess the suffrage, they can take political action to mitigate their plight; such a situation can lead, for example, to the adoption of new welfare programs. Given a major revolutionary breakthrough associated with the gaining of independence and/or the termination of feudalistic restrictions, economic development and gradual persistent institutional alterations may thus be effective in promoting the democratic way because of such interactions. Perhaps the evidence will one day permit us to speak not only of self-sustained development but of self-sustained movements toward equality as well.

2. The foregoing represents a capsule summary of the findings. The next undertaking is to review the major propositions in greater detail. For this it would be helpful to have a certain focus—some central issue that provides a framework for presenting the whole in something other than tried and true fashion. I propose that the center of the stage be occupied by per capita income, saving and investment, income distribution, and the components of aggregate demand. In terms of the previous section, D_2 and D_3 are to be highlighted along with the nearly inevitable inclusion of income and capital formation. Interest is to center on the relationship between demand and income distribution.

In discussing the problems of the poorer countries, particularly when analyzing their domestic difficulties, economists have generally had more to say about supply than demand. This is in large part understandable; the emphasis should probably be upon the conditions of supply. Yet there is acute danger in forcing demand to play an unduly subservient role. It is fairly easy to leap from such statements as "the average and the marginal propensities to consume in the poor countries tend to be very high" or "Say's Law tends to be relevant for the underdeveloped areas" to the conclusion that the adequacy of aggregate demand can more or less be taken for granted. A high average propensity to consume may simply characterize stagnation, while each of the other two propositions awaits a prior change. That is, the marginal propensity to consume does not matter unless there is a prior change in income, and supply does not create its own demand in the private sector until entrepreneurs foresee opportunities in growth-inducing activities. While shortages in the productive services frequently frustrate entrepreneurial plans, these plans do not come to the surface unless decision makers can look forward to adequate markets. It is to the credit of Paul Rosenstein-Rodan and Ragnar Nurkse that they made these points explicit.[4] In a much earthier fashion Andrew Carnegie reputedly asserted that he would rather own a market than a mill; with enough sales to count on, he felt, the task of assembling the necessary productive services would be relatively easy.[5] In effect, even in a poor country the inducement to invest is as much an ingredient of capital formation as is the adequacy of investment funds. More generally, adequate demand and available markets are a necessary condition during every phase of development.

However, the process of development generally requires a change in the relative importance of the several *components* of aggregate demand. There is, in fact, a significant linkage between the magnitude of inequality and the composition of demand. If economic growth benefits only a relatively small number at the outset, any increase in consumption is likely to have a fairly narrow base and to be concentrated in luxury goods. As an economy

[4] See Paul Rosenstein-Rodan, "Problems of Industrialization of Eastern and South-Eastern Europe," *Economic Journal*, 53 (June–September, 1943), 202–211; and Ragnar Nurkse, "Some International Aspects of the Problem of Economic Development," *American Economic Review, Papers and Proceedings*, 42 (May, 1952), 570–583.

[5] Stanford Research Institute, *Manual of Industrial Development, With Spe cial Application to Latin America*, p. 41.

continues to advance, however, its growth tends to affect a greater percentage of the population, which then demands more material enjoyments. Increasingly, consumption tends to occur on a mass basis, and insofar as the economy's markets are internal, production tends to follow suit. Without the inducement then provided by expanding consumption, aggregate demand, perhaps no longer bolstered by the components which thrived in the earlier periods, may flounder—and with it the economy's rate of growth. Measures designed to reduce income inequality can thus be beneficial, probably necessary, when the economy requires a changed composition of aggregate demand in order to advance at a regular pace.

The basic point, then, concerns the associations between demand and distribution during the course of economic development. The composition of demand appropriate for a given range of economic development may be functionally related to the degree of inequality of income distribution. The major purpose of this chapter is to explore the nature of these relationships. The chapter aims for some tentative generalizations, perhaps outrageously "bold hypotheses," regarding the changes in income distribution and in the investment, saving, and consumption behaviors that attend economic development. It thus involves an attempt to include income distribution and the components of aggregate demand in a single dynamic system.

The theory embraces Mexico's record of development and perhaps other experiences as well. Although it may possess rather broad applicability, several conditions limit its degree of generalization. One most difficult matter pertains to the social system used as a point of departure. The theory concerns nations which are at first encumbered by "feudalistic" trappings; that is, their societies are initially characterized by little mobility and rigid class relationships. Power may, however, reside essentially in a domestic elite, or it may be held by foreign interests in varying degrees. By the same token, institutional reform may then involve the shedding of colonial ties as well as some dispersion of domestic power. Moreover, relatively newly settled areas may never have been burdened by rigidities of class and status, so that the propositions initially do not apply to them. In brief, the initial social conditions may be quite varied, so that the difficulties of generalization are perhaps greatest in this range. Fortunately, this represents the phase of development which is least germane to the basic problems being examined.

The remaining assumptions can be quickly and easily stated. With the removal or mitigation of the institutional restrictions just mentioned, the nation tends toward a "mixed economy," wherein the private sector generates most of the GNP but the government nevertheless performs an important dynamic function by both inducing and undertaking investment activity.[6] Foreign trade constitutes a fairly significant percentage of over-all activity, although it tends to decline in relative importance over time. Capital-labor ratios are of course low at the outset. If land-labor ratios are similarly low and the rate of population growth is fairly high (some 2 per cent or more per annum), the problems discussed herein are intensified considerably. Given these conditions, let us observe the likely behavior of income distribution and of aggregate demand and its components as societies undergo economic development.

3. "Feudalism" provides the point of departure. Under this system the distribution of income (and wealth, status, power, and prestige) is of course very badly skewed toward the bottom. The society tends to be characterized essentially by two classes, and the top few per cent of the population may well enjoy more than 50 per cent of the total income received. In due time, as a result of a process that may last decades, the system experiences some corrosion, frequently brought on, or at least encouraged, by foreign contacts. A native middle class begins to exhibit some signs of strength. The distribution of income may then be affected, but only in minor fashion. The data, if available, should show some increase in equality at the very top of the income scale, perhaps for no more than the highest 2 or 3 per cent of the income receivers. For the rest, a somewhat greater inequality may now be found between the top group and the remaining income receivers, whose lot generally remains unchanged.

As the economy continues its mild and unspectacular advance,

[6] The greater the direct participation of the public sector in economic affairs the less income inequality matters on aggregative grounds, and in the limiting case of socialism it matters hardly at all. This argument cuts both ways. When additional savings are particularly necessary for economic advance, the government can call forth public saving without relying on income inequality. In turn,

the new entrepreneurial group finds itself hamstrung by the traditional institutions, particularly by an oligarchic government dedicated to the preservation of the status quo. The middle class is
frequently in the best position to institute a discontinuous, revolutionary type of social change in that it may be relatively powerful
as well as discontented. The serfs and peasants, who can generally
lay claim only to the latter and who may in the past have spilled
much blood fruitlessly because they lacked the former, may join
the new elite, and these have often made up the ingredients of a
successful rebellion. In the areas seeking national independence,
the new elite would probably be represented less by business men
and more by intellectuals and the military. In any event, the new
group has now attained the power and prestige which it sought,
while many among the rural masses may receive what they most
desire, namely, freedom from servile obligations and the ownership
of their own land.

The initial revolutionary changes, however, are largely political-
social rather than economic. The middle class and the peasants
each possess more freedom, mobility, and prestige, but the revolutionary and immediate postrevolutionary years tend to disrupt
much of the economic activity. Even if the revolution is quick and
relatively bloodless, the period of adjustment to new forms of economic organization and to new responsibilities is likely to reduce
the national product. The beneficiaries of the revolution thus frequently receive a greater share of a lessened total output during
and immediately following the period of change; their absolute
planes of living may therefore move in either direction during the
time. If a program of land reform is executed very slowly, the
rural masses may be worse off economically, both relatively and
absolutely. While the immediate effects on income distribution are
thus uncertain, the revolution does however serve as an instrument
for weakening other types of inequality.

4. With the elimination, or considerable mitigation, of feudalism, an economy remains too poor to tolerate rapid economic advances on all fronts. Postrevolutionary economic growth initially
graces a relatively small proportion of the whole. A Mexican econ-

income equality is of less moment should demand limitations ever arise, for the
government can again act to remedy the deficiency.

omist, Jorge Espinosa de los Reyes,[7] has offered some explanations of this early tendency toward increasing inequality. He lists among the contributing factors a relative decrease in agricultural productivity, a population growth which contributes to a rising supply of urban labor, a concentration of saving combined with a heightened demand for capital, monopoly and monopsony power in industry, high profits in recently created industries, and a lack of honesty in public administration. To this one might add rising price levels.

The experiences of Mexico tend to support this suggestion of rising inequality at the onset of more rapid economic development. An examination of the very many dimensions of economic inequality—the division of personal income by size, functional income distribution, sectoral income differentials, distribution by geographic zones, the behavior of real wages, the concentration of wealth, the incidence of savings, the composition of consumers' demand, and so on—yields an impression of growing inequality in the country during the twenties and thirties and a rather definite picture of sharply rising inequality in the forties combined with a nearly stabilized or moderately increasing degree of inequality in the fifties.[8] Espinosa de los Reyes has, however, concentrated on the approximate periods of increasing inequality for several of the currently advanced countries.[9] He views the process as having continued until 1850 in the United Kingdom, 1890 in both the United States and Germany, and the 1930's in Japan. In Prussia, for example, during 1854–1875 the income received by the top 5 per cent of the population climbed from 21 per cent to 25 per cent, while the incomes of the lower 90 per cent declined from 73 to 65 per cent of the total incomes received. In a recent work L. J. Zimmerman has employed Pareto coefficients to show that an ". . . increase in the inequality of income distribution is one of the attendant circumstances of economic development";[10] for both England and Germany (Prussia) the coefficients decreased until World

---

[7] Jorge Espinosa de los Reyes, "La distribución del ingreso nacional," in Universidad Nacional Autónoma de México, *Problemas del desarrollo económico mexicano*, pp. 161 ff.

[8] See chapters 5 and 6 of the present work.

[9] Espinosa de los Reyes, "La distribución del ingreso nacional," p. 177.

[10] L. J. Zimmerman, *Poor Lands, Rich Lands: The Widening Gap*, pp. 118–119.

War I. Simon Kuznets has of course performed monumental work in this field. In one source he has shown that the relative income distribution ceased to move toward greater inequality in England sometime before World War I and in Prussia about 1913;[11] elsewhere he has provided evidence of greater inequality in an underdeveloped country than in an advanced one;[12] and he has generally warned against the danger of confusing the dynamic approach of the first with the cross-sectional treatment of the second. This warning bears fruit in the case of India. Her income has not been unequally divided relative to that of the advanced countries, and during some selected years in the fifties her over-all distribution may have even become slightly more equal. On the other hand, during the same period, both capital formation and income inequality in the urban sector increased fairly substantially.[13] It is, of course, the behavior of income inequality within any particular country over time that is germane to the present analysis.

The "logic" of economic development apparently requires that the income distribution initially turn in favor of the rising upper middle income class, typically associated with urban pursuits, and against two other groups: the handful, perhaps 1 or 2 per cent, at the very top and the vast masses below. The process of economic development in effect can be viewed as a gradual swelling of the ranks and incomes of the middle class, a kind of pressing down on the Lorenz curve from the top right, until the middle group begins to embrace most of the gainfully occupied. By the same token an eventual arresting of the development process may be associated with an inability of the lower income groups to regain and then

[11] Simon Kuznets, "Economic Growth and Income Inequality," *American Economic Review*, 45 (March, 1955), 1–28, esp. 4.

[12] Simon Kuznets, "Quantitative Aspects of the Economic Growth of Nations: VIII, Distribution of Income by Size," *Economic Development and Cultural Change*, 11 (January, 1963), part 2, 1–80.

[13] See P. D. Ojha and V. V. Bhatt, "Pattern of Income Distribution in an Underdeveloped Economy: A Case Study of India," *American Economic Review*, 54 (September, 1964), esp. 714–715. To measure the degree of income inequality, the authors employ a concentration ratio which relates the area between a Lorenz curve and the diagonal to the total area under the diagonal. From the two fiscal years 1953–1955 to the two years 1955–1957 the concentration ratio concerned with personal income in the urban sector increased from 0.378 to 0.421.

surpass the relative position which they held around the time of the earlier institutional reforms. This blockage can result from the efforts of the newly privileged group to prevent any inroads upon its relative standing; like the aristocracy whose ranks it once fought so strenuously to enter, it may now struggle to uphold its enhanced position. Even if development proceeds smoothly, only in due time and after some progress has been experienced (probably a number of decades) will the total distribution exhibit greater equality.

This period of rising inequality of income distribution in turn makes the gains of the revolution appear illusory to many. On the one hand income inequality is required for incentives and growth-promoting behavior. This applies especially to entrepreneurs, managers, supervisors, and skilled workmen in the industrial sector whose services are in extremely short supply in the short run. If they are to be attracted to any particular productive activity, the marked inequalities must in all probability occur at least until considerable increases in supply can be forthcoming. On the other hand equality of opportunity (that is, personal freedom and the possibility of social mobility) affects the incentives of the less privileged. More generally, an open society tends to reduce the great disparities in productivity and earnings associated with rigidified non-competing groups.[14] As the Mexican Revolution well illustrates, great economic value attaches to a reduction in discrimination and an increase in social mobility. Thus a conflict in goals soon emerges which is difficult to resolve; it in fact continues to disturb the economically advanced countries, though to a lesser degree. The inequalities in income and wealth desirable for incentive purposes combat with the equalities of opportunity similarly desirable for incentive purposes. Moore's proposition that "a complex division of labor demands . . . at least an approximation to reward by merit"[15] can be interpreted as an argument for both inequality of income distribution and a greater equality of opportunity that encourages the development of one's talents. Mexico, as we have

[14] For the effects of class structure on achievement motivation, see David C. McClelland, "The Achievement Motive in Economic Growth," in B. F. Hoselitz and W. E. Moore, eds., *Industrialization and Society*, pp. 74–96.

[15] Wilbert E. Moore, "Theoretical Aspects of Industrialization," *Social Research*, 15 (September, 1948), 286.

seen, had barely completed her Revolution before she moved into what must have been an era of growing inequality of income distribution. Because of inheritance and similar factors, this in turn rendered the freedoms introduced by the Revolution of considerably less import. Only later, as Mexico gained in wealth, was her government in a position to reduce the inequality of income distribution and to improve the equality of opportunity somewhat, especially through education. The country's remarkable political stability assisted in reducing the potential seriousness of this conflict.

5. While much, perhaps most, of the earlier inequality is necessary for development—and any attempt to eliminate it would be tantamount to halting development—it is certainly not tenable that all of this inequality is necessary for or conducive to economic advancement. For the middle and lower upper income groups to gain relative to the very high income groups is, one would think, beneficial on almost all counts. That the former should also gain at the expense of the poverty-stricken seems only a mixed blessing. On the one hand the whole economy and at least one economic segment are advancing; it would hardly be preferable to have this one element stagnate and remain equal in poverty with the lower income groups. On the other hand there are obviously quantitative limits to the desirability of this type of change. Suppose, for example, that the highest 30 per cent received 95 per cent of the income. The avenues to additional expansion would probably be closed, or at least clogged, because of the implications for incentives, productivity, internal demand, and, in all probability, political stability.

The precise nature of the limitation to growing inequality is arbitrary, and it involves value judgments. Perhaps most observers would agree that an enhanced inequality is not a desirable aspect of economic development if accompanied by absolute declines in the personal incomes of the low income groups. Some might wish to take this one step further by proposing that some modicum of improvement for all income groups is advisable on economic, humanitarian, psychological, and political grounds. Since the underdeveloped world as a whole, including the relatively stagnant countries, has been expanding at a rate of at least 1 per cent per capita per year, a developing economy should be able to provide this modest improvement for the families below the median income level. If the distribution of income initially moves against the low income groups without their suffering declines in their planes of living, or perhaps even while they are gaining in absolute terms, it thus seems reasonable to regard the relative changes as potentially favorable for development. True, the absolute planes of living of the lowest income groups represent only the initial criterion to be employed in judging the value of enhanced income inequality at this point. At least two added criteria include the savings propensities of the favored groups and the eventual allocations of the investment funds. The inequality-saving-investment argument obviously holds only under these growth-inducing conditions, as Mexico's history, pre-1910 as well as post-Revolutionary, abundantly illustrates. However, these represent additional tests. The point at issue is simply that limits need to be placed upon the price paid by the low income groups for the advance of the entire economy.[16]

Why should many families fail to attain growth rates of at least 1 per cent a year? What, in effect, are the forces generally responsible for what may be deemed undue inequality? One explanation is certainly to be found in lagging productivity and is best illustrated by small scale agriculture. While one can hardly demand that full-blown irrigation projects appear throughout the length and breadth of the land in Year I, minor technical improvements can raise productivity and incomes and reduce inequality simultaneously. Unless such programs are quickly pursued, some elements in the rural sector can easily experience absolute declines in their living conditions.

Secondly, while an extremely popular pastime consists of dwelling upon and exaggerating the harms of inflation, rising living costs undoubtedly intensify the inequality of income distribution. If Mexico's experience can be trusted, the literature may be too harsh toward inflation and its effect upon economic development as such. Mexico's inflation was at least moderately associated with (though it did not necessarily "cause") private and public capital formation. Since Mexico's growth record gives fair support to inflation,

---

[16] See chapter 5, the section on personal income distribution, for an attempt to formalize this problem.

it strengthens the income inequality argument in the process. Investment in Mexico led to higher prices and a further skewness of income distribution, and these in turn apparently contributed to additional saving and investment, though not to the extent suggested by the forced saving thesis. On the other hand the rise in prices was quite severe, enough to lower the planes of living of many poor families. Mexico's history further suggests that inflation permits the profit recipients to gain relative to the wage earners—this part of the forced saving sequences is realized—but they may not devote their resources extensively to growth-inducing investment. Particularly high profits may occur in commerce, together with a high propensity to consume on the part of the recipients of property returns.

A third factor may be the degree of monopolization, again evidenced especially in commerce. Here, however, the terrain is difficult. The combination of technological requirements and limited markets may call for only a small number of firms in a given industry; monopolization helps reduce risk and uncertainty, a most important matter in a poorer country; and monopoly power may, in the spirit of Schumpeter, generate business saving. Much of monopoly power in a developing economy may simply be unavoidable. In manufacturing, especially, it may be best to settle for potential competition—that is, for the removal of artificial barriers to entry.

Finally, population growth plays its role. Here we are on more certain grounds than in the instance of monopoly, but perhaps less so than in the case of inflation. When population increases result from reduced death rates, as they now do typically, many of the consequences are highly attractive. Improved health, vitality, and longevity are some cases in point. Then, too, population pressures may, in Hirschman-like fashion, produce demands for action. Yet superior health can be enjoyed even more fully with lower birth rates, and pressure for action may emanate from proper planning, again, if need be, in accordance with Hirschman's prescriptions. Moreover, a high incidence of births strengthens inequality in the rural sector and, through migration, transports it to the towns and cities in the form of depressed real wages. Insofar as the technical relationships between labor and capital are highly substitutive, low wages not only contribute to inequality but discourage capital formation as well. Should the relationships between the productive services generally be complementary, growth and equality do not move in the same direction; a stand-by force may stimulate growth, while the combination of relatively high wage rates and open or concealed unemployment furthers inequality. However, even this latter case is one of degree. A redundant labor force is not advantageous when inadequate demand, particularly a retarded mass consumer market, becomes the major obstacle to development. For the most part, a high rate of population growth engenders a type of inequality not important for growth purposes.[17]

6. We note, next, that advances in mass production and mass consumption do not tend to associate themselves with the earlier phases of economic development. This is particularly true of these goods when they are new in the experience of the people. Admittedly there are some major exceptions to this generalization, probably best illustrated in the contemporary world by small radios, sewing machines, bicycles, and of course cheap textiles. Nevertheless the income elasticity of the demand for food and perhaps for improved housing on the part of farmers and nonfarmers alike is still relatively high, the incomes of most families have not tended to change a great deal and they remain exceedingly low, and the economy simply cannot progress in satisfactory fashion at this point if consumption rises posthaste. These factors spell constraints upon aggregate consumer demands, particularly for most manufactured goods.

Other components of aggregate demand, however, are in a position to provide the necessary markets. The government can certainly help sustain aggregate demand. This has been an integral part of the development of many of today's poorer countries, just as it characterized the economic advancement of Japan and Russia, among others. Governments are in a peculiarly good position to promote increases in aggregate demand, since they can circum-

[17] These arguments serve to throw light on the value of political-ideological labels. "Liberals" are allegedly interested in promoting greater equality. "Conservatives" are likely to look with favor upon higher productivity, general price stability, workable competition, and reduced birth rates. In the paragraphs just concluded, a list of things dear to the hearts of conservatives has been proposed as a means of furthering an objective similarity dear to the hearts of liberals.

vent some important market constraints having to do with risk, profitability, and sufficient credit. Another major source of demand is of course the external one. It is no difficult matter to document the role of foreign trade in spurring economic advancement, as in the case of the United Kingdom, or during the period beginning with World War II. The producers' goods industries may also stimulate each other, with their mutual demands being several times removed from the developments in some particular consumer goods industries. This source of demand, often associated with technological improvements, is again well illustrated by the early industrial growth of the United Kingdom.[18] A frequently experienced case in point has been the demand created for coke as a result of the expansion of an iron and steel industry. Finally, some particularized consumer demand may invigorate part of the economy for a time. This occurred in Mexico some ten to fifteen years after the onset of the Revolution. As the affluent flocked to the center in search of economic security they thereby instituted a tremendous construction boom in Mexico City and adjoining areas.[19]

These several illustrations perform the twofold function of indicating the importance of markets for economic growth and of demonstrating that advances in demand and output can occur without a strong mass consumption market. Yet when a nation seeks growth through industrialization and a greater reliance on domestic demand, it must eventually develop a mass market for its consumer goods as well as a productive apparatus consistent with such a market. This is true in part because the logic of the machine demands mass-produced, standardized commodities. It is true also because of the limitations of the other components of aggregate demand:

(a) Exports tend to be unreliable as a basis for prolonged sustained expansion. Economically they render the poor country— particularly the poor country of the post-World War I era— vulnerable to foreign changes in demand, in the availability of

---

[18] See, for example, Goran Ohlin, "Balanced Economic Growth in History," *American Economic Review, Papers and Proceedings*, 49 (May, 1959), 338–353.

[19] See Edmundo Flores, "The Significance of Land-Use Changes in the Economic Development of Mexico," *Land Economics*, 35 (May, 1959), 115–124.

goods, and in commercial policy. If export earnings continue un-abated, the affluence of the export sector in the midst of an un-satisfied hunger for consumption goods can create political-eco-nomic havoc because of the creation of a dual economy. When a relatively small economy does base its long run growth on exports, as in the too frequently cited instances of Denmark and New Zea-land, a combination of relatively secure markets and a series of reforms permitting eventual mass consumption appears necessary. The wage goods of course then originate in the flow of imports rather than in standardized production. As for the first require-ment, that of reducing the uncertainty attending foreign trade, the major substitute for a *modus vivendi* with a richer country as-sumes the form of cooperation with other poor countries, as in the case of trading blocs, customs unions, and regional developments. These devices for enhancing both the size and predictability of markets tend to lead, however, to precisely the standardized pro-duction here being advocated. The only remaining alternative for a small country is the relatively slow, haphazard, uncontrolled, export-based growth which most underdeveloped areas object to so strenuously. A larger country certainly cannot be expected to concentrate on such a model indefinitely.

(b) If luxurious and fairly particularized types of demand have initially carried the growth process, this by definition limits the scope of the economy's advancement. The resulting composition of demand simply cannot satisfy the needs of development. The market tends to direct resources to such activities as luxury hous-ing, services and the production of highly differentiated goods. Such items call for hand labor and/or the machine production of high priced, high profit margin, low volume goods.

(c) Technological change may support a satisfactory growth rate indefinitely, but to rely solely or largely on this source of investment is to burden it unduly. In the advanced economies this has been aided and abetted by the upward shifts in the analytical consumption functions associated with rising living standards.

(d) The government's demand for goods and services is in a rather unique position. If unwisely conceived and poorly executed, governmental activity may be so associated with waste and cor-ruption that it becomes politically and economically intolerable. Uncontrolled inflation and/or unduly high expenditures on the military establishment are two cases in point. On the other hand if the government's demand does serve to increase the wealth and productivity of the economy it almost certainly facilitates the appearance of a mass market because of multipliers and the effects on productivity and capacity. Under either set of circumstances the private sector is likely to resist unlimited expansion of the government's contribution to the economy.

Thus any one of the components of demand which had previously provided the markets for the economy's expansion may falter, whereupon the development of heretofore weak mass markets and the standardized production of consumer goods offer the soundest basis for further economic advancement. That the economy has arrived at this state is actually a token of its progress, for it has now just begun to acquire the properties of an "affluent society." It may yet remain transitional, however, with respect to its capital-labor ratios; that is, it may still experience capital shortages and disguised and/or open unemployment. This of course places serious constraints upon rising wage rates as sources of enhanced consumer purchasing power. Particularly is this true when the substitutability between capital and labor is highly limited, whereupon higher wages tend to depress capital formation and to add to open unemployment. These difficulties suggest the value of continuing to stabilize real wage rates in the capital intensive sectors and of minimizing vast disparities within the entire wage structure. (Among other things, this requires a consistent policy toward unionization on the part of the government.) Income distribution is to be rendered less unequal, and consumption stimulated, more through the expansion of employment opportunities in the highly productive industries than through an increase in wage rates as such. Considerably more so than in the advanced countries, the governments of the transitional economies must encourage structural changes in the work force through policies designed to stimulate capital formation and improve the quality of the work force. Heightened productivity in agriculture as well as the organization of rural labor, to the fullest extent possible, should prove rewarding. Despite optimum wage rates, however, the inducement to invest may be inadequate, because of weak markets. Insofar as exports grow and technological changes flourish widely, this problem is attenuated. If these fail to provide adequate support, the government's share of the national product must increase temporarily until the forces of change establish mass production. Public welfare measures may prove increasingly necessary. To the utmost of political feasibility, the authorities should heighten tax revenue and reduce the degree of regressiveness in the fiscal system.

In brief, the particular phases of a nation's development have implications for both the structuring of its aggregate demand and its degree of income inequality. The elimination of the existing capital shortage and labor redundancy need not signal the required change, since demand difficulties can easily arise beforehand. The relevant series to examine are those pertaining to income, consumption, private investment, and the other components of demand. If the growth rate of an economy has been rapid for several decades and then shows signs of receding, if the private investment coefficient, $\frac{I}{Y}$, and the rates of increase in investment, $\frac{\Delta I}{I}$, tend to stabilize or fall off, and if other major components of aggregate demand, such as investment based on technological borrowing, exports, or luxurious consumption, cannot continue their earlier pace, the time for altering the direction of income redistribution has in all probability arrived.

7. The several phases of development just discussed can be represented in a diagram and then in a model. The concepts included in the diagram are the familiar ones of income or output, saving, and investment, though with some slight variations. Each is corrected for price changes. Gross output per head appears on the horizontal axis; aggregate income or output could also be utilized, but per capita concepts lend themselves more readily to international comparisons. The per capita incomes occurring later in time generally appear further to the right on the axis, but given occasional recessions this need not always be the case. Ex ante per capita saving and investment each appear on the vertical axis; the investment variable reflects opportunities for which the anticipated profit rates are at least "normal." Each variable pertains to indigenous activities, but either may be influenced by international capital flows. For example, direct foreign investment shifts the investment function upward if it introduces new commodities which domestic entrepreneurs may exploit or downward if it

concerns established and competitive goods. Similarly, foreign enterprises may influence expectations and therefore the propensity to save. However, these effects are indirect. International capital flows ar not represented directly in the function but rather act as instruments of adjustment when disparities between investment opportunities and saving occur.

The shortage of saving in an exceedingly poor, virtually stagnating country is probably exaggerated. This is evidenced by the surplus typically available for such noneconomic and/or unproductive ends as the accumulation of precious metals, the maintenance of armies, and the observance of religious rituals. Saving therefore need not expand markedly with the first signs of significant economic progress. Initially the saving function may be quite flat and exhibit a rather low, albeit positive, second derivative. Thereupon it proceeds to take on the properties of long run savings functions in the more advanced economies and approaches linearity—a sign, of course, of its close dependence on income. The investment curve, on the other hand, lies relatively close to the income axis when the economy is very poor because of inadequate investment opportunities. This function responds quite sharply to the removal of feudalistic restrictions and the appearance of a government committed to economic development. The second derivative then tends to be not only positive but relatively high. The curve continues to climb rapidly as superior foreign techniques are assimilated, the government contributes social overhead, and exports and/or a particularized consumption demand create additional demands for capital goods. In due time, as the best available opportunities are exploited, the investment curve tends to fall off with further increases in income. The first derivative may still tend to be positive, but the second can easily adopt a minus sign at this point. If the function levels off sufficiently within this range it can retard, even arrest, the growth process. A redistribution of income in favor of the lower income groups may then preserve the expansion of investment. By the same token such income redistribution would rotate the saving curve downward, but since the resulting increase in income should make for a more rapid movement along the saving function, the net effect on absolute per capita saving should be positive.

These propositions give rise to the functions depicted in Figure 5.

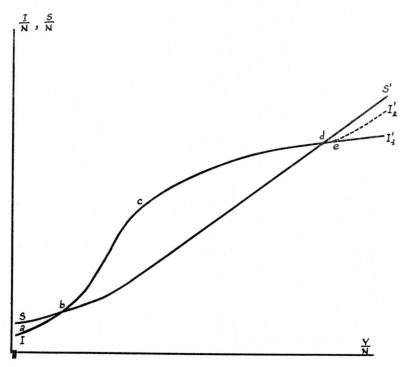

Figure 5. Proposed Relationship between Per Capita Income and
Per Capita Investment and Saving

The *II'* curve shows the investment opportunities per head as a function of per capita income, while *SS'* indicates the relationship between saving and income, again in per capita terms. For middle income countries the savings function tends to be the lower of the two;
for the very poor and the rich countries it is the *II'* curve that lies
below. The lower curve places the constraints upon capital forma-
tion and determines the ex post investment coefficient, $\frac{I}{Y}$ $(= \frac{I}{N} / \frac{Y}{N})$.
While ex ante per capita saving and per capita investment each de-
pend upon the level of per capita income, the rate of increase in
the income variable is thus in turn governed by the function that
lies closer to the income axis. Given a constant output-capital ratio,
the lower function determines the pace at which the economy can

move, and, as long as its slope is positive, introduces a higher plane of living in the next period. It will also be noted that the II' and SS' functions intersect at two points. These certainly have nothing to do with static equilibrium, since a change in per capita income normally occurs in either case. If "equilibrium" is at all appropriate at the intersection of $\frac{I}{N}$ and $\frac{S}{N}$, it is an unstable dynamic equilibrium in which the two variables are equal in contributing to, and placing constraints upon, the growth process. Whether this position is to be acclaimed or deplored depends primarily on the given levels of $\frac{I}{N}$ and $\frac{S}{N}$. If both were higher, then irrespective of their equality or inequality the economy would grow more rapidly, assuming the capital-output ratios as given at that point. A wide disparity between $\frac{I}{N}$ and $\frac{S}{N}$ does, however, denote either a considerable waste of economic surplus, when $\frac{S}{N} > \frac{I}{N}$, or a loss of opportunities for development, when $\frac{I}{N} > \frac{S}{N}$. The optimum is thus represented by a relatively high level equality of $\frac{I}{N}$ and $\frac{S}{N}$.

Several other properties of these functions also invite comment —of as brief a character as the material permits.

(a) One might wish to go beyond ex ante domestic saving and embrace all potential sources of investment funds, such as the creation of money by domestic institutions and the procurement of funds from abroad. This would give rise to a new function, evidently lying above SS' and in all probability sloping upward more sharply to the right. Since these added sources of funds help relieve the saving bottleneck in the middle income range, they should reduce the time period of required growing income inequality. On the other hand, insofar as they also contribute to inflation they may well render the income inequality more intense unless, and until, the low income groups find a way of hedging against inflation.

(b) It is further tempting to play with the possibilities of lags. Does the investment opportunities curve depend on current per capita income, as described, or is it to be related to increases in income over the past period, as most acceleration theories would have it? Accelerator models which relate investment to incomes of past periods generally imply a certain pessimism, or at least conservatism, on the part of investors, who perpetually order capital goods on the basis of bygone levels of incomes. This is not the kind of behavior to be anticipated from investors in a young, rapidly growing economy. Entrepreneurs expect income to move ahead and they invest accordingly. Under these conditions it is highly respectable to assume investment to be a function of current, rather than lagged, income. This is tantamount to employing an accelerator of the type $I_t = v (Y^E_{t+1} - Y_t)$, where Y^E_{t+1} represents the expected income of the coming period. In effect, by investing in this period (induced investment is a function of to-day's income), firms are counting on rising incomes and sales in the next period. Once the investment opportunities curve begins to fall off, the kind of thinking implied in most accelerator models begins to predominate, and the introduction of lags is probably desirable. Since the assumption that I is a function of Y is the simpler one and lends itself more easily to the employment of data, since it does imply an accelerator of a certain type, and since, finally, it is relevant in a growing economy no less frequently than the more common form of the accelerator, it is accepted here. Similar arguments appear in the saving case. Undue complications, such as those attending the technical problems of dating, would arise if savings were made to depend upon last period's income.

(c) The graph is fairly useful for an analysis of growth forces and necessary institutional changes. However, it fails to depict the basic underlying dynamics of change, which may be thought of as a mutual interaction among the variables strategic for development—what Gunnar Myrdal has referred to as cumulative causation.[20] Figure 5 does not emphasize this type of movement. Income does affect investment opportunities and the supply of savings, but the counterinfluence of these two variables on income is only implied. To give graphic representation to the mutual interplay that occurs in successful development, one can readily employ a system of four quadrants, as in Figure 6. The upper right quadrant depicts the now familiar saving and investment function. Moving counterclockwise, the graph in the upper left quadrant has the ex post equalities of saving and investment on the horizontal axis and traces the behavior of these variables. Since this curve always reflects the behavior of the smaller of the two ex ante concepts, it

[20] Gunnar Myrdal, *Rich Lands and Poor*, chapter 2.

initially rises at an increasing rate (a portion of II' and then SS'), then approximates linearity (the SS' influence), and finally continues upward at a decreasing rate (the effect of the II' curve again). The third, lower left quadrant features the realized $\frac{I}{N}$ and $\frac{S}{N}$, as before, on the horizontal axis and $\frac{Y}{N}$ on the vertical one. The function in this case is the reciprocal of the incremental capital output ratio, here assumed to be linear. Then realized $\frac{I}{N} \cdot \frac{\Delta Y}{\Delta K}$ equals the rise in $\frac{Y}{N}$ in the forthcoming period, which can be indicated on the vertical axis. To it may be added the current level of $\frac{Y}{N}$ thereby yielding the per capita income in the next period. That is, the $\frac{Y}{N}$ of the following period is given as $\frac{Y+\Delta Y}{N}$. (If one also wished to take account of population growth, this could be done by introducing ΔN exogenously. Thereupon the new $\frac{Y}{N}$ would be given by $\frac{Y+\Delta Y}{N+\Delta N}$.) Finally, this may be transferred to the horizontal axis of the upper right quadrant by means of a forty-five degree line that cuts through the lower right quadrant. Tomorrow's per capita income thereby becomes today's per capita income and affects $\frac{I}{N}$ and $\frac{S}{N}$ anew.

8. While the introduction of four quadrants highlights the interplay between income growth and capital formation, it still fails to give adequate representation to the influence of income distribution. This variable merely assumes an exogenous role; when it alters, the functions in the upper right quadrant shift their positions. More attention needs to be given also to the components of aggregate demand. It thus seems advisable to construct a relatively simple model that includes these and other variables. This exercise shall then allow some arithmetic illustrations that are useful for further elucidation.

The system calls first for several groupings. In keeping with a long established tradition, the instruments of production may be classified simply as either labor or capital. Nothing is specifically assumed about "the" production function, except that there is less substitutability between the two inputs in urban pursuits than in agriculture. The private portion of national income may be broken down into wages, W, and property returns, P. The economy may further be divided into investment and consumption or saving and consumption as the case may be. Yet another breakdown is given by the private and the public sectors.

The categories of course overlap. Both the private and govern-

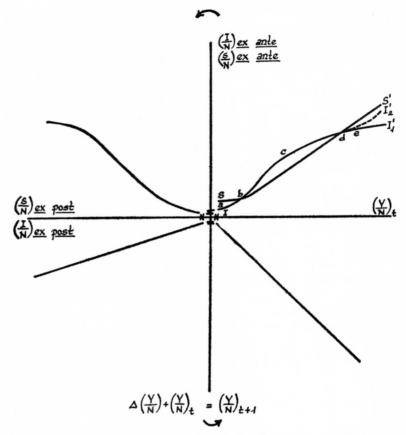

Figure 6. Proposed Mutual Interaction between Per Capita Income and Per Capita Investment and Saving

mental sectors employ labor and capital, and both engage in invest-ment and consumption. The total national product, Y, thus equals the sum of I_g, I_p, C_g, and C_p, where g represents government and p indicates the private sector. The two sets of public activities, I_g and C_g, are given to the system. Private and governmental investment bear a fairly constant relation to one another, so that $I_g = iI_g$. The two investment categories expressed as percentages of the national product each tend to rise during stage two (the range from b to d in Figure 5) and then level off during stage three (beyond d). Governmental consumption, as a percentage of the total product, $\frac{C_g}{Y}$, rises by a few percentage points throughout the course of development.

National output, the capital stock, and per capita income each grow over time, as given, respectively, by $\frac{\Delta Y}{Y} = \frac{S}{Y} / \frac{\Delta K}{\Delta Y}$, $\frac{\Delta I}{I} = \frac{\Delta S}{\Delta Y} / \frac{\Delta K}{\Delta Y}$, and $\Delta\left(\frac{Y}{N}\right) / \left(\frac{Y}{N}\right) = \frac{\Delta Y}{Y} - \frac{\Delta N}{N}$. Total saving S equals $S_p + (T - C_g) + F$, where T indicates tax revenue less transfers, F represents foreign investment funds, and each is given exogenously. The marginal propensity to save $\frac{\Delta S}{\Delta Y}$ exceeds the average $\frac{S}{Y}$, and it increases less than the average over time. The two population variables N and ΔN are also exogenous. While the rate of population growth can evidently be related to changes in per capita income, the model focuses upon the alterations in per capita income which can be traced primarily to the developments in the income variable.

The national income is further divided among wages and property returns, inclusive of public transfer payments, and taxes net of transfers. The relative shares in turn exercise a strong influence of saving and consumption behavior. Thus ex ante per capita saving $\frac{S_a}{N}$ is a function not only of $\frac{Y}{N}$, as in Figures 5–6, but also of $\frac{P}{Y}$ and deliberate public policies and other exogenous forces, X. The latter two of course shift the SS' curve. Alternately, private savings can be related to property and wage incomes and therefore to Y and X, and the results may be divided by Y or N as one wishes. To retain the concepts of the relative shares, let us write $\frac{S_p}{Y} = m\frac{P}{Y} + l\frac{W}{Y}$ and, by the same token, $\frac{C_p}{Y} = (1-m)\frac{P}{Y} + (1-l)\frac{W}{Y}$, where m is the propensity to save out of property income and l represents the propensity to save out of labor income. Labor's propensity to save l may reasonably be assumed to be zero, particularly in stages one and two, but Mexico's experience points to the foolhardiness of presupposing that the propensity to save out of property income is 1. Nevertheless, in stages one and two only the recipients of property incomes by assumption engage in private saving, and in stage three they are responsible for the lion's share. Hence, as a first approximation the propensity to save in the private sector depends upon their income share and their saving propensity; that is,

$\frac{S_p}{Y} = \frac{S_p}{P} \cdot \frac{P}{Y}$ and $\frac{\Delta S_p}{\Delta Y} = \frac{\Delta S_p}{\Delta P} \cdot \frac{\Delta P}{\Delta Y}$. The average propensity to save out of property income tends to rise over time as does the marginal but to a lesser degree. The wage and property shares in the national income depend not only upon X, that is, the public policies and a complex of exogenous institutional arrangements, but also upon $\frac{Y}{N}$. Thus $\frac{P}{Y}$ tends to expand during stages one and two and to contract during stage three; while $\frac{W}{Y}$ behaves conversely.

Of considerable significance for the model is what might be deemed a stages theory of investment constraints. The major objective of public policy is the most rapid annual advance of per capita income, although in the everyday world this will have to be tempered by judgments regarding the tolerable limits of unemployment, inflation, political unrest, and similar causes of concern. The advances in per capita income depend upon the increases in capital formation per head, ex post. The latter in turn are constrained at different times by limited inducements to invest (stages one and three) and limited resources for capital formation (stage two). When saving and investment are thought of in ex ante or functional terms, $\frac{S_a}{N} > \frac{I_a}{N}$ in stages one and three and $\frac{I_a}{N} > \frac{S_a}{N}$ in stage two, as noted in the discussion of Figure 5. Over the course of stage two $\frac{S_a}{N}$ restricts the expansion and determines realized $\frac{I}{N}$, while during the first and third stages $\frac{I_a}{N}$ imposes the limits upon development and determines realized $\frac{S}{N}$. $\frac{S_a}{N}$ and $\frac{I_a}{N}$ each depend upon $\frac{Y}{N}$ and the various exogenous forces X, but in addition $\frac{S_a}{N}$ is a function of $\frac{P}{Y}$ and $\frac{I_a}{N}$ is also functionally related to the rate of increase of per capita consumption in the private sector, $\Delta(\frac{C_p}{N})/(\frac{C_p}{N})$. According to the hypotheses, this last factor assumes particular significance in stage three. It in turn is related to $\frac{W}{Y}$.

Let us now trace the possible developments of these variables by appealing to Mexico's economic history whenever it is helpful to do so. The specific magnitudes will of course vary among countries; indeed sometimes, as with the ratios of tax revenues or governmental expenditure to national income, they will vary to a considerable extent. Under such circumstances the directions of change of the variables and the interrelationships among them should still prove interesting.

Of considerable significance is the behavior of $\frac{s_p}{Y}$. Once the necessary institutional reforms have occurred and the economy has passed into the second stage, the wage earners refrain from saving, as heretofore, but the recipients of property incomes exhibit some tendency to increase their saving. Let us assume that their average propensity is 0.15 and that their marginal propensity to save equals 0.2. Hence $\frac{s_p}{Y}$ must advance over time, since the margin exceeds it. Further, it should increase as the margin itself rises to some degree and as $\frac{P}{Y}$ also rises. Initially permit $\frac{P}{Y}$ to equal 40 per cent. Thereupon $\frac{s_p}{Y} = 0.06$. If the incremental capital-output ratio $\frac{\Delta K}{\Delta Y}$ and the rate of population increase $\frac{\Delta N}{N}$, respectively, equal 3 and 0.02, then insofar as the private sector alone contributes to growth, $\frac{\Delta Y}{Y} = 0.02$ and $\Delta\left(\frac{Y}{N}\right)/\left(\frac{Y}{N}\right)$ is reduced to zero.

This of course still leaves public investment unaccounted for. In keeping with Mexico's record, let the government's investment comprise two-thirds of private realized investment. During the course of stage two this constant ratio between the investments in the two sectors implies that a rise in the property share increases the public investment coefficient $\frac{I_g}{Y}$ as well as the private coefficient $\frac{I_p}{Y}$; but perhaps more so, an expansion in $\frac{I_g}{Y}$ raises $\frac{P}{Y}$ and increases $\frac{I_p}{Y}$. Also, domestic private and public saving should be supplemented by a trickle of foreign funds, F, shared equally by government and private industry. Thereupon $\frac{I}{Y}$ in the aggregate rises to just over 0.1, and, given a $\frac{\Delta K}{\Delta Y}$ of 3, the national output expands at an annual rate of $3\frac{1}{2}$ per cent. In turn, the rate of increase in investment, $\frac{\Delta I}{I}$, is influenced by the marginal propensity to save for the entire economy, which can be determined simply from $\frac{\Delta S}{\Delta Y} = \frac{\Delta S_p}{\Delta Y} + \frac{\Delta(T-C_g)}{\Delta Y} + \frac{\Delta F}{\Delta Y}$. For the private sector, $\frac{\Delta S_p}{\Delta Y} = \frac{\Delta S_p}{\Delta P} \cdot \frac{\Delta P}{\Delta Y}$, where, as already indicated, $\frac{\Delta S_p}{\Delta P}$ is 0.20 and $\frac{\Delta P}{\Delta Y}$ can be assumed to be 0.45. Then $\frac{\Delta S_p}{\Delta Y}$ is 0.09. The marginal propensities do not exceed the average by the same proportion for the remaining sources of saving (so that the government deficit as a percentage of national income should rise). Let $\frac{\Delta(T-C_g)}{Y} + \frac{\Delta F}{\Delta Y}$ be 0.06. Thereupon $\frac{\Delta S}{\Delta Y}$ is 0.15, and $\frac{\Delta I}{I}$ equals 0.05, or $1\frac{1}{2}$ percentage points in excess of the rate of increase in income. Finally, it is possible to determine the rate of

Concept	% At the Onset of Stage 2, Beyond b in Figure 5. ($\$150 > \frac{Y}{N} > \$100$)	At the Onset of Stage 3, Beyond e in Figure 5. ($\$325 > \frac{Y}{N} > \$250$)
I/Y	10.5	16.5
I_g/Y	4.2	6.5
I_p/Y	6.3	10.0
C/Y	89.5	83.5
C_g/Y	3.0	4.5
C_p/Y	86.5	79.0
T/Y	7.0	10.5
P/Y	40.0	38.0
W/Y	53.0	51.5
$m(=S_p/P)$	15.0	25.0
$I\ (=S_p/W)$	0.0	2.0
S/Y	10.5	16.5
S_p/Y	6.0	9.5
$(T\text{-}C_g)/Y$	4.0	6.0
F/Y	0.5	1.0
$\Delta Y/Y$	3.5	5.5
$\Delta N/N$	2.0	3.0
$\Delta(\frac{Y}{N})/(\frac{Y}{N})$	1.5	2.5
$\Delta S/\Delta Y$	15.0	16.5
$\Delta I/I$	5.0	5.5
$\Delta C_g/C_g$	1.0	5.5
$\Delta C_p/C_p$	3.4	5.5
I_a/Y	>10.0	16.5
S_a/Y	10.0	>16.5

* Throughout, the marginal capital-output ratio is assumed to be as high as 3.
This may be somewhat on the conservative side, and hence it may understate
the rate of increase in income associated with any given $\frac{I}{Y}$. In column 2, for example, the $\frac{I}{Y}$ of 16.5 per cent could well give rise to a $\frac{\Delta Y}{Y}$ of at least 6 per cent.
It is to be stressed that while the relative shares in column 2 approximate
those in column 1, they have altered considerably during the interval between
the beginning of stage two and the early phases of stage three. Thus $\frac{P}{Y}$ may have
exceeded 50 per cent during its peak while $\frac{W}{Y}$ dropped as low as 40 per cent.
Mixed incomes would either be prorated or divided equally between capital and
labor.

The symbols are explained in the text. The ones that may not be immediately
evident are p, g, P, and N, which, respectively, represent the private sector,
government, property income, and population.

increase in private consumption, once the growth in government consumption is given, by assigning appropriate weights to the rates of increase of the various components.[21] The annual rate of increase in private consumption, $\frac{\Delta c_p}{c_p}$, then registers at 3.4 per cent. (See Table 57, column 1, for a summary of the various computations.)

The economy is now well on its way as it moves along within the second stage. The distribution of income becomes less equal as a result of the process of development (note the effects of differences in productivity, inflation, high supply prices, and so on), together with exogenous shocks favorable to profits (such as demands associated with warfare) and perhaps the adoption of deliberate public policies. Insofar as the latter are required they should not be difficult to implement on the expenditures side. The public sector, in Mexico as elsewhere, initially tends to emphasize tangible capital. Thereupon

. . . the entrepreneurial class is likely to derive benefits at least in proportion to its income from such social overhead capital as highways, communications, and improved port facilities. These social capital facilities are likely to widen the range of profitable investment opportunities and thus compensate the entrepreneurs for their increased tax burden.[22]

On the revenue side the governing point is that the consumption activities of profit earners tend to hamper economic development as much as the consumption of any other income recipients. This suggests a tax system that favors the profit recipients in their capacity as savers and investors. Personal income tax rates can be made fairly progressive, for example, while various deductions and allowances, such as accelerated depreciation, are permitted for investment activities. As noted, Mexico was for a time remiss in these respects.

Let $\frac{P}{Y}$ continue to climb until it attains, let us say, the relatively high ratio of 0.5. Further $\frac{S_p}{P}$ has risen, since it is less than $\frac{\Delta S_p}{\Delta P}$; let

[21] The expression in question is $\frac{\Delta Y}{Y} = \left(\frac{c_p}{Y}\right) \cdot \left(\frac{\Delta c_p}{c_p}\right) + \left(\frac{c_g}{Y}\right) \cdot \left(\frac{\Delta c_g}{c_g}\right) + \left(\frac{I}{Y}\right) \cdot \left(\frac{\Delta I}{I}\right)$, where everything but $\frac{\Delta c_p}{c_p}$ is known.

[22] John H. Adler, "The Fiscal and Monetary Implementation of Development Programs," *American Economic Review, Papers and Proceedings,* 42 (May, 1952), 600.

the new average propensity to save out of property income be 22 per cent. As a result $\frac{S_p}{Y}$ equals 11 per cent, $\frac{I}{Y}$ rises to nearly 18 per cent, national income expands at a rate of 6 per cent a year, and, insofar as $\frac{\Delta P}{\Delta Y} > \frac{P}{Y}$ and $\frac{\Delta S_p}{\Delta P} > \frac{S_p}{P}$, $\frac{\Delta I}{I} > \frac{\Delta Y}{Y}$, amounting to 7 per cent or more a year. These rates of expansion resemble those experienced by Mexico during the fifties, although the investment coefficient here is considerably higher than in the actual case. However, the economy cannot employ this path of economic development endlessly. Assume that $\frac{P}{Y}$ continued to rise until it reached 60 per cent, while $\frac{S_p}{P}$ attained nearly 30 per cent because of the influence of a higher margin. This would imply, on the basis of the assumed relationships, a private investment coefficient of 18 per cent, a total investment coefficient of 30 per cent, and an income growth rate of 10 per cent, results not easily sustained in the everyday world. Further, in an economy advancing so rapidly, recipients of property incomes could well be both willing and able to raise their marginal savings propensities, while the favored earners of wages and salaries could raise their propensities to save above zero. In sum, the time would come when the economy would possess a remarkable capacity for generating saving, given the continuation of the trends in income distribution and per capita income in stage two. The issue would then become one of the *purposes* of capital formation. What would be the incentive to invest if the capital stock rose in this fashion? Under the circumstances the realized investment coefficient would undoubtedly fall (and/or the capital stock output ratio would rise), leading to reduced rates of growth in output of about 3 or 4 per cent a year and to little change in per capita income.

More rapid rates of increase in the per capita consumption of wage goods hardly provide a complete solution to these problems, but they would certainly be of assistance. Income distribution should now become more equal, as represented by a rising $\frac{W}{Y}$. Economic development may itself furnish some of the sources of this reversal; for example, capital formation may raise labor productivity and wage incomes in particular industries. But the modifications brought about through "natural" processes tend to promote greater equality over one range of the Lorenz curve and less over another, as with the changes in productivity associated with occupational shifts. More seriously perhaps, they tend to be gradual and continual in character. Public policy must therefore provide a supplement, and more so than in the second stage. The government can, for example, step up its expenditures on education in order to improve labor's productivity. Admittedly, outlays on general education also do not bear fruit for some time, but this is not necessarily true of vocational training at the intermediate levels. This can also become the occasion for a greater concern with productivity in low income agriculture or with the degree of monopoly power in industry. Further, the government can expend its welfare–social security programs sufficiently to relax the principle of self-support and, as in the economically advanced countries, utilize subsidies and transfer payments as a means of bolstering aggregate demand.

These policies help shift the investment function upward, raise the total realized investment coefficient to 16 per cent or more, and advance the average over-all growth rate to about 6 per cent a year. As the economy moves past e within stage three, then insofar as the Mexican case offers guidance, I_p approaches 10 per cent of the gross national product, I_g constitutes at least 6 per cent, C_g lies in the vicinity of 4 per cent, and C_p makes up the remaining 80 per cent or less. (The last two magnitudes reflect Mexico's relatively low military expenditures.) The rates of increase of these various categories tend to be equal. The national income is further divided so that wages, property income, and tax revenue net of taxes, respectively, account for more than 50 per cent, less than 40 per cent, and about 10 per cent of the total. (See Table 57, column 2 for a more detailed presentation.) The economy thereby sustains its advance.

9. It will be noted that the II' curve in Figures 5 and 6 possesses two inflection points at a and c, a highly probable inflection point at e, and two points of intersection with SS', b and d. Each tends to be associated with institutional changes which permit movements along the function and, consequently, advances in per capita income. These points call not only for a description of the institutional changes which must be effected but also for some account of the manner in which the alterations may be introduced.

The changes most difficult to introduce are likely to occur at *a*—though, as previously mentioned, some newly settled communities may be fortunate enough to avoid it altogether and begin in the vicinity of *b*. The modification at *a* is the one that at least reduces the major feudalistic privileges, and it can well exact bloodshed before it becomes successful. In Western European experience it was directed by the middle class. This is the most likely source of leadership, since no strong labor movement has yet emerged, and the peasants, serfs, and peons tend either to remain passive or to fail when they become restive and disrespectful. The U.S.S.R. and Communist China lend themselves less readily to these generalizations regarding the role of the middle class, but even in these cases communism hardly sprang forth in full bloom after a mitigation of feudalism. Russia experienced its emancipation of the serfs, the 1905 reforms, and considerable capitalistic development prior to 1917. In China, communism arrived almost four decades after the 1911 Revolution, with little increase in per capita income during the interim. Graphically, Chinese history between 1911 and 1949 can be represented in both the shapes and positions of the *SS'* and *II'* curves. That is, the several points of inflection and intersection are clustered together over a small range along the horizontal axis, while the curves tend to shift inwardly over time in response to population growth. In any event, while a heretofore stagnating feudalistic society can conceivably find itself under the leadership of the extreme Left as it begins to experience economic growth, history supports a generalization favoring non-Communist, typically middle-class direction both during and after the alleviation of feudalism. In more recent years the leadership has increasingly emanated from the military and the intellectuals, in large part because the revolution has frequently involved the attainment of national independence. In these instances, also, the newly created countries have not tended toward communism in order to achieve their national goals.

The dating of *a*, and then of the range *ab*, is generally not a facile task. For Mexico *a* is represented by the Revolution of 1910–1920; while *ab* is of much shorter duration. The more effective the changes at *a*, the more rapidly an economy can experience growth (and its initial attending income inequality) and the less it need linger in the vicinity of the per capita income represented by *ab*. Be that as it may, the range *ab* tends to be of relatively short duration and the per capita income alters little over its course.

The institutional changes required at *b* are least likely to occasion difficulty. The nature of political-economic power is such that its possessors should somehow manage to bring about the necessary increase in income inequality. If this is not accompanied by serious absolute declines in planes of living and if the previous changes have been fairly sweeping, then the combination of the recency of reforms, the lag in the populace's awareness of the relative changes in income and wealth, and the probable spurt in economic activity can render the phase represented by *bc* a period of relative political calm and stability. Further, the more radical groups require some time to augment and cement their forces. The atmosphere should be one of considerable unity fostered by favorable and rising expectations, given the above conditions.

In some instances in history the remaining turning points have occasioned the greatest difficulty and have eventually erupted into violence and radical change. It is in this neighborhood that communism is most likely to appear. The range from *c* to *d* can be extremely troublesome, since it calls for some delicate maneuvering. Inequality should still be increasing, but at a decreasing rate. To aim for this is to pose the possibility of alienating virtually all segments of society, especially the new group of industrial and commercial entrepreneurs on the one hand and a rising progressive group concerned with the betrayal of the reforms or the revolution on the other. The government would be wise at this juncture to protect the society from future upheaval by taking steps that will greatly affect the economy potentially but only to a minor extent at present. A revision of the tax structure constitutes an exceedingly important illustration. The introduction of a progressive tax schedule that touches relatively few income receivers in the current period but affects an increasing number as the economy becomes richer accomplishes the triple purpose of promoting consumption later, furthering saving now, and propagandizing now that the government is interested in distributive justice and the welfare of all. At least three problems accompany this type of program, however. One is the difficulty of recognizing point *c*. Yet even if the government miscalculates by several years, particularly if it acts somewhat prematurely rather than tardily, the matter should not be a serious one. The important policy change must come shortly after d, when I as a percentage of Y becomes constant and $\frac{\Delta I}{I}$ declines, and c may be recognized when $\frac{I}{Y}$ begins to increase at a decreasing rate or $\frac{\Delta I}{I}$ levels off. The second problem, infinitely more serious than the first and one that occurs from point c onward, concerns the resistance on the part of the upper income groups. They should possess considerable political power and much of the nation's economic advance depends upon them, but they may refuse to tolerate any changes which they regard as leading to a deterioration in their relative positions. It is of course just this type of recalcitrance which can lead to further revolutionary change. The third matter may be the growing impatience of the disadvantaged, in part countered by propaganda and by the policy that merely sets the stage for a later redistribution. All this is not without its Machiavellian properties, however. It involves the perpetration of a deception upon the masses, who are led to believe that the government is intensely devoted to their welfare and committed to the ideal of equality. When all citizens are proclaimed equal, the current inequalities cannot only be enhanced but also made to appear transitory.[23]

A second means of alleviating political tension in the neighborhood of cd, in fact from point b on, is considerably less disingenuous. This concerns the actual introduction of programs that will keep the growing inequality within tolerable and necessary limits. We have already noted several aspects of this, such as the prevention of absolute declines in planes of living and the maximum control of inflation consistent with economic growth. In addition this can embrace whatever programs of assistance, social welfare, and social security the economy can afford at the time. Such measures should not be lumped together as "welfare statism" and dismissed as items that unreasonable peoples wish to enjoy, cannot afford, and receive only at the expense of further economic development. Welfare measures need to be disaggregated into several components to determine which ones may be compatible with the earlier phases of economic development.

[23] Frederick C. Turner, *The Dynamic of Mexican Nationalism, passim.*

A third vehicle for relieving political tension is economic development itself. This implies that the government must further investment in the broadest sense of the term, whether it be public or private or whether it be fixed capital formation or include some economic activity more conventionally classified as consumption. Economic development ought to strengthen political stability in a variety of ways. For one thing the faster its rate the shorter may be the period of increasing inequality that need be experienced. Further, the effects of economic advancement are likely to trickle down to the lower, though not necessarily the lowest, income group. Then, too, the middle class, which tends to support the government, is likely to gain economic strength. Yet these points serve to remind us again of the dangers of this period. The growing strength of the middle class can bring forth not only stability but a rigidity that heightens resistance to change; the "trickling down" process can give rise to resentment because of a decline in relative standing while aspirations mount considerably more rapidly than actual attainment; and the period of growing income inequality may not only be shortened but by the same token be made more intense.

Fourth, and finally, political unrest is positively correlated with the magnitude of foreign control of the economy. Resentment against increasing income inequality is certainly aggravated when the beneficiaries of the process are outsiders who "exploit" the economy for their own ends. If, on the other hand, foreign domination is relatively minor, the government avoids the criticism that comes from economic subservience to a foreign power. Instead it can emphasize the nationalistic elements of economic change. The popular pride in the nation's achievement tends to reflect on the government itself and to lend an element of stability to it because of such an association. In foreign economic relations the economically advisable may thus partially have to give way to the politically feasible.

At point d and beyond, the problem is that of effecting reforms which reverse the trend toward income inequality. The economic circumstances are then likely to be serious because of the shape and position of the investment function. If growth slackens and income inequality continues to increase, the political situation can easily deteriorate, particularly if foreign influences continue to predominate. This, apparently, is the phase during which a communism rooted in domestic difficulties (as opposed to one introduced by military conquest) is most likely to appear.[24] It has been fashionable to argue that Marx was wrong in believing that capitalism led to communism, since the latter has appeared in the poorest countries; hence, it has been felt, a nation might "skip" capitalism and move directly from feudalism to communism. True, communism is strongest in the poorer countries with per capita incomes ranging from fifty dollars to several hundred or perhaps as much as one thousand dollars per year, where it promotes rapid economic growth by allocating resources to productive capital formation. It does not follow that the world's poorest countries, just on the verge of shedding feudalism, are the most likely candidates for communism. The Communist countries are not necessarily the very poverty-stricken ones, and they certainly do not tend to be nations that have just revolted against feudalism. Rather, one detects in their histories a sequence of feudalism, a quasi and abortive capitalism, and communism. Marx thus emerges as partially right in his stages thesis.

Significantly, few observers regarded Mexico as ripe for communism in the early sixties. Despite the considerable freedom permitted them, the Communists had made little progress in attracting the masses, and their major function seemed to be that of enhancing Soviet prestige in the cold war.[25] Over a period of twenty-five years, during the stage of rising income inequality, Mexico had performed relatively well in the areas of social assistance, economic growth, and Mexicanization. Nor had her government been delinquent in heralding the achievements of the Revolution. Hence, among the policies here being advocated to relieve political tension, particularly over the range *cd*, Mexico was somewhat remiss only in altering her income distribution. By the early sixties, however, Mexico had instituted various programs to bring about the discontinuity at *e*. These included an expansion of social

---

[24] While communism may appear essentially because of the weaknesses of the social system, the strains and disorders of war can still serve as a catalyst.

[25] Karl M. Schmitt, "Communism in Mexico Today," *Western Political Quarterly*, 15 (March, 1962), 111–124.

security, an enhanced emphasis on training and education, fiscal reform, a resurgent public investment, and an apparent control of severe inflation.

The modifications at *e* require one final comment, although it does not have a marked bearing on the Mexican case. Communism is not the only perilous "ism" a nation may have to contend with as it enacts its economic development. Assume that a country has made considerable economic progress over the range *bd* and that it is now confronted with the necessity of introducing reforms, the mere prospect of which is displeasing to many elements within the community. Or the country may successfully implement some of the reforms and in effect experience the discontinuity in the *II'* function at point *e*. Thereupon the society and the economy proceed to alter with considerable rapidity, a rapidity, in fact, which is again distasteful to many members of the community. The latter might include small artisans and shopkeepers, the meagerly trained white-collar workers, and the possessors of concentrated economic power. If these elements are sufficiently resentful to act, and, if in having acted they are successful (as they are particularly likely to be during the aftermath of a major war), they may bring in a regime of the extreme Right. While communism is a threat primarily when countries are in the low income group, it is here suggested, fascism is a danger essentially in the middle income communities. Whether it actually materializes is obviously as much a matter of a nation's history and culture as of its plane of living.[26] The dictator of the Right who may come to power at this relatively advanced economic level hardly resembles his near relative, the status quo dictator near point *a*. In particular, the new man may raise the *II'* function because of government demands associated with policies of militarism and external aggression. These several remarks suggest another way of interpreting the discontinuity at *e*. While prolonged stagnation before *e* is always a possibility, the major issue is typically not whether *II'* will recover, but under whose auspices—the extreme Left, the extreme

---

[26] In Mexico fascism has been represented by the Sinarquistas, who organized around 1937 in order to establish an authoritarian clerical state. While they have survived, they have only represented a relatively small minority.

Right, or the moderate reform groups. If the last named have their way at all, they will probably do so with some lag. If they fail even in this much, we must be prepared to drop the assumption of the mixed economy as the term is conventionally used.

10. In sum, a community that emerges from centuries of economic stagnation and adopts a mixed economy finds it necessary to experience two waves of institutional reform. The first of these can be relatively brief and abrupt. It is generally directed against a system that is committed to the status quo and will not compromise with change. The more cleanly it breaks with the past, the easier should be the implementation of the second reform movement. Sandwiched between the two periods of reform is an interval of enhanced income inequality. The second reform movement, in contrast to the first, is more frequently a gradual, long-continuing process. In part this results from the continual adjustments required in a developing economy, but it is further necessary because resistance may now stem from a group whose cooperation furthers economic change; insofar as this group blocks the necessary reforms, the economy's growth rate tends to suffer. As noted, the second period of reform should witness a trend toward greater equality of income distribution.

The alterations in income distribution and the political-social modifications are in turn significant economically because of their effects upon investment behavior, however broadly the term may be conceived. The initial group of reforms makes the exploitation of additional investment opportunities feasible; under the proper conditions, the second period, that of rising inequality, encourages the saving to finance these opportunities; and the series of ensuing reforms promotes a more rapid rate of increase in mass consumption and in induced capital formation. Development thus involves overcoming a series of investment constraints, with saving providing the major obstacle during the second or intermediate stage and inadequate investment opportunities posing the major difficulties in the first and third stages.

Finally, these variables bear a relationship to the components of aggregate demand. Particularly important is the role played by mass-produced consumer goods, or wage goods, during the course of development. These cannot, and do not, bulk large in the early periods of economic advancement. During stage one and especially stage two, foreign buyers, the government, other firms, and relatively affluent consumers provide much of the markets. The capital formation that then occurs is for the purpose of providing for these sources of demand. In stage three, however, the increase in the consumption of wage goods takes on particular significance for both capital formation and economic growth.[27]

---

[27] The foregoing view of economic development can probably be regarded as one of the many extensions of Keynesian economics. While Keynes admittedly did not analyze the composition of aggregate demand in detail, he did focus his attention upon the relationships between institutional change, aggregate demand, and national income. The present work also resembles Rostow's theory to some degree. For example, the slopes of the saving and investment functions beyond *b* suggest the period of take-off, while in the range *de* the society must decide among several alternatives, including that of mass consumption. The present scope is much narrower, however. In addition, in these pages the instances of discontinuous change number two at the utmost, nothing matches the phase of self-sustained growth, and there is much less endeavor to make a case for stages as such. Finally, the present approach of course has classical overtones because of its stress upon the relationship between growth and income distribution, but the predictions voiced here are considerably more optimistic and have little to do with the retardative effects of rising rents.

Bibliography of Sources Cited

BOOKS

Agarwala, A. N., and Singh, S. P. *The Economics of Underdevelopment.* New York: Oxford University Press, 1963.

Benham, Frederick Charles, and Holley, H. A. *A Short Introduction to the Economy of Latin America.* London: Oxford University Press, 1960.

Bird, Richard, and Oldman, Oliver. *Readings on Taxation in Developing Countries.* Baltimore: John Hopkins Press, 1964.

Bruton, Henry J. *Principles of Development Economics.* Englewood Cliffs, N. J.: Prentice-Hall, 1965.

Cline, Howard F. *Mexico Revolution to Evolution: 1940–1960.* New York: Oxford University Press, 1962.

———. *The United States and Mexico.* Cambridge, Mass.: Harvard University Press, 1953.

Combined Mexican Working Party, The. *The Economic Development of Mexico.* Baltimore: Johns Hopkins Press, for The International Bank for Reconstruction and Development, 1953.

Cosío Villegas, Daniel, ed. *Historia moderna de México*, vol. 7, parts 1 and 2, *El porfiriato: La vida económica.* Mexico, D. F.: Editorial Hermes, 1965.

Dávila Reig, Lorenzo. *La estructura de federal impuestos en México.* Mexico D. F.: Universidad Nacional Autónoma de México, 1962.

Delgado Navarro, Juan. *Desarrollo económico y justicia social en México.* Mexico, D. F.: Universidad Nacional Autónoma de México, 1961.

Domar, Evsey D. *Essays in the Theory of Economic Growth.* New York: Oxford University Press, 1957.

Domingo Lavin, José. *Inversiones extranjeras.* Mexico: EDIAPSA, 1954.

Fernández y Fernández, Ramón, and Acosta, Ricardo. *Política agrícola.* Mexico, D. F.: Fondo de Cultura Económica, 1961.

Flores de la Peña, Horacio. *Los obstáculos al desarrollo económico: El desequilibro fundamental.* Mexico, D. F.: Universidad Nacional Autónoma de México, Escuela Nacional de Economía, 1955.

Flores Márquez, Miguel. *La distribución del ingreso en México.* Mexico, D. F.: Universidad Nacional Autónoma de México, 1958.

Glade, William P., Jr., and Anderson, Charles W. *The Political Economy of Mexico.* Madison: University of Wisconsin Press, 1963.

González Santos, Armando. *La agricultura: Estructura y utilización de los recursos.* Mexico: Fondo de Cultura Económica, 1957.

Gruening, Ernest. *Mexico and Its Heritage.* New York: Appleton-Century, 1928.

Hagen, Everett E., ed. *Planning Economic Development.* Homewood, Ill.: Irwin, 1963.

Hansen, Alvin. *Economic Issues of the 1960's.* New York: McGraw-Hill, 1960.

Harvard University, International Program in Taxation. *Taxation in Mexico.* Boston: Little, Brown, 1957.

Hirschman, Albert. *The Strategy of Economic Development.* New Haven: Yale University Press, 1958.

Hoselitz, Bert F., and Moore, Wilbert E. (editors of papers delivered at the North American Conference on the Social Implications of Industrialization and Technological Changes, Chicago, 1960). *Industrialization and Society.* New York: UNESCO, 1963.

Joint Tax Program [of The Organization of American States, The Inter-American Development Bank, and The Economic Commission for Latin America], Conference on Fiscal Policy (Santiago, Chile: December, 1962). *Fiscal Policy for Economic Growth in Latin America.* Baltimore: John Hopkins Press, 1965.

Kindleberger, Charles P. *Economic Development.* New York: McGraw-Hill, 1958.

Kuznets, Simon. *Six Lectures on Economic Growth.* Glencoe, Ill.: Free Press, 1959.

López Rosado, Jorge. *El productor marginal y la distribución del ingreso nacional.* Mexico, D. F.: Universidad Nacional Autónoma de México, 1959.

Matthews, R. C. O. *The Business Cycle.* Chicago: University of Chicago Press, 1959.

Meier, Gerald M. *International Trade and Development.* New York: Harper and Row, 1963.

México: Cincuenta años de revolución, I, La economía. Mexico, D. F.: Fondo de Cultura Económica, 1960.

México: Cincuenta años de revolución, II, La vida social. Mexico, D. F.: Fondo de Cultura Económica, 1960.

Moore, Wilbert E. *Industrialization and Labor.* Ithaca, N. Y.: Cornell University Press, 1951.

Mosk, Sanford A. *The Industrial Revolution in Mexico.* Berkeley: University of California Press, 1950.

Myrdal, Gunnar. *Rich Lands and Poor.* New York: Harper, 1957.

Navarrete, Ifigenia Martínis de. *La distribución del ingreso y el desarrollo económico de México.* Mexico, D. F.: Instituto Mexicano de Investigaciones Económicas, 1960.

Noriega, Alfonso, Jr. *México debe bastarse a sí mismo.* Mexico, D. F.: Confederación de Cámeras Industriales, 1956.

Parkes, Henry B. *A History of Mexico.* Boston: Houghton Mifflin, 1950.

Pepelasis, Adamantios; Mears, Leon; and Adelman, Irma, eds. *Economic Development.* New York: Harper, 1961.

Poblete Troncoso, Moisés, and Burnett, Ben G. *The Rise of the Latin American Labor Movement.* New York: Bookman, 1960.

Ruiz, Ramón Eduardo. *Mexico: The Challenge of Poverty and Illiteracy.* San Marino, Calif.: Huntington Library, 1963.

Schlarman, Joseph H. L. *Mexico: A Land of Volcanoes.* Milwaukee, Wis.: Bruce, 1950.

Scott, Robert E. *Mexican Government in Transition.* Urbana, Ill. University of Illinois Press, 1959.

Silva Herzog, Jesús. *El agrarismo mexicano y la reforma agraria, exposición y crítica.* Mexico, D. F.: Fondo de Cultura Económica, 1959.

Simpson, Eyler N. *The Ejido: Mexico's Way Out.* Chapel Hill: University of North Carolina Press, 1937.

Stanford Research Institute. *Manual of Industrial Development with Special Application to Latin America.* Stanford, Calif., 1954.

Tannenbaum, Frank. *Mexico: The Struggle for Peace and Bread.* New York: A. A. Knopf, 1950.

Turner, Frederick C. *The Dynamic of Mexican Nationalism.* Chapel Hill: The University of North Carolina Press, 1968.

Universidad Nacional Autónoma de México, Escuela Nacional de Economía. *La intervención del estado en la economía.* Mexico, D. F.: 1955.

———. *Problemas del desarrollo económico de México.* Mexico, D. F.: 1958.

Vernon, Raymond. *The Dilemma of Mexico's Development.* Cambridge, Mass.: Harvard University Press, 1963.

———, ed. *Public Policy and Private Enterprise in Mexico.* Cambridge, Mass.: Harvard University Press, 1964.

Viner, Jacob. *International Trade and Economic Development*. Glencoe, Ill.: The Free Press, 1952.
Whetten, Nathan. *Rural Mexico*. Chicago: University of Chicago Press, 1948.
Wythe, George. *Industry in Latin America*. New York: Columbia University Press, 1949.
Zimmerman, L. J. *Poor Lands, Rich Lands: The Widening Gap*. New York: Random House, 1965.

PERIODICALS

Adler, John H. "The Fiscal and Monetary Implementation of Development Programs," *American Economic Review, Papers and Proceedings* 42 (May, 1952), 584–600.
Aubrey, Henry G. "Structure and Balance in Rapid Economic Growth: The Example of Mexico," *Political Science Quarterly* 69 (December, 1954), 517–540.
Bach, Federico. "The Distribution of Wealth in Mexico," *The Annals* 208 (March, 1940), 70–77.
Ball, John M. "Some Comments on Mexico's Population," *Journal of Geography* 61 (October, 1962), 296–301.
Baltra, Alberto, "La reforma agraria y el progreso económico," *Revista de Economía* 23 (January, 1960), 6.
Belshaw, Michael H. "Aspects of Community Development in Rural Mexico," *Inter-American Economic Affairs* 15 (Spring, 1962), 71–94.
Bernstein, E. M., and Patel, I. G. "Inflation in Relation to Economic Development," *International Monetary Fund Staff Papers* 2 (November, 1952), 363–398.
Beteta, Mario Ramón. "Notes on Foreign Investment in Mexico," *Comercio Exterior de México* 8 (August, 1962), Supplement.
Bird, Richard. "Economy of the Mexican Federal District," *Inter-American Economic Affairs* 17 (Autumn, 1963), 19–51.
Brandenburg, Frank R. "Organized Business in Mexico," *Inter-American Economic Affairs* 12 (Winter, 1958), 26–50.
Brandenburg, Frank R. "A Contribution to the Theory of Entrepreneurship and Economic Development: A Case of Mexico," *Inter-American Economic Affairs* 16 (Winter, 1962), 3–23.
Calderón, Guillermo. "Las inversiones extranjeras y el ahorro interno," *Revista de Economía* 21 (June, 1958), 148–153.
Calderón M., A., and Suárez C., A. "Impuesto sobre la renta," *Revista de Economía* 16 (December, 1953), 372.
Campos Salas, Octaviano. "Economic Panorama of Modern Mexico," *Comercio Exterior de México* 9 (February, 1963), Supplement.

Carrillo Flores, Antonio. "Mexico and the Indian," *Américas* 16 (February, 1964), 9–16.

——. "Mexico Forges Ahead." *Foreign Affairs* 36 (April, 1958), 491–503.

Castañeda, Jorge. "Revolution and Foreign Policy: Mexico's Experience," *Political Science Quarterly* 78 (September, 1963), 391–417.

Castillo, Carlos Manuel. "La economía agrícola en la región del Bajío," *Problemas Agrícolas y Industriales de México* 8 (July–December, 1956), 111

Ceceña, José Luís. "Inversiones extranjeras directas en México," *Revista de Economía* 15 (October, 1952), 317.

Chenery, Hollis B. "The Application of Investment Criteria," *Quarterly Journal of Economics* 67 (February, 1953), 76–96.

Cook, Robert C., ed. "Mexico, the Problem of People," *Population Bulletin* 20 (November, 1964), 173–203.

Cruz, Oscar René. "Estudio comparativo de los principales planes revolucionarios de México," *Revista de Economía* 23 (June, 1960), 175–176.

Davis, Kingsley. "Institutional Patterns Favoring High Fertility in Underdeveloped Areas," *Eugenics Quarterly* 2 (March, 1955), 33–39.

De Durand, Josefina Poulat. "Trabajo femenino a domicilio," *Revista de Economía* 20 (May, 1957), 121–124.

Dowsett, C. P. "Agriculture and Economic Development: Mexico," *Australian Quarterly* 34 (March, 1962), 62–68.

Emery, Robert F. "Mexican Monetary Policy Since the 1959 Devaluation," *Inter-American Economic Affairs* 12 (Spring, 1959), 72–85.

Equihua, Clementina Z. de, and Navarrete, Ifigenia M. de. "El desarrollo económico de México y la mujer," *Revista de Economía* 20 (May, 1957), 117–120.

Flores, Edmundo. "The Significance of Land Use Changes in the Economic Development of Mexico," *Land Economics* 35 (May, 1959), 114–124.

Flores de la Peña, Horacio, and Ferrer, Aldo. "Salarios reales y desarrollo económico," *El Trimestre Económico* 18 (October–December, 1951), 617–628.

Gellner, Marianne. "Mexico: New Frontiers of Progress," *World Today* 20 (December, 1964), 523–532.

German Parra, Manuel. "Un programa reaccionario para la Revolución Mexicana," *Siempre*, No. 171 (October 3, 1956), 16–17.

Golden, Hilda H. "Literacy and Social Change in Underdeveloped Countries," *Rural Sociology* 20 (March, 1955), 1–7.

Gurley, John G., and Shaw, Edward S. "Financial Aspects of Economic

Development," *American Economic Review* 45 (September, 1955), 515–538.

Hilton, Stanley E. "Church-State Dispute over Education in Mexico from Carranza to Cárdenas," *The Americas* 21 (October, 1964), 163–183.

Kuznets, Simon. "Economic Growth and Income Inequality," *American Economic Review* 45 (March, 1955), 1–28.

———. "Quantitative Aspects of the Economic Growth of Nations: VIII, Distribution of Income by Size," *Economic Development and Cultural Change* 11 (January, 1963), part 2, 1–80.

Lampman, Robert J. "Recent Thought on Egalitarianism," *Quarterly Journal of Economics* 71 (May, 1957), 234–266.

Langnas, I. A. "Mexico Today; Aspects of Progress Since the Revolution," *World Today* 17 (April, 1961), 158–167.

"La nueva ley del impuesto sobre la renta," *El Mercado de Valores* 25 (January 11, 1965), 13–36 and 49.

Lewis, Oscar, "México desde 1940," *Investigación Económica* 18 (Second Quarter, 1958), 185–256.

———. "Mexico Since Cárdenas," *Social Research* 26 (Spring, 1959), 18–30.

Lombardo Toledano, Vicente. "The Labor Movement," *The Annals* 208 (March, 1940), 48–54.

López Hurtado, Julio. "Repercusiones de las características generales de la industria en la capacidad productiva," *Revista de Economía* 17 (November, 1954), 305.

López Romero, Adolfo. "Desarrollo económico de México," *El Trimestre Económico* 29 (January–March, 1962), 30–68.

López Rosado, Diego G., and Noyola Vázques, Juan F. "Los salarios reales en México, 1939–1950," *El Trimestre Económico* (April–July, 1951), 201–209.

Macrae, Norman. "Mexico Shows the Way?" *Economist* 216 (September 25, 1965), xii–xx.

Maddox, James G. "Economic Growth and Revolution in Mexico," *Land Economics* 36 (August, 1960), 266–278.

"Mexican Import Controls; Policy Permits," *Economist* 212 (August 8, 1964), 578.

"Mexico: Booming Urban Economy," *Hispanic American Report* 17 (July, 1964), 594–596.

Moore, Wilbert E. "Theoretical Aspects of Industrialization," *Social Research* 15 (September, 1948), 277–303.

Mosk, Sanford A. "Discussion" [of H. G. Aubrey's "Industrial Investment Decision . . ."], *Journal of Economic History* 15 (December, 1955), 355–359.

Moyo Porrás, Edmundo. "Repercusiones de las características generales de la industria en el comercio exterior," *Revista de Economía* 17 (November, 1954), 294.

Mueller, Marnie W. "Structural Inflation and the Mexican experience," *Yale Economic Essays* 5 (Spring, 1965), 145–194.

Mújica Montoya, Emilio. "Repercusiones de las características generales de la industria en los precios," *Revista de Economía* 17 (September–October, 1954), 284.

The Nacional Financiera, Department of Financial Studies. "Tax Incentives for New Industry," *Mexican American Review* 29 (December, 1961), 59.

Navarrete, Ifigenia Martínis de. "Naturaleza de la reforma fiscal," *Comercio Exterior* 12 (March, 1962), 138–142.

Needler, Martin C. "The Political Development of Mexico," *American Political Science Review* 55 (June, 1961), 308–312.

Nurkse, Ragnar. "Some International Aspects of the Problem of Economic Development," *American Economic Review, Papers and Proceedings* 42 (May, 1952), 570–583.

Ohlin, Goran. "Balanced Economic Growth in History," *American Economic Review, Papers and Proceedings* 49 (May, 1959), 338–353.

Ojha, P. D., and Bhatt, V. V. "Pattern of Income Distribution on an Underdeveloped Economy: A Case Study of India," *American Economic Reviews* 54 (September, 1964), 711–720.

Parks, Richard W. "The Role of Agriculture in Mexican Economic Development," *Inter-American Economic Affairs* 18 (Summer, 1964), 3–27.

Prebish, Raúl. "Commercial Policy in the Underdeveloped Countries," *American Economic Review: Papers and Proceedings* 49 (May, 1959), 251–273.

Quint, B. "Cleaning Up the Border," *Mexican American Review* 29 (September, 1961), 3.

Randall, Laura. "Labour Migration and Mexican Economic Development," *Social and Economic Studies* 11 (March, 1962), 73.

Redfield, Robert. "The Indian in Mexico," *The Annals* 208 (March, 1940), 132–143.

Reston, James. "The Biggest Story on the World," *The New Republic* 148 (May 4, 1963), 15–17.

Retchkiman, Benjamin. "Distribución del ingreso," *Revista de Economía* 21 (August, 1958), 224–230.

Ríos G., Vicente. "Tendencia de la industria en México," *Revista de Economía* 17 (November, 1954), 301–304.

Robinson, Elizabeth H., and Warren C. "Rural-urban Fertility Differentials in Mexico," *American Sociological Review* 25 (February, 1960), 77–81.

Rosenstein-Rodan, Paul. "Problems of Industrialization of Eastern and South-Eastern Europe," *Economic Journal* 53 (June–September, 1943), 202–211.

Schmitt, Karl M. "Communism in Mexico Today," *Western Political Quarterly* 15 (March, 1962), 111–124.

Shelton, David H. "Mexico's Economic Growth: Success of Diversified Development," *Southwestern Social Science Quarterly* 41 (December, 1960), 304–319.

Singer, Hans W. "The Distribution of Gains Between Investing and Borrowing Countries," *American Economic Review, Papers and Proceedings* 40 (May, 1950), 473–485.

Solís M., Leopoldo, *et al.* "La distribución del ingreso y el desarrollo económico de México," *Comercio Exterior* 11 (February, 1961), 89.

Strassman, Paul W. "Economic Growth and Income Distribution," *Quarterly Journal of Economics* 70 (August, 1956), 425–440.

Sturmthal, Adolf. "Economic Development, Income Distribution, and Capital Formation in Mexico," *Journal of Political Economy* 63 (June, 1955), 183–201.

"The Fiscal Reform," *Comercio Exterior de México* 11 (January, 1965), 3–4.

"The Mexican Economy in 1961." *Comercio Exterior de México* 8 (April, 1962), 2 ff.

"Three-Fifths Mexican." *Economist* 213 (December 12, 1964), 1282.

Urquidi, Víctor L. "Problemas fundamentales de la economía mexicana," *Cuadernos Americanos* 114 (January–February, 1961), 69.

Wagner, Philip L. "Indian Economic Life in Chiapas," *Economic Geography* 39 (April, 1963), 156–164.

Washington, S. Walter. "Mexican Resistance to Communism," *Foreign Affairs* 36 (April, 1958), 504–515.

OTHER

Banco de México. *Informe anual*. Mexico, D. F.: Selected years.

Banco Nacional de Comercio Exterior. *Comercio Exterior de México*. Mexico, D. F.: Selected years.

Banco Nacional de México. *Review of the Economic Situation of Mexico*. Mexico, D. F.: Selected years.

Botsford, Keith. "Mexico Follows a 'Solo Camino'," *New York Times Magazine*, April 26, 1964, pp. 20, 64, 67.

Cámara Nacional de la Industria de Transformación. *Viente años de lucha, 1941–1961*. Mexico, D. F.: 1962.

Committee for Economic Development. *How Low Income Countries Can Advance Their Own Growth*. New York: September, 1966.

Dirección General Estadística: México. *Compendio estadístico*. Mexico, D. F.: Selected years.

Dirección General de Estadística, Secretaría de Economía. *Ingresos y egresos de la población de México en el mes de octubre de 1956*. Mexico, D. F.: 1956.

Hernández Delgado, José. "The Contribution of National Financiera to the Industrialization of Mexico." Mexico, D. F.: Nacional Financiera, August 1, 1961.

Instituto Mexicano del Seguro Social. *Ley del seguro social*. Mexico, D. F.: 1962.

International Bank for Reconstruction and Development. *Mexico's Public Investment Program, 1957–1958*. Report No. WH-59, July, 1957.

International Monetary Fund. *International Monetary Statistics*. Washington, D.C.: Selected years.

Kennedy, Paul P. "Mexico Launches Education Drive," *New York Times*, May 5, 1963, section 1, p. 4.

Nacional Financiera. *El Mercado de Valores*. Mexico, D. F.: Selected years.

Nacional Financiera. *Informe anual*. Mexico, D. F.: Selected years.

Nacional Financiera. *Mexican Economy: Selected Economic Indicators*. Mexico, D. F.: 1961.

Organization for Economic Cooperation and Development, Third Study Conference on Problems of Economic Development. *Government Finance and Economic Development*. Athens, Greece: December 12–19, 1963.

Secretaría de Economía. *Memoria*. Mexico, D. F.: 1958.

Secretaría de Hacienda y Crédito Público. "Ley federal del impuesto sobre le renta." *Boletín Oficial* 8 (February, 1962), 197–270.

Secretaría de Hacienda y Crédito Público, Dirección General del Impuesto sobre le Renta. *Ley del impuesto sobre la renta*. Mexico, D. F.: 1954.

Secretaría de Industria y Comercio. *Anuario estadístico de los Estados Unidos Mexicanos, 1960–1961*. Mexico, D. F.: 1963.

Secretaría de Industria y Comercio. *Memoria*. Mexico, D. F.: 1960.

United Nations. *Private Foreign Investment*. New York: 1958.

United Nations, Department of Economic Affairs. *Progress in Land Reform*. New York: 1954.

United Nations, Department of Economic and Social Affairs. *The Demographic Yearbook*. New York: Selected years.

United Nations, Department of Economic and Social Affairs. *The Latin American Common Market*. New York: 1959.

United Nations, Economic and Social Council. *World Economic Survey*. New York: Selected years.

United Nations, Economic Commission for Latin America. *Economic Survey of Latin America*. New York: Selected years.

United Nations, Economic Commission for Latin America. *Human Resources of Central America, Panama and Mexico, 1950–1960, in Relation to Some Aspects of Economic Development*. New York: 1960.

United Nations, Economic Commission for Latin America. *Inflation and Growth: A Summary of Experience in Latin America*. New York: 1960.

United Nations, Economic Commission for Latin America. *Labor Productivity of the Cotton Textile Industry in Five Latin American Countries*. Mexico, D. F.: 1951.

UNESCO. *Seminar on Urbanization Problems in Latin America*. New York: 1960.

UNESCO. *External Disequilibrium in the Economic Development of Latin America: The Case of Mexico*. New York: 1957.

UNESCO, Economic Commission for Latin America. *Recent Events and Trends in Mexico*. New York: 1950.

United Nations, Statistical Office. *Statistical Yearbook*. New York: Selected years.

United Nations, Technical Assistance Administration. *Taxes and Fiscal Policy in Under-developed Countries*. New York: 1954.

Urquidi, Víctor L. "La inflación en México." Unpublished.

———. "Tres lustros de experiencia monetaria en México: Algunas enseñanzas," *Memoria del segundo congreso mexicano de ciencias sociales*, vol. 2. Mexico, D. F.: Banco de México, 1940.

Wilhelm, Marion. "Mexicans Hand Reds Stiff Rebuff at Polls," *Christian Science Monitor*, July 11, 1961, p. 12.

Index

accidents: 253, 259

Agency for International Development: 115

aggregate demand: performance of, 161–167 *passim*; 173, 174, 176–179, 296; and income, 161; and investment, 163, 195; and inflation, 189, 209; and devaluation, 204; components of, 243, 281, 282–283, 292–293; Keynes on, 317 n.; mentioned, 301

Agrarian Code of 1934: 57

agricultural extension services: 250

agriculture: statistics on, 6, 138; productivity of, and economy, 8, 17, 18, 39–44, 61–62, 138, 173, 177, 286, 290, 295, 309; background of, 15; helped by Cárdenas, 17; and exports, 42–43, 205; problems in development of, 48–50; and technology, 44, 50, 58, 62, 252; and the Revolution, 55–56, 118; credit for, 63, 64, 197; under López Mateos, 65; and income distribution, 138, 140–149, 150, 178; effect of, on domestic markets, 168; and population growth, 172; effect of inflation on, 185–186; taxes on income from, 214, 218, 225, 230, 232; and urban migration, 262; government aid to, 244–245, 250, 252, 275.

Alemán, Miguel: 58

Alliance for Progress: 113, 115, 231

anomie, of urbanites: 259

army: 118. SEE ALSO military

Aubrey, Henry G.: on industry, 18, 20 n.; on agriculture, 43–44, 144; on income, 135, 144; on investment, 180–181

Aztecs: attitude of, toward women, 84

balanced growth: and institutions, 47; and public investment, 91; and income, 144

balance of payments: and government aid, 92, 93; and credit from Nacional Financiera, 94; and economic health, 96, 243; and tariffs, 100–101; and tax exemption, 101; and foreign investment, 105; and capital, 172; effect of inflation on, 201–209; effect of prices on, 201–202, 203; and imports, 205; and devaluation, 207, 208, 209

Banco de Crédito Agrícola: 63

Banco de México: extended credit, 17; and money policy, 96; and functional income distribution, 138; on real GNP, 171

Banco Nacional de Comercio Exterior: on GNP, 171–173

Banco Nacional de Crédito Ejidal: 63–64

Bankers Association of Mexico: 237

banking: statistics on, 6; developed under Díaz, 16; and economic problems, 96, 173–174

Beneficiencia Pública, La: 254

Benham, F., and H. A. Holley: on economic diversity, 37–38

Bernstein, E. M., and I. G. Patel: on inflation, 185–186

birth rates: 29, 31–35 *passim*

Bloque de Unidad Obrera (BUO): 67–69

bonds: from Nacional Financiera, 97; interest rate on, 107; and commodity prices, 199–201

bracero: 103

business: under Cárdenas, 17; and

DATE DUE

DATE DUE			
FEB 11 '74			
MAY 7 '75			
GAYLORD			PRINTED IN U.S.A.